leslie

white planet

A MAD

DASH THROUGH

MODERN

GLOBAL SKI

CULTURE

GREYSTONE BOOKS
D&M PUBLISHERS INC.
Vancouver/Toronto/Berkeley

For Myles,
who has the keys to the kingdom.

10 11 12 13 14   5 4 3 2 1

Greystone Books
An imprint of D&M Publishers Inc.
2323 Quebec Street, Suite 201
Vancouver BC Canada V5T 4S7
www.greystonebooks.com

Cataloguing data available from Library and Archives Canada
ISBN 978-1-55365-479-7 (pbk.)
ISBN 978-1-55365-646-3 (ebook)

Editing by Lucy Kenward
Copyediting by Lara Kordic
Cover and text design by Jessica Sullivan
Cover photograph © Chase Jarvis/Getty Images
Printed and bound in Canada by Friesens
Text printed on acid-free, 100% post-consumer paper
Distributed in the U.S. by Publishers Group West

We gratefully acknowledge the financial support of the Canada Council
for the Arts, the British Columbia Arts Council, the Province of British
Columbia through the Book Publishing Tax Credit, and the Government
of Canada through the Canada Book Fund for our publishing activities.

Mixed Sources
Cert no. SW-COC-001271
© 1996 FSC
FSC

CONTENTS

"There is nothing ordinary about the mountains, nor about the people who seek meaning and beauty in them."
—THE MOE BROTHERS, co-founders of *POWDER* magazine

ACKNOWLEDGMENTS

THANKING everyone I should be thanking is a daunting prospect. After twenty-plus years of trekking the globe with dozens of ski freaks, meeting hundreds more wherever I've touched down, and being helped daily in this ever-more-fractious quest by everyone from ski areas to tourist bureaus to people apologetically pointing guns in my face because, well, they were just doing their jobs, the task is clearly impossible. So I'll just do what I can.

My mother, as you will read, sent—OK, forced—me to go skiing for the first time. The experience I had that day could have turned into a lifetime of resentment. Fortunately, it went the other way.

Merl, Rat, Cleary, Skihoe, DeCaen, Kalisz, Altec, and Motz were my high school ski buddies, meaning they most frequently formed the phalanx of frozen jeans, wine, and weed that was my alpine baptism. I met Mary Eberle, my first love, on a ski trip, and my best memories of our times together—whether the posh trappings of Aspen or sleeping in the snow at Tuckerman Ravine on Mt. Washington—revolve around skiing. My biology teacher, Roman Fedorowicz, ski-trip organizer and delinquent ski-team coach (tasks taken on, in true ski-bum fashion, solely to afford more skiing), influenced the course of my life in more ways than, in retrospect, even I am shocked to recall. Stephen "Merl" Connolly was the good friend and co-conspirator in pretty much everything of consequence—from art to music, rock-climbing, streaking, and various other forms of subversion—that I launched into the ski abyss with. In Waterloo, Christopher J. Hart, who otherwise supervised my lab work in an aquatic entomology course, opened the doors of perception when he introduced me to telemarking.

Stuck knee-deep now, I'll cover the rest in categories. These are people I've benefited from knowing or traveling with, or who have delivered me of something important— whether insight, influence, understanding, admiration, or a simple laugh in the snow. There will be many oversights for which I pre-beg forgiveness.

Jackals, powderhounds, athletes: Mark Abma, J.P. Auclair, Jenn Berg, Micah Black, El Fucking Bobby, Rob Boyd, Darian Boyle, Wendy Brookbank, Sarah Burke, Greg Campbell, Sammy Carlson, Danny Caruso, Johnny "Foon" Chilton, "Sergeant" Jim Conway, Chris Davenport, Claudio y Orlando Dias, Vinnie Dorion, Mike Douglas, Simon Dumont, Chris Eby, John Falkiner, Wendy Fisher, Dana Flahr, Alison Gannet, Sebastian Garhammer, Shane Gould, Tanner Hall, Hugo Harrisson, Mike Hattrup, Drew Heatherington, Chad Hendron, "Coloro" Herman, Jeff Holden, J.T. Holmes, Per Huss, Troy Jungen, Craig Kelly, Lisa Korthals, Steve Kuijt, Joseph P. Lammers III, Jon Larsson, Pierre-Yves LeBlanc, Ricky Lewon, Kristen Lignel, Sverre Lillequist, Noel Lyons, Ian McIntosh, Charlotte Moats, Brant Moles, Steve Mooz, Ian Morrison, Seth Morrison, El Punto Negro, Shawn "Smiley" Nesbitt, Jeremy Nobis, Paul Parker, Lee Ann Patterson, Eric Pehota, Gordy Peifer, Dominique Perret, Kye Petersen, Bryce Philips, Les Trois Philippes, Kina Pickett, Glen Plake, Philou Poirier, Kasha Rigby, Carla Rizutto, Chris Rubens, Joe "The Dog" Sagona, Frank Salter, Chad

Sayers, T.J. Schiller, Richie Schley, Scott Schmidt, John Smart, Ptor Spricenieks, Shane Szocs, Johnny Thrash, Dan Treadway, Kristen Ulmer, Rex Wehrman, Karin Weinberger, Henrik Windstedt, Chris Winter, Saifon Woozley, Eduardo Chichero Xaffon, Kaj Zachrisson. Special nods to the departed: Alan Bard, Matt Brakel, Brett Carlson, Doug Coombs, C.R. Johnson, Shane McConkey, Trevor Petersen, Hans Sari, and Dave Sheets.

Prima donnas, photographers, cinematographers: Kevin "Feet" Banks, the late Dick Barrymore, Christian Begin, Eric Berger, Hide Chiyasu, Lee Cohen, Damian Cromwell, Hank deVre, Mattias Fredriksson, Scott Gaffney, Henry Georgi, Bill Heath, Dave Heath, Ilja Herb, Bryn Hughes, Blake Jorgenson, Ace Kvale, Dustin Lindgren, Therese Lundgren, Ace MacKay-Smith, Scott Markewitz, Wade McCoy, Flip McCririck, Paul Morrison, Pat Morrow, Ben Mullin, Nate Nash, Nolen Oayda, Steve Ogle, Christian Pondella, Bruce Rowles, Magali Roy, Mark Shapiro, the late Carl Skoog, Beat Steiner, Greg Stump, Travis Tetreault, Murray Wais.

Bullies, editors, writers: Mike Berard, Bruno Bertrand, Tom Bie, Fredrik Boberg, Jake Bogoch, John Bresee, Kevin Brooker, Keith Carlsen, Steve Casimiro, Robert Choquette, John Crawford-Currie, Bruce Edgerly, Colin Field, Porter Fox, David Goodman, Bill Kerig, Tove Lillequist, James Little, Ian Macmillan, G.D. Maxwell, Steve Metcalf, Sam Moulton, Jules Older, Hiroshi Owada, David Reddick, Lisa Richardson, Ben Sadavoy, Mitchell Scott, Rob Story, Derek Taylor, Steven Threndyle. Westwood Creative Artists and Nancy Flight at Greystone Books fastened wheels of one form or another to this chattering vehicle; my editor, Lucy Kenward, deserves huge thanks for engineering its currently sleeker lines and driving so adeptly.

Criminals, madmen, visionaries: Ken Achenbach, Christian Begin, Alan Bard and Tom Carter, Team Clambin, Giorgio Daidola, Marc Deschamps, Mike Douglas, Lhotse

Hawk, Geny Hess, Jill and Pete, Carole and Brad Karafil, Dolores LaChapelle, Pelle Lang, Pete "Swede" Mattson, the late Shane McConkey, Dan McDonald, Dave and Jake Moe, Glenn Noel, Dave and Doug Perry, Trevor Petersen and Eric Pehota, Glen Plake, Greg Stump.

Crystal balls, blueprints, films: Ski the Outer Limits (Roger Brown and Barry Corbet, 1968), *Winter Equinox* (Bill Burks, 1974), *Blizzard of Aahhhs* (Greg Stump, 1988), *Loco Motion* (Christian Begin, 1995), and the collective works of Matchstick Productions (MSP), Teton Gravity Research (TGR), Poor Boyz Productions (PBP), and Free Radicals.

Tabloids, employers, magazines: bits, bites, and a few choking mouthfuls of dozens of articles, essays, and columns have been liberally sprinkled, repurposed, and undergone DNA-like recombination in the service of weaving this romp through modern global ski culture. These originally appeared, among other places, in *Åka Skidor, explore, POWDER, Ski Canada, SKIER,* and *Skiing.*

Friends, family, lifesavers: As usual, thanks are due Mary and the girls at Starbucks Creekside, as well as those who kept my head and health above water during the dark and trying winter of 2008–09. I owe you all so much: Jake Bogoch, Caroline Carnerie, Caroline Cossette, Mike Douglas, Lina Edvinsson, Caleigh Garland, Myles Emily Garland, Aki Kaltenbach, Stephen Madigan, Julia "Gabe" McCabe, Paul and Gail Morrison, "Agedashi Tofu" Mullin, Lisa Richardson, Kristen Rust, Grant Stoddard, Elin Sylvan, and, most fondly, "Coach" Laura Robson.

And finally, props to the fortuitous merger of plate tectonics, gravity, and atmospheric chaos that forms the happy template for this collective madness. That means you, too, Ullr. I know you're struggling hard with climate change and all, but thanks for the continued magic of snow, whenever and wherever you deliver. Nothing can compare.

Nothing.

PROLOGUE:
LEGEND

Skiing... is positively thrilling no matter how
well or poorly you've mastered it. From the...
moment you begin to slide over snow, feel the
tug of gravity pull you downhill, your heart and
spirit exults. It is pure thrill. There are, to be sure,
more than a few moments of frustration... But
even during that painful period, there is a constant thrill... Once the basics have been reduced
to muscle memory, skiing is a non-stop celebration of how good life can be when you live it at
the edge of your self-defined envelope, be that
envelope green or double black.
G.D. MAXWELL, *Pique Newsmagazine*,
April 9, 2009

I CAN BARELY remember what I did yesterday, but I clearly remember my first
day of skiing. Well, maybe not clearly—more like an old
Super 8 movie—but you get the picture.

Housebound on a gorgeous spring-break day sometime
in the late sixties, my hyperkinetic friend Mike and I were
driving my mother nuts with loud Hot Wheels races and
house-wide G.I. Joe battles. In a fit of desperation, she
insisted we take some dusty ski equipment that was lan-
guishing in the garage—unused since the early fifties—to

the nearby Don Valley Ski Centre, a riverbank operation in one of Toronto's newly minted suburban wastelands, and give it a whirl.

"It'll be more fun than tobogganing," she said, pretty much selling us.

We wrapped chubby hands around wooden, enamel-painted skis with bear-trap bindings, bamboo poles, and boots far too big for grade-school feet, and schlepped it all to the hill. It was an arduous journey of an hour or so, and when we arrived, impatient and excited at the sight of people zipping down the slope, we still had to figure out how all this equipment worked.

We struggled with the stiff, cumbersome boots, cables, springs, and myriad straps for what seemed an eternity. The bindings seemed to defy any law of engineering gleaned from Meccano sets, Lego bricks, or tabletop hockey, but when the forward throws on the cable finally snapped down, it seemed the boots were attached to the skis. It didn't last. With each tentative step the bindings would let go, leaving us ski-less and frustrated. Only through the sympathetic intervention of adults who witnessed our comic plight (tsk-tsking over what kind of parent would cast neophyte children adrift like this) were we eventually affixed awkwardly to the planks.

We quickly mastered shuffling ahead on the skis, and eagerly got in line for the tow. As we waited our turn, I watched the fat hemp rope whiz around a small truck wheel driven by a chugging diesel engine and studied the loading procedure. It seemed simple: tuck your poles under one arm, place one hand ahead of your body, another behind your back, and grab the rope. Which was just what I did. My arms were practically ripped from their sockets as I saw snow, then sky, then snow again. I could hear the slurping, wet whoosh of a body being dragged through snow, the clack-clack of skis clapping together, and Mike's hysterical laughter. My eyes, nose, and mouth filled with snow. Finally, I'd let go of the rope.

I felt sick. The tow operator picked me up and shepherded me back to the line, where I had the satisfaction of watching the same fate befall Mike. Each of us tried a second time, with a similar result. Beaten, we sniveled around like wounded puppies until, again, someone offered to help. When we eventually made it to the top, it was like we'd been airlifted from hell to well ... we weren't sure what.

The speed of sliding downhill was dizzying and intoxicating, the frequent wipeouts brutal and instructive. We continued to have our arms yanked numb by the speedy rope tows, fall backward off a platter lift—a spring-loaded metal pole with a plastic disc you tucked through your crotch to pull you along, itself a novelty—and skid helplessly downhill upside down, we plowed full-speed and out of control into hay bales, and generally took a massive beating from the tiny 115-foot vertical. The most vivid frames from this flickering film, however, are not of motion but notion—how it all looked and felt to my uninitiated senses.

Between runs, we sipped scalding hot chocolate from a rancid-smelling machine and queued with tanned, sunglass-adorned hedonists who reeked of coconut and spoke of Collingwood and the Laurentians, the Alps and Banff. Everyone but us—clad in jeans with flannel pajamas dangling below the cuffs—wore sleek, black stretch pants that disappeared into their boots. Smart knit sweaters, turtlenecks, and headbands out-polled jackets, scarves, and hats, making a James Bondian damn-the-elements fashion statement. European labels were legion—Piz Buin, Snik, Vuarnet, Carrera, Arlberg. This leitmotif created the very real sense of *mountains,* something I knew only from picture books. Amid a monotonous suburban landscape we discovered a window onto a world apart. I stared long and hard, not realizing I was viewing a tiny corner of a world-wide diaspora, an entire galaxy of alpine travel, history, and endeavor.

Mike and I were too battered to walk home, and we sheepishly used our last dime to call my mother. She cried when she saw us: we were broken, bruised, and bloodied, our pajamas shredded by rusty ski edges, the palms of our mitts torn out by the rough hemp of the rope tow. Consumed by guilt, she overlooked our shit-eating grins and did what any conflicted parent would: screamed at us for not calling her sooner.

"It's OK, mom," I smiled, unaware that I'd just experienced the closest a human can come to flying without leaving the Earth. "We had fun."

a
gathering
storm

1 | SMOKE AND MIRRORS

> "There's nothing really can touch skiing, is there?"
> Nick said. "The way it feels when you first drop
> off on a long run." "Huh," said George. "It's too
> swell to talk about."—ERNEST HEMINGWAY,
> *"Cross-Country Snow,"* 1925

THIS STORY starts with a volcano. Or maybe it's that one story ends there and another begins. Or maybe it's just that a volcano, with an umbilical attachment to the core of the Earth, is the perfect metaphor for a gateway to another world. Either way, if there's one thing you can usually count on with a volcano, it's a hole on top.

This Mexican version, however, was proving maddeningly elusive. The lip of fractured ice wavering above us like salt crystals ringing a margarita glass had got no closer in the last hour. Was it that the slope was steepening? Or was it the moonwalk we were executing to make certain our crampons found firm footing on the glacier's marble surface? Was it our zigzagging around the blue yawn of each small crevasse and resting, so it seemed, every thirty seconds? Or was it simply due to failing brain function at

18,000 feet, an altitude few accomplished skiers would ever contemplate and most North American mountaineers would never encounter and the fact that my friend Merl and I—hitching along with no clue, no rope, frozen feet, and hallucinogenic half-breaths—were neither?

Very likely. As in, all of the above.

Still, when there was enough oxygen to formulate the thought, I figured we *should* be making progress. And then suddenly, progress appeared. We were staring into the crater, the mix of ice and lava underfoot now more like the salt-and-peppered rim of a Bloody Mary, I thought, in the abstract way you entertain irrelevant ideas when you are high—or very high. And I could see why gaining this purchase had seemed too slow: the crater's edge wasn't level but sloped radically at some thirty degrees. Stumbling through the crevasse field, we'd actually been contouring the volcano in the direction of its rising rim. We'd breached it on a false summit about halfway around; far below to our left was the lower margin of the crater, its adjacent snow-field a mess of ashen streaks, volcanic dribble on a white bib, while above to our right was the summit. Which meant more climbing. Which probably wasn't a good thing given the nausea, violent headaches, and dizziness we were experiencing—but really, how much farther could it be?

An hour later we were finished, literally and figuratively. Just shy of the rim's highest point—a crenulated mannequin of brick-colored lava—we were too cold, hypoxic, and exhausted to go farther. Merl was talking but he sounded like Donald Duck, or someone sucking on helium. I couldn't understand and laughed hysterically at him, which made my head hurt so badly I wanted to cradle it. He thought I understood perfectly and laughed back. Then he threw up. That's what I remember, but maybe it didn't happen; by that point I was already beginning to hallucinate. We took a picture—one of those photos climbers are famous for, with the camera held out at arm's length and aimed toward our conjoined faces. I pulled an inscribed Frisbee from my pack and hucked it far into the crater to honor a friend who'd died in an oil-rig disaster off Newfoundland the year before. In the rarified air, the disc arced across the crater for an awfully long time before spiraling down into the toxic miasma rising from a vent encrusted in lurid yellow sulfur.

That seemed right: a petroleum-based product swallowed by the very earth that generated it; a fitting farewell for someone who'd been in service of that substance when he slipped quietly into hypothermic slumber, bobbing in the roiling North Atlantic, never to be found, returning to the sea from whence we all came.

These were the kinds of thoughts I had while skiing.

THE VARIOUS TRAILS I'd followed to the summit of Pico de Orizaba—Mexico's highest mountain and North America's loftiest volcano at 18,504 feet—had started in my parents' living room as an adolescent. Years after my first time on skis, I'd come across a unique juxtaposition in a coffee-table book about Mexico: a full-page, black-and-white photo of an old Spanish church with a massive, snow-covered volcano—pulled preternaturally close by a telephoto lens, I now know—looming behind. Snow in Mexico? Wow. Could you *ski* on something like that? It planted a seed of secret desire.

In high school I'd taken up skiing in earnest with Merl and a few other friends. The lift-serviced partying that essentially defined the sport in the hard-packed conditions of Eastern Canada was for us both social activity and healthy conduit to dissipate teenage energy. We'd jumped in just as the ever-evolving sport's context was shifting yet again.

In the late sixties and early seventies, North American youth challenged every aspect of the status quo. Nothing was sacred, even the supposedly footloose sport of skiing, longtime poster child of the hedonistic, jet-setting nouveau riche. An overzealous, corporate-minded ski industry was focused on lifts, groomed runs, and fancy condos at the expense of the gravity-driven, wind-and-snow-in-the-face sensations that attracted people in the first place, and young skiers railed against this packaged experience. They rejected the strictures associated with alpine racing and constipated European ski technique, innovating with mogul skiing, aerial maneuvers, and ski ballet (later re-branding it "acro-skiing" didn't postpone its extinction), a troika collectively known as "freestyle."

Freestyle skiing essentially put the boots to technique—damning convention and embracing invention—liberally fueled by the passing of weed and jugs of wine. This fit with the rebel-id of every teen, and our bedrooms were papered with requisite posters of freestyle antihero heroes like Wayne Wong, "Airborne Eddie" Ferguson, Suzy Chaffee, and Scott Brooksbank sporting short, colorful skis, science-experiment bindings of questionable security, and sloppy, equally questionable rear-entry boots (back-buckling boots that made it easier to slip your foot in but that destabilized the overall boot structure). We also dressed and acted the part by skiing gang style in logo-adorned lab coats, bright-green gaiters, and the occasional top hat, executing ridiculous tricks like Tipstands and Wongbangers (a front flip between your poles) in lift lines where they were sure to effect maximum annoyance. We rode our skis in the backseat (i.e., on their tails), eschewing style in favor of simply wiggling our asses to turn, built illegal jumps in full view, got upside down off them when we could, and, for our considerable trouble, were thrown off every mountain we visited. If freestylers were skiing's punks, we'd aimed to be the Sex Pistols.

Ardent rock climbers and canoeists, Merl and I also shared a more conventional outdoor interest that had been piqued by school ski trips to the American West's larger mountains. There we'd gazed longingly at the bowls and faces staring back from beyond the ski-area boundaries. We weren't alone: skiers were ducking ropes, climbing peaks, and taking helicopters and snowcats into the great white beyond to rediscover the joys of fresh, untracked snow that had begotten the sport. We thus found ourselves with eyes widening simultaneously toward the open rebellion of freestyle and the quieter freedoms of open backcountry. Like Alice through the looking glass, I eventually stumbled across a perfect portal into both on a magazine rack in the Toronto subway system one slushy day in the mid-seventies.

In 1972, David and Jake Moe, Seattle brothers living in Sun Valley, Idaho, set out to capture the new vibes flowing through ski country with an experiential, literary, and visual homage called *POWDER: Journal of the Other Ski Experience*. Despite bad poetry, stream-of-consciousness writing, and a surreal cover depicting skiers tracking up the moon, the magazine would redefine the sport in the eyes of many. As Steve Casimiro, *POWDER* editor from 1987–98, put it in his introduction to the twentieth anniversary issue:

> *POWDER* embodied the soul of skiing and the spirit of those fighting commercialism and searching for lost ideals. To understand its impact in 1972, you have to understand what came before: not much. Other ski magazines were boring and bland—establishment publications that mirrored the mainstream and painted the world in black and white. *POWDER* ripped the lid off. All of a sudden

there was a world in Technicolor, a world of backcountry lunacy, of powder so deep you choked, of speeds so fast you could die. It was a world alive, a world that existed in the acts of madmen and idiots, a world that seethed and surged and finally found legitimacy in a weird little publication from Sun Valley.[1]

Leafing through a copy of what had since become POWDER: The Skier's Magazine, I was captivated by its unique ethos, embodied literally and figuratively in the title. The issue's cover featured a close-up of a wool-toqued hippie, snow crystals constellating his hat, ice clinging to a beard encircling open-mouthed joy that clearly said "best run ever." It was unusual fodder for an action-sport magazine but brilliant and effective: I instantly wanted whatever it was the dude had just experienced. I was also impressed by the magazine's focus on the unexpected places (both mental and physical) that skiing could take you, including, in another issue, a colorful story about climbing and skiing Mexico's highest volcanoes by the infamous (I was soon apprised) American ski-adventuring duo of Tom Carter and Alan Bard. Whoa.

The long-buried seed began a silent, stealthy sprouting.

AFTER A YEAR at southern Ontario's University of Waterloo—undertaken mostly to convince our parents we were serious enough to possibly return—Merl and I executed a familiar ritual for young eastern skiers: heading west for a winter in the Rocky Mountains. We spent the first part of the ski season cringing at −40°F on the slopes of Banff, Alberta, then road-tripped in our converted van around the western states well into spring. Following our freestyle heros in cutting a swath of beer, bongs, babes, and bumps (our passion was moguls at the time), we had the adventure we'd hoped for and more. But after landing dutifully back in school, we found our newly minted alpine savvy constrained by funds and time. To continue our love affair with snow, we took up cross-country skiing and telemarking—the latter an arcane but rapidly re-popularizing downhilling technique that uses Nordic-style freeheel bindings in which your boot is anchored only at the toe. (Alpine bindings have lock-down heels.)

Freeheel alpine skiing, as this combination is more correctly referred to (the telemark is simply a drop-kneed turn accomplished on any freeheel ski), was suddenly the new freestyle, attracting skiing's always edgy and inventive fringe. Ski freaks flocked to it in droves, tweaking, reinventing, and putting a twentieth-century stamp on the genre, propelled by *POWDER* and the growing popularity of ski videos. Freeheel equipment was light, maneuverable, and versatile, turning tiny hills of any stripe into challenging—albeit wobbly—descents and allowing skiers to climb freely (physically *and* financially) up the slopes at commercial areas and ski down. It was, however, a rural backcountry knob that became the center of our nascent freeheel universe: a mere grassy pimple rising from surrounding cornfields, an oblong blip on a 1:25,000 topographic map, Killer Hill nevertheless loomed large in local mythology.

KILLER HILL POPPED up about ten thousand years ago, when the retreating terminus of a continental glacier hesitated long enough for meltwater to deposit a load of silt into a massive ice cavern. When the glacier moved on, a mound remained where the cavern had been. Geologists called it a kame; local ski-touring guru Chris Hart used another name.

No one had actually died there, but several people *had* seen God—and there wasn't always smoke or wine involved. We were hard-pressed to squeeze three turns down its miserly, sixty-foot flanks, and yet Killer Hill held its own innate challenge. The icy boilerplate snow of the perpetually scoured windward side could send us rocketing out of control, legs akimbo, at the slightest provocation. The more desirable and usually powdery lee side was overhung by a massive cornice, and the bottom of the hill ended in an electrified barbed-wire cattle fence that, depending on snow depth, stood ankle- to knee-high, incapacitating more than a few unfortunate skiers.

Starved for downhill turns in this soporific landscape, we'd taken—with trepidation—to these skinny cross-country boards and their three-pin bindings (three upright metal pins fit into three holes under the boot's toe, clamped together by a pathetic metal bail). However, on my first outing with Hart one November, he'd climbed me up all 300 feet of Mt. Chicopee, the still-shuttered regional ski area, linked my arm through his for balance, said "just do what I do," and led me on a hitherto unheard-of telemark descent through the pulsating mists of snow guns.

"*That*, grasshopper," he'd intoned didactically at the bottom, "is where it's at."

And so it was. We dug into old ski literature to learn more about the technique, analyzing grainy photos of pipe-smoking gentlemen in tweed jackets genuflecting over heinously long and heavy wooden planks. Then we set out to plumb the paltry powder stashes of the countryside on our "pins"; our thirst for vertical undiminished, we merely added it up in smaller denominations. Maybe we were drawn to Killer Hill's isolation, appearing as it did on the horizon no matter from which direction we approached. Or maybe it simply represented the essence of skiing as we'd come to understand it: getting out there and manufacturing fun with some element of risk—even if the danger was only a couple of strings of rusted barbed wire.

I'd also learned from Hart how folks crouched atop Killer Hill in every season, the burning-hay incense of homegrown marijuana curling skyward while they watched maples bud into spring, sway green through the torpid days of summer, morph into fall's familiar colors, then drop the entire palette in a clamor of wind and rain to leave silver branches naked and frosted and reaching. Waiting, as we all were, for snow.

There was a collective belief—of the type exacerbated by incense—that truth and beauty dwelt on Killer Hill. Or that its vistas of farm, forest, and fence somehow formed a crucible of creative realization—like the shallow summit depression we mythologized as a meteorite crater. Atop it, picnicking with a date on a halcyon summer day, I'd find myself anticipating a winter that couldn't return soon enough. Daydreaming of downcast TV weather forecasters visibly unhappy over the arrival of Arctic outflows they were reporting, I joyously imagined those same air masses bearing down, plucking moisture from the Great Lakes (proving these polluted water bodies were still good—er, *great*—for something), forming flakes, and enveloping this very spot. I thought about the phone call that would inevitably come on a crisp morning after a heavy snowfall. "Hey," Hart would mumble in the low, conspiratorial tone that was his wont, "I know you've probably got work to do, but why don't you blow it off and we'll go out to Killer Hill?" Inevitably, the girl I lay in the grass with would catch my preoccupation.

"What are you thinking about?" she'd whisper.

Whiteout. A swirl of flakes blowing drifts across a cornfield and obscuring my vision. Cold air stinging my nostrils. Squinting along fence rows, straining through the blizzard for Killer Hill's looming, lopsided form. It was always there, hovering in the howling distance.

"Nothing," I'd reply with a grin that started somewhere back in the Pleistocene era of high school ski trips and stretched into whatever adventure the future held. "Just hills."

CHASING GRAVITY WAS our food; finding it the flavor. Being only a bite-sized thrill, however, Killer Hill kept us hungry, and our appetites increased in kind. By autumn 1983, a year into a master's degree, I'd photocopied the volcano from my parents' book and mailed it to Merl, labeling it with one word: December. Some form of affirmative drifted back. Then we waited for a green light: the first snowfall.

For me, those first flakes that fell each year were cause to run (often embarrassingly) onto a porch or into the street screaming. The Zen of Winter started with eagerly tracking a lone flake to Earth, then another, and another. I was mesmerized to see how and where these crystals found purchase: leaning against a tiny pebble on the road, deliquescing on the hood of a car, wedged between two blades of grass. At night I'd pull a chair to the front window to watch snow explode in every direction, dramatically illuminated by the glow of streetlamps. I enjoyed and even sickly craved driving at night in heavy snow, flicking on my high-beams to create an even more disorienting effect. I thought cable television's new Weather Channel—with its enthusiastic, meteorologically savvy hosts and blinking red warnings—was the best fucking invention *ever*.

It was all about snow, man, and snow was special. Not so much for nonskiers though, who more often dreaded a big snowfall's travel delays and traffic gridlock, and the effort required for its removal. They did have a point: snow could sometimes be a yin-yang proposition.

On the day we were to leave for Mexico, a blizzard descended. Merl and I were, as usual, enthusiastic about the snow in a late-night, beery kind of way—until it dawned on us that we could be trapped. Already people's cars were sealed in their driveways, and we needed to drive several hours to make our flight. We'd have to start early. In the dark, we knocked on my neighbor's door. Our plight unspoken, Kenny the Snowblower simply nodded understanding, disappeared inside, then reemerged adorned in his Toronto Maple Leafs toque and windowpane glasses to release our truck from its tomb with his new machine. It was a task he relished, and, honor among snow men, we saluted him as we fishtailed up the street into the maelstrom.

AFTER FAILING TO recruit Hart or other local adventurers for the Mexico mission, Merl and I had zeroed in on the two highest volcanoes on Mexico's Central Plateau and gathered what beta we could. We'd made sketchy photocopies of even sketchier road, climbing, and ski routes. We raced stairs, ran distances, lifted weights, and practiced crevasse rescue on ropes hung from trees. The latter exercise proved moot: we accidentally left the rope at home in the mad, hungover, pre-dawn rush to get to the airport.

"I thought you said *you* had the rope," became our instant running joke.

According to Aztec legends, Popocatépetl is a warrior god. According to everyone else, it's a big frickin' volcano: North America's fifth-highest peak at 17,802 feet. In either case, it has inspired many to ascend its lava and ice flanks: the Aztecs threw human sacrifices into the smoldering maw; Hernán Cortés lowered men into the crater to fetch sulfur for gunpowder; climbers use the easily accessed high altitude to train for Himalayan expeditions; and, every once in a while, adventurous skiers turn up at the orange-roofed Vincenzo Guaretta hostel at 13,000 feet. Picture a 150-bed Howard Johnson motel with picnic benches at Everest Base Camp, and you can see why it's a good place to acclimatize and make friends with people who have acute altitude sickness and digestive problems. We settled in to eat fiery *huevos rancheros* and drink cheap beer, the country's only certifiably safe liquid.

After a couple days, our heart rates below two hundred beats per minute (barely), we were ready to climb the volcano. Six hours later we were at the top. From the POWDER article, we knew it to be a challenging but exhilarating descent down almost 2,000 feet of forty-degree slope. Could we keep our wits about us? In fresh snow it would be a heavenly plunge, but our introduction to volcano skiing didn't quite measure up.

To start, it hadn't snowed in months. Our chattering, popcorn-light, first-generation telemark skis were never meant for such tired, rock-hard surfaces—though having learned to ski them on eastern Canadian ice offered some hope of salvation. Falling in these conditions would mean a high-speed slide and eventual launch onto the razor-sharp vestiges of a lava-edged glacier. The upper slope was veneered in volcanic dust, and the sulfur-redolent plume rising from the crater billowed downward to engulf us. But, young and foolish, we were ready for anything that even remotely resembled skiing.

On top of unpleasant respiratory conditions, we'd picked the most popular climbing day of the year to be on Mexico's most popular summit. The feast of Our Lady of Guadalupe is a national holiday on which scores of weekend *alpinistas,* oblivious to the thin, odiferous air, pilgrimage up the *vólcan*'s icy slopes brandishing homemade crampons and ice axes. Half of Mexico was on top of Popo that day, and all of them were watching in disbelief as we stepped onto our skis. Separated from the lava fields by bulletproof ice and pock-marked, sun-crusted snow, we adjusted our equipment, readjusted our nerves, and pushed off. Gasping for air and unsteady on my toothpick skis under a massive, swaying pack, I felt like I was skiing for the first time ever. Merl, too. He tripped up within a few turns, immediately rocketing down a lava-studded snow patch toward certain mincing. Climbers are trained to self-arrest such falls by digging the tip of an ice axe or other equipment into the snow, but Merl somehow stopped himself by dragging his fingers. Warned, we composed ourselves and continued the descent.

The skiing was difficult, and we really only adjusted to it as we neared the bottom of the pitch. Puzzled brown faces peered down from the crater rim while below, tan desert rose to meet us; there would be no lift-line backslapping at the end of this run. Eventually we stood in the lava field, dazed, hearts racing, altitude headaches replaced by adrenalin buzzes. To the east and barely visible stood Pico de Orizaba.

After conquering Popo we beat a hasty retreat, bouncing our rental car east down the mountain on streambed roads to the edge of the Caribbean slope and Tlachichuca, a mining town whose walls still display the bulletholes of Emiliano Zapata's socialist revolution. We dodged piles of garbage and raced tumbleweeds down dusty streets to the home of Joaquín Canchola Limón. As the owner of the only four-wheel drive truck in town, Joaquín was in the business of ferrying climbers to a small stone hut at 14,000 feet on Orizaba's northern flank. We pitched our tent in his yard for the night, then as we enjoyed (for the moment) his wife's special Our Lady of Guadalupe tamales, Joaquín pointed out a notation in his dog-eared register by none other than Alan Bard and Tom Carter, who'd first conquered these peaks on pins in the late seventies.

"Sharpen your edges *and* your minds," it read simply.

The entry seemed pertinent; it was only two weeks old.

"It doesn't say anything about a rope," Merl offered.

In the hut on Orizaba we endured a fitful, heart-pounding, rodent-ridden night. At some point I dreamed I was with Cortés's men when they'd descended into Popo's crater.

"Señor, can you throw me a rope," a silver-helmeted *conquistador* cried up to me as I gazed down from the rim.

"I thought *you* brought the rope," I called back through cupped hands.

In the cold dark of 4 a.m., we tamped down ominously churning bellyfuls of intestine-eroding tamales with raisin-and-rat-turd-peppered oatmeal, then started our summit bid.

We climbed through a spectacular fuchsia sunrise, not a sailor-be-warned portent of any approaching storm but merely the supercharged murk of distant Mexico City's ever-lapping smog. Reaching the toe of the glacier around 6 a.m., we changed from (freezing) canvas running shoes into (freezing) leather telemark boots and ill-fitting crampons and began the long, upward slog toward Orizaba's ragged rim. As we stood wobbly atop the volcano around 10 a.m., we looked east to the blue of the Caribbean, while behind us, reclining elegantly in cinnamon sheets on the western horizon—smoking seductively—lay Popocatépetl.

We stood there for what was only a moment but seemed like forever, foolishly enjoying the dangerous hubris of having ascended with no rope, before one of us came to our senses.

"Let's get the fuck down," said Merl.

Our wheezy breathing and occluded thinking were possible signs of deadly high-altitude pulmonary and cerebral edema, and it was indeed clear we had to get lower in a hurry. Moving fast, however, was neither possible nor a particularly good idea: mountain descents—whether by foot or on skis—are notorious for exploiting and claiming victims of exhaustion, inattention, and, particularly, hubris.

My crampons were strapped onto my boots in a series of figure eights, and fumbling them off with frozen hands took forever, stowing them an eternity. Bending to slip the toe of one flimsy telemark boot into the always difficult rat-trap ski binding, I nearly blacked out and had to sit down. Merl was having similar difficulties. Getting our skis on was like repairing a watch while drunk. When we were finally ready, maybe, we checked each other for loose objects. Sanity seemed the only thing not locked down tight.

I had the honor of going first this time and was determined not to repeat Merl's fall on Popo. But Orizaba was a different story; its extra 1,000 vertical feet of glacier were steeper by far. My first few turns on its linoleum surface were on close to a fifty-degree incline that dropped me mockingly into a crevasse field. I made one heart-pounding hop turn, then two, followed by a quick but unsteady traverse to avoid a couple of crevasses. Legs shaking, I stopped to hang over my poles and catch my labored breath. Another *vuelta* and then... disaster. Setting up for the next turn, I caught the edge of my inside ski on a tiny, unyielding piece of rock embedded in the ice and was thrown off balance; before I could react, the weight of my pack carried my center of gravity past my feet and tipped me over, downhill. Just like that I was sliding headfirst out of control.

Damn, we should have been skiing on a rope here!

Of course it was too late for that kind of thinking—or any thinking, really. Instinctively I wormed my body around on the snow, working to get my head uphill and my feet below me. Even with that accomplished, the edges of my skis found no purchase on the slick surface. With no ice axe at the ready to self-arrest with, I struggled a mittened hand out of its pole strap and slid it down the pole's metal shaft, grasping it above the basket with both hands, rolling onto my belly, and digging the metal point in with all the strength I could muster. My clothing bunched up, exposing my stomach to the abrasive ice and rock, but I could feel myself slowing, giving me impetus to dig even harder by pulling myself toward the pole basket with flexing elbows. And then, miraculously, I simply stopped and it was silent.

I lay hanging onto the pole, huffing lips pressed to the snow as if, somehow, more oxygen might be found there. I had the presence of mind not to try changing positions, pending evaluation. Looking down, I saw that my ankles and skis hung over the edge of the crevasse that, while not large enough to disappear into completely was big enough to snap a leg.

Merl skied down tentatively.

"Touché," he said in the understated way naïve idiots often respond to anything of consequence. We were *Dumb and Dumber* before it was even fashionable: still alive in spite of ourselves.

After this incident, things improved. The slope mellowed below the crevasse field, the skiing became easier and our turns wider. The surface had softened enough in the muted sunlight to send small sprays off the tails of our boards as we arced slowly toward the toe of the glacier. Our frozen feet, pounding headaches, and dizziness evaporated at around 17,000 feet, and back at our starting point, we suddenly felt strong again. When we took off our skis and looked back at our tracks—kindergarten finger-wiggles through the soft icing of the lower glacier—a huge sense of accomplishment enveloped us. Bard and Carter may have been here first, but we were the first Canadians to descend Orizaba on freeheel gear, and second best was always good enough for us.

Back at the hut, Joaquín awaited, as promised, with cold beer. It was Miller time, Mexican-style. Bouncing toward Tlachichuca in the back of his truck, I stared after the massive form of Orizaba hunched on the horizon, and all I could see was Killer Hill's gentle shoulders. Skiing really could take you from your backyard to something that approximated the moon. After a long, winding, snowy road of some ten years, the seed planted by my parents' coffee-table book had come to fruition. A quest fulfilled.

Or had it only started?

2 | A BUM'S RUSH

What I really feel is that, if on a pair of skis...
I forget everything except the joys of living...
Well, why in God's name not stay on skis?
VISCOUNT ANTHONY KNEBWORTH *in a*
letter to his father, Earl of Lytton, 1924

IN THE morning after a heavy rain, Santiago, Chile, was sort of like the basement of paradise. Its ubiquitous smog had been washed down gutters, the acrid smell of diesel exhaust replaced by musty garden scents and flowers. On downtown *paseos*, businesspeople rushed from coffee and morning papers toward whatever *encuentro* awaited. In surrounding neighborhoods, distant horns crowed over eager milkmen pushing ancient, squeaking carts and clanging bells to rouse customers. Towering above the city to the east loomed snow-capped heaven: when you could see them like this, the Andes formed a monolith of surreal scale.

It was usually magical anticipation that followed me out of the city on such a day, but that morning found me glancing over my shoulder at the sound of every footfall, certain I was being pursued. Shouldering my pack, I fought my way onto a bus and out to the police barrier that marked the start of most mountain roads in this country, seeking a ride up to Farrellones, the ski town I then called home. After my passport was approved by a couple of grim-looking *carabineros*, I joined a sightseeing Israeli couple in a *collectivo* taxi on the familiar heart-stopping ride up the canyon. Settling back in my seat, I shut my eyes and wondered how things could have got so crazy. What the hell was I doing there?

Part of the answer was easy: I was a ski bum in South America.

IN SOME WAYS, the previous few months had been a classic traveler's saga; in others, the quintessential search for myself. Mostly, however, they'd served up a sensory overload.

Starting at the southern tip of the continent in late March, I'd hiked and skied alone through Patagonia's Torres del Paine National Park, where I was followed by a puma for two days. I never saw or heard it but had only to retrace my steps a few hundred feet to see its eerily massive prints overlaying my own. Mid-May found me in the southern port of Punta Arenas on the Straits of Magellan, hunkered down in a bar. The soccer on television was interrupted by a report of massive snowfalls, road closures, catastrophic avalanches, and death in the Andes near Santiago. The bar patrons were universally horrified and glad they weren't there—a disaster zone was the last place you'd want to be. But not me.

Ski bumming is a dedication to snow-sliding strong enough to make you ignore danger, shirk responsibility, eschew common comforts, and live near the bottom of the food chain, all in the name of making turns. I'd had my tastes of this time-honored rite of passage—skipping class in university whenever there was a big dump of snow, the overly freezing winter stint in Banff and subsequent tour of the Rockies with Merl in our van—but I'd always longed for something beyond the packed slopes and posh trappings of the home experience. The prospect of an adventure longer than the week I'd spent in Mexico had lured me to the Southern Hemisphere.

Upon completing my undergrad degree, I'd decided to reward myself with the delinquency of a summer of skiing. With only two reliable choices—South America or New Zealand—I'd flipped a coin that came up *cabezas*. So off I went, in the North American spring of 1982 (austral autumn), with more gear than the Austrian alpine team, alone, unilingual, and not just a bit naïve. After all, when you're a twenty-five-year-old product of pampered Western culture, the world is still one big friendly place and you're indestructible, the realities of life's inherent fragility yet to sink in. A lesson that foreign ski bumming is unusually adept at teaching.

When the snow started falling in Chile, I headed north from Patagonia and eventually talked my way into a job at a ski area within a couple of hours' drive of Santiago. Bunking in a large, wood-and-stone *refugio* high in the Andes with a happy-go-lucky crew of international instructors and patrollers seemed just what I was after. But all was not well in the area. Tension lingered from the 1973 American-backed coup that had ousted freely elected communist president Salvador Allende; military patrols of the infamous mass-murderer General Augusto Pinochet's ruling junta ranged the slopes with unholstered guns (they were poor skiers and, so the locals said, even poorer shots). Whether or not they were simply maintaining a show of force or searching for subversives among a jet-set crowd dominated by wealthy Brazilians, diplomats, and Pan Am flight attendants was never clear, but they seemed oblivious to the gun-running, cocaine smuggling, and extortion around them.

This I knew from having an unwelcome ear to the ground. In addition to working on the mountain, I ended up running the boutique/bar in the ski shop. It was the social hub of the resort, the place to gather after a frenzied day on the slopes, and it was there that I finally learned Spanish (I'd been passed—barely—in a high school course only after promising the instructor *never* to take Spanish again).

The sunny days above treeline on the resort's wide-open slopes were long and heady, the patio perpetually full of fashion-conscious types power-drinking white wine and shucking fresh mussels hauled from a coast that could be seen from the mountain on rare, smog-free days. Everything was larger than life there, including the people.

Characters were everywhere, starting with the *chanchos de cadenas* (chain pigs), a bedraggled, barefoot lot that stumbled like zombies along the shoulders of the approach road during snowstorms, and that for the equivalent of two cents affixed chains to your vehicle's tires with broken tools. There was the platoon of American instructors in the ski school, a French-Canadian who lived in a snow cave above the first chairlift, a handful of down-and-out pro racers from Europe. The ambience was both international (the ghost of racer Spider Sabich ruled the slopes; the celebrated and once-frequent visitor had been shot dead in Aspen, Colorado, by actress Claudine Longet) and, like all foreign ski destinations, uniquely local (drunk on *pisco*, the mountain manager rolled the new $150,000 German grooming machine on its first day of operation).

There was history. I learned that Norwegian and British engineers introduced skis here during the construction of the trans-Andean railway in 1910. Public consciousness of the sport caught up in 1913, when a Chilean diplomat

who'd lived in Norway organized a ski tour to the popular
Maipo volcano; then Germans and Austrians in conjunc-
tion with well-to-do Chileans, started the Ski Club of Chile,
and used mining roads to build cabins at Farellones and
shape the first resorts, like Portillo. A gaggle of French skiers had more or less built this place by hand during Chile's
sweltering summers.

The weather? Apparently no North American knew what
El Niño meant the year I was in Chile, but I had a front-row
seat: as I'd seen on television, the first storm of the year
had sparked unprecedented flooding in Santiago, destroy-
ing *barrios* and upscale neighborhoods alike, carrying people away in the process. At Portillo, the storm dropped
nearly ten feet of snow onto otherwise dry slopes; it all slid,
killed some police in a patrol shack, destroyed a lift, and
submerged the road under twenty-five feet of icy cement.
It took weeks to clear. This pattern was repeated all winter, with ski areas closed for days at a time. At mine, life
rose and fell around the single *máquina* available to clear
all roads and parking areas. Snow blew in so hard during
one hellacious three-day *tormenta* that the bull wheel of the
main chairlift was actually buried; the lift cable and suspended chairs emerged from the snow as if from underwa-
ter. A man trying to uncover his car ended up so deep that
by the time he reached the vehicle's roof he had to be rescued from the snow pit he'd dug.

Frequent earthquakes tended to shake snow loose from
all but the most tenacious slopes, heightening avalanche
conditions. When the glasses hanging over my bar started
rattling, someone would yell *terremoto!* and we'd all run outside to safety. Just as often, we would exit only to discover
that the shaking was a military helicopter coming to evacu-
ate another victim of a peculiar local trend: people regularly
skied into lift lines out of control at outrageous speeds, and

injuries abounded. My on-mountain activities were dominated by shoveling off flat roofs, placing bamboo poles
where someone was likely to hit them, and removing the
doors from various structures to use as backboards to strap
down the latest lift-line victims. Out of bounds? There was
no such thing. We could go where we wanted, and people
did, followed by a squadron of hopeful Andean condors.

And yet, so much was great. The endless sunshine
between storms, the endless western view in the mornings, and the endless nights—which seemed bottled, ready
to be uncorked at will. You had but to say the word *fiesta*
and a party would happen. The people were warm, friendly,
sincere, and only occasionally dangerous, especially the
smiling, tanned, oh-so-intense women—married ones in
particular.

The skiing was beyond my wildest expectations, and
the frequent closures meant we often had the mountain to
ourselves. Bottomless powder could be found days after a
storm on the right slope. There was the 1,000-vertical-
foot couloir above the area, a pilgrimage we made on full-
moon nights so that you could drop into the slot just as *la
luna* pulled directly overhead. On such occasions, things
often had an electric-blue halo around them, an artifact of
ingesting magic mushrooms shipped north from Chile's
austral rain forests. It was full-tilt crazy but also endear-
ing: a culture struggling to preserve itself on one hand and
trying to emulate the materialistic trappings of *norte amer-
icanos* on the other. For a rube ski fanatic with little to compare it to, it delivered the experience of a lifetime.

The very reason for ski bumming.

AS EVEN NONSKIERS know, skiing can be a consuming
passion. Just *what,* then, is the shape of this fixation? Start
here: instructors and coaches obsessed with technique;

gearheads beset over the minutiae of equipment and design; other skiers simply and singly preoccupied with the various attributes of terrain (piste, moguls, steeps, chutes, glades) or jargon-laden meteorology (orographic precipitation, upslope storms, pineapple expresses, katabatic winds). Some ski writers are consumed with the physics of snow itself, penning columns on crystal formation and configuration and the temperatures at which it happens; water content and related phenomena like rime, graupel, and sleet—even the angle at which the Earth leans away from the sun in order to cause winter (known as axial tilt, it's 23.5 degrees). There are abundant places in which to explore these notions, including some twenty national and international ski and snowboard titles that clutter magazines racks in North America alone—more publications than those devoted to surfing, skateboarding, hiking, and climbing.

Evidence of this peculiar mania lies in a glut of "I've been there" me-bris: ski gear and roofboxes adorned with resort-logo stickers; hats constellated with ski-area pins; jackets hung with clattering collections of weather-worn lift tickets. Likewise, there's no end to the bizarre collateral that says "I'm a Skier." Bumper stickers announce, "I ♥ Big Dumps" and "If Hell Freezes Over I'll Ski That, Too." Auto knick-knacks like license-plate brackets and seatbelt covers scream "Ski Utah" or "Ski Tahoe," turning vehicles into rolling chambers of commerce for the mountain ranges of their drivers' fancy.

What is it about this particular badge—one rarely encountered in other individual sports like surfing or climbing—that so appeals to skiers? Here's a clue: since you don't see stickers claiming "I've been to Rogers Pass" or other favored lift-free snow stashes, perhaps it has to do with skiing's conspicuous infrastructure and the fact that ski resorts are—or once were—built to attract like-minded individuals. While in some cases skiing was merely grafted onto pre-existing mountain locations, in others whole towns have sprouted *solely* because of the sport.

Society makes it hard to live simply and in the moment, so ski aficionados of all stripes are usually making some kind of sacrifice to get their fix. Which is why ski bums take perverse pleasure in the identity of a couch-surfing, dumpster-diving existence; the greater the sacrifice, the richer the reward. Some hang onto the ideal their entire lives, proudly wearing it on their sleeves, while others cover it up with the onion skins of career, family, and other facets of existence. But like a jungle tribe suddenly forced to relocate to a city and wear suits, true ski bums never lose a sensitivity to the perceived threats to their simple traditions. The kind of threats that progress and development ultimately deliver.

Mike Berard, a writer, photo contributor, and one-time editor of Canada's *SKIER* magazine, still has a self-confessed obsession with the ski-bum life that almost always finds its way into his columns and features.

"This rootsy, cool, vibrant part of my life really stands out now that everything's more complicated," he says, alluding to ski-bumming's Peter Pan qualities. "When all you had to do was ski, or wake up to a shitty job you were only doing so you could ski, life was carefree and simple.

"I met a construction worker in Fernie, [British Columbia] who exemplifies the ski-bum dichotomy," Berard continues. "He snowboards all winter, and in the off-season wants a job that lets him bank enough money to keep doing it. New construction projects give him that *but...* he doesn't want to see too much new business bringing more tourists to town to steal his fresh tracks. Only it's too late—the change is already there and he's participating in it. Fernie has expanded a ton, and more citizens and tourists are what keep the mountain operating for guys like him."

This unsettling trade-off is the new reality for most mountain towns, and it drives the most obsessed skiers into the unfettered realm of the backcountry, or to remoter towns where the tide of change hasn't risen too high. "Itinerant" is part of the credo: ski bum and ski gypsy were always one and the same.

These notions are mined endlessly in ski media, and though much of skiing has become the aegis of the wealthy, even these folks can relate. Connecting with the ski-bum ethos is maintaining contact with the grass roots; celebrating the core and its dedication to gravity. Above all there is this: ski-bumming's essence—the compelling human arc of struggle and survival to achieve a certain idealistic end—never grows old as a storyline.

The National Film Board of Canada's 2002 *Ski Bums,* shot in and around Whistler, British Columbia, follows an eclectic cast of oddly nicknamed characters from their resort life to the high-alpine world beyond the ropes to investigate the attitudes and emotions of those for whom snow-riding isn't just a *way* of life, but life itself. Although much is gleaned from the subjects' candid comments, including how and why they regularly walk a tightrope between life and death in the mountains, the movie's true charm lies in its depiction of cliché: an indigent ski bum living in a van or squat, eating peoples' unfinished food in the lodge cafeteria; making soup from the free hot water, ketchup, and crackers available; and poaching the bathing facilities of high-class hotels.

Almost predictably, the filmmakers are ski bums themselves. Portraying this lifestyle is nothing new. Dick Barrymore's 1969 movie, *Last of the Ski Bums,* followed a tradition begun by ski-film icon Warren Miller, who built a multimillion-dollar empire on the movies he churned out each year in Sun Valley, Idaho (where David and Jake Moe were also stationed when they started the ski bum's bible,

POWDER). Miller and his ski-bum buddies lived in tents and trailers, hunted (with guns) for food, and made pocket money where and when they could by instructing, shilling books of self-penned ski cartoons, and, eventually, touring Miller's celebrated annual movies through ski towns. Though Warren is no longer personally involved, the fall classics bearing his name now play to thousands in every major city on the continent.

Ski bumming's storied history reaches well back into the sport's literary tradition and possibly as far as its modern roots. As author Peter Shelton has noted, "ski bum"—a decidedly postwar phrase first mentioned in *Ski* magazine in 1948 ("Inside Report: Ski Bums Wait Table, Ogle Heiresses") and immortalized in a 1950 *Life* magazine pictorial set in Sun Valley ("*Life* Visits Some Ski Bums")—quickly acquired succinct definition: anyone who wanted to ski so badly they were willing to give up anything to do so.[2]

"The word bum came out of the Depression, but the meaning took a turn after World War II," Miller is quoted as saying. "A lot of people hit the road then, and it was almost a badge of honor not to be locked into the 9-to-5... The words freedom and ski bum are inextricably intertwined."

In 1962, when skiing was still considered a fringe activity, *Sports Illustrated* published "The Oldest Ski Bum in the World" about New York–based Leon Vart, a Russian artist whose path began when he found a discarded ski in Moscow at age thirteen. He may or may not have been the oldest person, but his was a story emblematic of an esoteric subculture barely on the public radar as skiing and resort development entered their Golden Age:

'Because I am poor, I must live among the rich.' At 73, [Vart] can afford such candor. It's about all he can afford, since ski bumming is a hand-to-mouth life... He relies on ingenuity (the next best thing to money) to get around and stay comfortably lodged. His lean, tall figure moves with ease and grace, though his blue eyes are faded from the glare of snow and sky... he has bartered his services as a painter, translator, correspondent, waiter, baby-and-dog-sitter, and ski instructor for the privilege of skiing in Europe, Asia, Africa, Australia, New Zealand and across the United States and Canada.[3]

Readers at the time likely saw Vart as a Beat Generation holdover, but today's skier—rich or poor—would have little trouble recognizing a kindred spirit.

Arnold Lunn, an early doyen of British mountaineering who first skied in 1896 in Chamonix, France, made much of the superior sensations afforded by sliding down a mountain, an act he believed could turn even the tamest terrain into acceptable challenge if not sheer, heart-thumping terror. Although the terminology never arises in his abundant and erudite writings, a ski-bum mindset was at the heart of it for Lunn and the cadre of well-to-do, sport-mad Brits who became the unlikely promulgators of skiing's recreational birth in the Alps. Unbelievably, in the preface to the 1949 second edition of *The Mountains of Youth*, Lunn is already mining the raw-to-this-day lament of ski-bumming's purist soul as an innocence lost to the march of progress, infrastructure, and organization (which, ironically, he contributed significantly to), offering up his own prose as a glue to hold the tribe together:

Ski-ing, as I have tried to show... illustrates the Spenglerian distinction between culture and civilization. Every great cultural cycle begins when a nomad tribe settles down... It is the economy of the farm, the village and the small city which gives birth to great Art... It is from Nature, from Homer's 'life-giving' earth that Art draws its inspiration, the inspiration which vanishes in the giant cities of a dying civilization. Ski-ing has passed through the Spenglerian cycle. It began as a culture in contact with Nature. In the Gothic phase of our sport we skied on snow moulded only by the natural agencies of sun and wind, frost and thaw... In those days, we skiers were as scattered as the primitive communities in which culture is born. Today we struggle in *télépheriques* and funiculars as crowded as the slums of our megalopolitan civilization, and the surface on which we ski is nearly as hard and quite as artificial as the city pavements which mask the kindly earth...

For the ski-runner the snow is no inert mantle on the hills... It is alive with a multiple personality. He learns to love the snow as a friend and to wrestle with it as an enemy... The genuine initiate of the mountain brotherhood has always been in the minority, and I doubt if the multiplication of Ski-hoists and Chair-lifts has either increased or decreased his numbers. Those for whom this book was written will always escape from the pistes. Mountaineering is not a substitute for religion but it has some of the characteristics of a devout cult. The true initiates recognize each other not only when they meet in the flesh, but also when they meet through the medium of the printed word.[4]

Where Lunn beat around the bush with lofty prose, however, others simply lit it on fire. As the literary world's best-known ski bum, Ernest Hemingway was the patron saint of the genre. In the mid-twenties, Hemingway spent two winters in Schruns, Austria, inculcating a serious ski addiction and subsequently popularizing the mindset in stories like "Cross-Country Snow":

"When have you got to go back to school?" Nick asked.

"Tonight," George said. "I've got to get the ten-forty from Montreux."

"I wish you could stick over and we could do the Dent du Lys tomorrow."

"I got to get educated," George said. "Gee, Mike, don't you wish we could just bum together? Take our skis and go on the train to where there was good running and then go on and put up at pubs and go right across the Oberland and up the Valais and all through the Engadine and just take repair kit and extra sweaters and pyjamas in our rucksacks and not give a damn about school or anything."

"Yes, and go through the Schwarzwald that way. Gee, the swell places."[5]

The swell places indeed. Oh, and is it coincidence that Papa Hemingway eventually moved to Sun Valley to finish out his days? (Not that most ski bums end up blowing their brains out; mountain living is generally mind-blowing enough.) Still, Hemingway had it right: ski bumming was at its best and most raw when you were on the move in a foreign land; this was adventure by its very nature.

IN CHILE I'd landed in an outlaw life where everybody looked out for themselves and took nothing for granted. Things there were generally weird enough to debase anyone, but life took a decidedly stranger turn when I came to work one day to find that the shop owner had been replaced by his ex-partner, whom I'd been told was dead. In reality he'd been doing time in the Caribbean—having taken the fall for a larger group in some drug-smuggling scam and losing a wife and young child in the process—and now he was back to claim his share of the business that had been stolen from him. He was a warm, charming man whom I instantly liked more than his predecessor, and with good reason: the latter eventually sent a gang of coked-up, gun-toting fruitcakes and a five-ton truck to reclaim the boutique by cleaning it out in broad daylight.

"What can we do?" I'd asked the head gunman, hoping that if I helped him he'd leave the staff alone.

"Have a drink," he'd laughed, handing me a bottle of whiskey and turning back to supervising his thugs.

Just then the new boss came in and was knocked unconsciousness with a metal pipe. This was so surreal that it was like watching a movie instead of a real act of almost murderous violence. There was a lot of blood and we were more than scared. It was then that my last ounce of innocence soaked into my polypropylene longjohns, along with the contents of my bladder.

So the taxi ride up the mountain with the Israelis was the denouement to this ski-bumming chapter of my life. I'd gone down to Santiago to see the boss in the hospital. He lay there with stitches in his head and a lost-looking grin on his face. He'd probably be OK, they said, but I knew I would never be the same.

My reflection was interrupted when we rounded a hairpin too closely and swerved to avoid an oncoming truck. With the driver braking hard, the vehicle slid through the dirt toward the unprotected embankment, hundreds of feet above the river below. With a loud *thunk,* we stopped with our front wheels overhanging the edge like some *Looney Tunes* Coyote–Road Runner cartoon. The Israelis clutched each other and mumbled prayers as the driver and I clambered into the backseat with them to stabilize the car. We all exited safely through the rear doors. The driver, to his credit extremely apologetic, not-so-much to his credit pledged that he would charge us only the half fare. Anyone else would have kicked him in the junk, but I paid without hesitation, perhaps in an unconscious effort to buy my way back to normalcy. I left them all standing on the road and walked the four steep hours back to the ski area. Mortality of every description was closing in.

Later, I sat on my bed wondering what to do, a mountain of gear and clothing adding to the mental claustrophobia. With the present snowpack, there was at least two months of good skiing left, and I'd come a long, lonesome way for it. Did I really need to leave? Was my drive to ski strong enough to conquer my paranoia? Ski-bumming of the Warren Miller car-camping style was one thing, but this was something apart. I looked out the window at golden canyons colored by the uneasy partnership of descending sun and rising smog. I picked up a pair of socks and tossed them into an open bag. Two days later I left the country.

Like a summer romance, Chile has never left me, and I recall the craziness with a fondness borne of an experience that can never be adequately described. Though much of the wildness of those days is long gone, some memories will never be dislodged: the vastness of the Andes, their wide-open slopes, legendary snowfalls, and cobalt skies; and, always, circling high overhead, the condors, reminding one that life in the mountains is a fragile proposition. And a strangely welcome struggle.

ONE OF THE hallmarks of snowhounds is how shared passion and communal endeavor can, under the right conditions, so easily be bent to the will of the id. Flash-forward twenty-eight years. These days I live in Whistler, where I make my living writing. A certain number of hours per day will deliver the required number of words by a specific deadline. I usually write from 6:30 to 10:00 a.m. in a local coffee shop. But inevitably, from mid-November through the end of April, if it has snowed any measurable amount the previous night and the 6 a.m. snow report looks promising, I will be in the Creekside Gondola line-up by 7:30 a.m. for an 8:15 opening. Rarely am I the first. A similar affliction apparently interferes with many other lives: however employed (or not), whatever façade of respectability is being maintained (or not), we are, one and all, ski bums in heart, soul, and mind.

Many in the morning line-up work nights specifically so they have mornings free *in case* it snows. There's helmet-cam George and pro-snowboarder Dave and his brother. There's perennial racer boy with his weird goggles and absurdly side-cut shape skis, and also seventy-year-old curmudgeon guy with the Austrian accent, who always gets in a shouting match about the fairness of the singles line. Anonymous tall dude rolls up alone with a beaten pair of fat skis and peers conspiratorially over the rim of a coffee that he hopes to stretch until the lift opens. Finally, a skein of painfully sleepy, dreadlocked dirt-bags drift in from parking-lot vans and hippie hovels after a long night of drumming and incense.

This crowd, as stickers announce from the surface of several snowboards, is the Creekside Crew, a frontline phalanx of powder mavens that guards the gates to the kingdom when there's even a whiff of potential face-shots (in ski-bum parlance, snow deep enough to fly up your nose when you turn in it). Some have assembled here for over twenty years; to them, those of us who've joined the fray in the last few anni are mere tourists. But we've nevertheless formed a bond, sharing the anticipation as a family—a family that meets only very early on certain mornings and likely will not see each other after the ride up. Like other family gatherings and the ski world in general, it's hard to discern where the various airs of obligation, ritual, and tradition begin, end, or overlap.

Obligation. We all know that the eight inches of new snow being reported is, due to wind-loading, likely double that on the upper mountain, three times that in the favored stashes we'll each head to.

Ritual. Predictably, no one shares the exact location of those stashes.

Tradition. In the communal, hedonistic world of the ski bum, where few things are sacred, one aphorism rings loud enough to merit cliché: there are no friends on a powder day.

This last is the loudest of skiing's many paeans to obsession—and contradiction. There's nothing quite as fun as navigating the preternatural world of powder with friends, but when push comes to shove—literally, in lift lines or along some traverses—it means that getting to *your* line, *your* turns, *your* face-shots will take precedence over anything. And if you have to barge ahead, losing your friends in a cloud of cold smoke only to find them at the bar at the end of the day to celebrate your respective triumphs, well then, that's the way it's got to be.

3 | INTO THE DEEP

> One can never be bored by powder skiing
> because it . . . only comes in sufficient amounts
> in particular places, at certain times on this
> earth; it lasts only a limited amount of time
> before sun or wind changes it. People devote
> their lives to it "for the pleasure of being so
> purely played" by gravity and snow.
> DELORES LACHAPELLE, *Earth Wisdom*, 1978

THREE HOURS earlier I'd been asleep on a bunk in a Christchurch youth hostel. Now I stood atop a ridge overlooking the steep, snow-choked bowls of New Zealand's Mt. Hutt, the once so-called "ski field in the sky." Hovering 6,000 feet above the town of Methven and the green and brown patchwork of the Canterbury Plains, I watched as surf-raised punk Maoris bedecked in wetsuits and zinc warpaint zigzagged through swinging T-bars (drag lifts on which two riders are pulled uphill on an inverted "T") on waves of Southern Alps snow. On the lodge decks, sheep farmers in generations-old gear tipped back quarts of Steinlager amid the screams of obnoxious keas, the eagle-like mountain parrots best described as green ravens with even more attitude and smarts. Visible from Mt. Hutt's precipitous ridges were several small ski areas lodged in surrounding high-alpine cirques. These "club fields"—thrown up and populated by the most core of NZ's hardcore ski families—were places you couldn't even imagine placing a lift, though each was strung with a single T-bar, poma, rope, or, in some cases, cable that you wore a belt to hook into and that was locally referred to as a "nutcracker." I blinked, filing away the exotic tableau, and dropped into two feet of the only kind of snow that really matters.

My final ski-bumming stint (discounting, many would argue, my current job) was another summer sojourn between university degrees. This time I'd gone looking for powder on the neglected side of that initial coin toss. Alone again, burdened by less and lighter gear (I was now exclusively a telemarker), I'd landed on the South Island one September and hitchhiked, bused, and ferried my way around the country. I skied volcanoes on the North Island, spent a hungry week in a mountain hut waiting out weather in an attempt to climb and ski NZ's highest peak, Mt. Cook, and traipsed through most of the nation's major ski areas. But oddly—or perhaps not—my biggest adventure came on the road.

After news of a big snowfall in the resort hubs of Queenstown and Wanaka, I hitchhiked south from Christchurch, catching my first ride through the folded-cardboard landscapes of the South Island with a sheep rancher. He dropped me in the middle of nowhere, then headed west on what seemed barely a road toward a vast sheep station in the foothills of the Southern Alps. How big was his holding? He rounded up his sheep with a helicopter. I watched the diminishing dust cloud marking the retreat of his rattling pickup for a long while.

After an hour, a car finally materialized on the horizon. It appeared to be bouncing down the road at high speed. It was a dirty-gold, American-made station wagon (most cars

in NZ were British or Japanese); the back was stuffed with
ski bags, duffels, and assorted gear; random items like a
boot, a glove, or a beer bottle were pressed against the windows like a storefront sale. The two occupants seemed to
be fighting with each other over the steering wheel as they
blew past at well over sixty miles per hour. But just as I
dejectedly dropped my thumb, the car screeched to a halt,
then backed up, burning rubber. A couple of long-haired,
smiling faces beamed out.

"Sorry mite, didn't see ya skeeez theea..."

"Yeeh, we wuz wristling..."

"... but then Jiff heea sees 'em lyin' in the greevel, heh?"

"... yeeh, and so I scream 'skeea!', and Geerrett heea..."

"... pulls over, so..."

"... hop een!"

There's a fine line between the ride you'll never forget
and the ride you wish you'd never taken. That line was
somewhere in Geoff and Garrett's car, but as with everything else in the vehicle, no one quite knew where.

The hyperkinetic pair were speed skiers on the NZ
national team. Of skiing's numerous insane disciplines,
speed skiing is by far the most certifiable. In the sport's
equivalent of drag racing, racers squeeze into aerodynamic
suits and helmets, don long, heavy skis, then hurtle down
a steep, straight track until they reach maximum velocity
and pass through an electronic speed trap. Where the track
flattens—the beginning of the long glide to a stop—skiers
are often going so fast that their bodies can't handle the
sudden compression. So they crash. Sometimes they catch
an edge on the track. And crash. Sometimes the air gets
under their skis and lifts them off the snow like a hydrofoil
so they lose control. And crash. Sometimes they crash...
just because. In any case, skiers can be torn apart, breaking
bones that only the tight suit (similar to motorcycle leath-
ers) keep in place.

Conversation revealed that these guys were friends with speed skier Steve McKinney, one of my favorite POWDER mag heroes. Where thrills were concerned, McKinney had done it all: first to break the 200 km/h barrier (125 mph; it has since pushed past 250 km/h, or 150 mph), summited Denali, paraglided off Mt. Everest.

"The faster my body travels, the slower my mind seems to work. In the crescendo of speed, there is no thought, no sound, no vision, no vibration. It is simply instinct and faith,"[6] McKinney famously offered of the womb-like calm inside his self-designed Darth Vader helmet.

Recalling this might have told me what I was in for.

Geoff and Garrett were drinking beer and showed me how they made the car bounce by simultaneously jostling up and down in their seats. Then some high-powered NZ marijuana appeared. I tried not to imbibe, but it was useless: the car was seriously hotboxed and one hit was more than enough. Which made it that much more intense when, at the top of a several-mile downhill, with no warning, Garrett climbed out the passenger window and crabbed across the windshield to the driver's side, reaching in to hold the wheel while Geoff slid across the seat and also went out the passenger window to lie on the roof facing forward. Garrett then positioned himself similarly on the driver's side roof, with his left arm still holding the steering wheel. Both were laughing like hyenas. I was alone in the backseat of a car hurtling down a mountain.

Clearly practiced, the maneuver took wordless seconds to execute, and there was no time to be scared. I'd passed instantly through a state of terror into acceptance of whatever fate was in store. Kind of like falling off a building.

Were near-death experiences the way these guys pumped up for a speed-skiing meet, I wondered? I was aware of the absurdity of posing this question while hanging out of the car with one arm propped in the window and the other arm on the roof. I was also aware that neither of them was watching the road while answering.

"Ow, weea not gowin' to anee speeed-skeeing thingie..."

"Now, weea gowin' to Wanaka..."

"...to geet in a heelicopta..."

"...and skee some powda."

Of course. Even skiing's most depraved shared the thirst.

WHEN DOLORES LaChapelle died in Silverton, Colorado, in January 2007 at the age of eighty-nine, the hagiography began immediately. And why not? Sure, you wouldn't find any cheesy dashboard figurines of the woman with the long silver braid and beatific smile offering blessings to acolytes in ski-town souvenir shops, but she was still the closest thing powder skiing would ever have to a patron saint.

Fêted and remembered everywhere, LaChapelle's considerably charmed life was rewoven in obituaries around the continent. Suddenly, a lot of people who'd never heard of the author, mountain sage, and driving force in the deep ecology movement, knew who Dolores LaChapelle was. Equally suddenly, many who'd never had cause to ponder such things learned that "powder"—the catch-all euphemism for unconsolidated, preferably deep snow—was a relatively new concept.

Deep ecologists consider humans an integral part of the environment and value human and non-human life equally. In this view, skiers who claim, "It's all about powder," are referring not simply to a substance but to their movement through, and thus relationship to, that substance. LaChapelle, who was ground zero to the idea's development and philosophized extensively on the subject, saw this relationship in purely Zen terms: the snow's molecules over here, your little clump of molecules over there, no difference between you and a tree, you and a table, you and frickin' Madonna.

Most ski stories begin with or center around the quest for powder, and once again, Arnold Lunn, in *The Mountains of Youth,* presciently describes why:

> The true skier... is not confined to a piste. He is an art-
> ist who creates a pattern of lovely lines from virgin and
> uncorrupted snow. What marble is to the sculptor, so are
> the latent harmonies of ridge and hollow, powder and sun-
> softened crust to the true skier. By a wise dispensation
> of providence, the snow, whose beauty has been defaced
> and destroyed by the multitude of piste addicts, does not
> record the passage of the [racer]. It is only soft snow that
> records the movements of individual skiers, and it is only
> in soft snow that the real artist can express himself.[7]

Art and science are indeed inseparable when it comes to powder, for its every aesthetic is based in chemistry and physics: the basic shape and geometry of flakes; the loft and water content of newly fallen snow; the downy hoar crystals that grow on powder's surface in cold weather; the sweep of a drift in a swirling wind; the shadowed compression of a ski track; the contrail of vaporized crystals billowing behind a skier.

Indeed, no substance on Earth is as transformative as snow, which, perhaps, isn't surprising given that no other element has the chameleonic properties of snow's precursor, water. And no other type of snow has the mutative capacity of powder. It is there and then it is not, settling, consolidating, moving with the breeze, deliquescing in the sun. Morphing all too quickly, it reminds us that the two-million-year-old blue ice on a glacier's face was once the stuff of face-shots.

Nothing on Earth compares to walking through falling snow. And gliding effortlessly through it? Well, you're crossing the welcome mat of an entire book devoted to why this prospect is such a powerful psychological trigger for skiers. Something about tumbling flakes draws you out, teases the id into consciousness. This is the trait we most appreciate; doubtless anthropological in nature, it is a Paleolithic holdover buried somewhere in our Cro-Magnon genes. You're aware of a hovering desire to *do* something, be *part* of it. Think snowmen and toboggans. At the same time, this new and subtle beauty seems to steer your attention from mundane concerns and make fast the moment with a host of new sensations. There's the cold, fresh, metallic smell and the sudden pervasive quiet. That which is typically invisible is revealed: footprints, animal tracks, and the eddying currents of wind. And the ultimate paradox of the world's familiar tracings becoming more apparent only because they've disappeared beneath an entirely new iconography: drooping hats adorning posts, mounds bowing over branches, and the white-lipped geometry of urban skylines; it is a land where, suddenly, every angle is curved, every curve flattened, and every flatness mute.

It's not just art and science, but music and math as well.

When Canada's prime ministerial *enfant terrible* Pierre Elliott Trudeau famously contemplated his (first) retirement while walking in an Ottawa blizzard one night, not a single Canuck of any political stripe thought it a stupid or unconsidered way to make a decision: we'd all been there, we all understood. Snowflakes both speak and listen. Making decisions in a snowstorm is our birthright.

Powder, then, is inarguably transformative to the human spirit. As skiers, powder is our medium, and the medium, as Marshall McLuhan pointed out, is the message. Descending in powder offers an indescribable sensation that clearly speaks to a primitive pleasure center of the brain, for it instantly demands more in a classic addictive cycle. And yet, unlike water, powder is fundamentally changed when you pass through it: just as there is no

concept of untracked water, so is there no concept of invio-
late powder. This isn't just philosophy, but morality as well;
snaking someone else's powder line—an irreplaceable commodity—is considered a contravention of skier decorum.

Let's back up a bit. Powder wouldn't exist if someone
hadn't figured out a way to ski it. It could just as easily have
been a failed experiment, maybe not as bad as Evel Kniev-
el's attempted motorcycle jump across the Snake River
Canyon, but still a natural phenomenon that no human tool
or technique could conquer. Before humans deigned to sub-
categorize it, in fact, the white stuff falling from the sky
was all just snow. Even if they're variously affected by the
depth, weight, and water content of the snow that's falling, mountains, forests, and waterways have no capacity
to differentiate. Humans, however, can and do: the Inuit
famously (or mythically) have many words for snow, to
describe its worth in construction and travel and to predict whether you're about to fall through it into the Arctic
Ocean. And though skiers have no word for "snow mixed
with the shit of a sled dog," we've developed a similar
snowcabulary. Simply put, skiers *invented* powder, imagin-
ing it into existence from the stacks of crystals piling up on
mountainsides around the world.

Ironically, it was a ski *racer* from Dartmouth College,
New Hampshire, named Dick Durrance who, in 1940,
started the modern powder ball rolling in Alta, Utah. Having opened a resort and started a ski school, he was dealing
with the local overabundance of snow and a glut of terrain
on which stemming (in which one ski at a time was pushed
into a turn) wasn't possible. It was clear that regular skiing—as practiced preferentially to this point on packed
snow, pistes, and racecourses—wasn't going to cut it here.
Alternate techniques were required, so Durrance invented
the short-swinging, up-down "dipsy-doodle" powder turn,
which quickly became the resort's signature export.

Meanwhile, a young Dolores Greenwell was skiing around Loveland Pass, Colorado, on a pair of six-foot-plus hickory skis. From 1947 through 1950, she taught skiing in Aspen, developing a nose and a preference for the untracked snow away from the lifts. In 1950 she made the first ski ascent of Mt. Columbia, second-highest peak in the Canadian Rockies, and the first ski ascent of Snow Dome, the continent's hydrographic apex. After she married Ed LaChapelle, a Canadian geophysicist she met on that trip, the couple spent time at the avalanche institute in Davos, Switzerland, before moving to Alta, where Ed was stationed on the U.S. Forest Service's avalanche and snow research team. Dolores, naturally, was there to ski. In 1956, she and Jim Shane were the first to dipsy-doodle down Alta's infamous Baldy Chute—in powder so deep they disappeared.

FOR MANY PEOPLE, skiing is a sphere of perpetual freedom into which they can step at will, and the sweet spot—that which instantly expands the sphere in every dimension—is powder. Whether one is in it or simply wants to be, powder is a realm of constant challenge. It is about words, but being unable to speak; about telling, but being unable to describe. It is sensations and memories. Silence amplifying a heartbeat and the rasping of breath. Involuntary grunts of effort and unconscious squeals of delight. Inspiration. Bad poetry. Broken marriages. Magazines. Movies. Grins. Silliness. Frozen toes and ice cream headaches. Magical turns and occasional smacks off a hidden hazard. First tracks. Lost skis. Trudging, navigating, and skiing over, through and around boilerplate, sastrugi, crust, slab, crud, and other snow-junk just to get to the good stuff. A way of feeling. A way of thinking. A way of life. A way, period. *Tao.*

"Our culture has no words for this experience of 'nothing' when skiing powder," LaChapelle put it in 1993's *Deep Powder Snow: 40 Years of Ecstatic Skiing, Avalanches, and*

Earth Wisdom. "In general the idea of nothingness or nothing in our culture is frightening. However, in Chinese
Taosit thought, it's called "the fullness of the void" out
of which all things come... My experiences with powder
snow gave me the first glimmerings of the further possibilities of mind."[8]

She was onto something.

It has been said that if joy is the response of a lover
receiving what they love, then this is the joy we feel skiing
powder with friends. Overflowing gratitude indeed seems
to paint the absolutely absurd grins flashed at the bottom
of a run. You *never* see such grins elsewhere—not on a tennis court or a golf course, not on a podium or in a dance
club. No flush of physical victory compares to the ineffable
euphoria of a journey through powder. It isn't just shared
fun but, as LaChapelle also notes, a sense of life fully lived,
together, "in a blaze of reality."

In the end, powder isn't about an outer experience
but an inner one, a crucial intersection of mind and body
where thinking and feeling cannot be teased apart. This is
where immersion and affliction, submergence and addiction live, forever invoking powder's unique spirituality as
religion. Yet this sport's recently canonized angel would
loudly eschew any traditional doctrine in favor of making
no distinction between the universe at large and anything
within it; no distinction, for instance, between saints and
sinners, powder snow and powder-snow seekers, the places
you look for it and the places it is found.

When—as I'd found in my travels—you got right down
to it, the essence of skiing is best summed by the equation:
soul/x = people + places + powder. Surely there was some
kind of heaven on Earth where this equation was always
solved.

4 | THE BIG EMPTY

Everything is an experiment.
Red Bull Snowthrill of Alaska book, 2003

AN INTERESTING set of circumstances had led to the Red Dog Saloon in Juneau, Alaska, where I stood in Birkenstocks, my rain-soaked socks caked in sawdust and peanut husks.

The trail had started in Toronto, bouncing through L.A., Seattle, and totem-poled Ketchikan before landing in Juneau. And now, surrounded by bad taxidermy, orange life-preserver rings, and beer mugs the size of pitchers, it seemed I might find whatever it was I was looking for.

Certainly the concept was evolving. Already there'd been the blind girl with a broken ankle on the plane who was content to tap her way onboard without help, the senator's aide at the former brothel we were bunking at who'd handed me a self-penned story about a surfer's life in land-locked Fairbanks, and the bales of salmon jerky the town seemed constructed from. Disparate images to be sure, they all pointed to something that ultimately embodied a spirit of self-reliance and wildness that seemed very Alaskan and not altogether unrelated to, well... say, skiing.

POWDER, where I was now a contributing editor, had sent me to Alaska on a quest. In fact, five writer/photographer teams had shown up at airports around the continent to receive envelopes stuffed with air tickets and these instructions: find the soul of skiing.

Really?

Others had been sent on discovery missions to the Vermont mega-resort of Killington, molehills of the Midwest, venerable Aspen in Colorado, and Washington's Mt. Rainier—North America's almost perennial record-holder for snowfall. These places all had well-known histories and hardcore habitués: "the known," if you will. I'd been sent to what was, in 1992, "the unknown," the big empty: Alaska.

With too many mountains to name and too few people to care, the outpost of Alaska had suddenly come onto the global snowsports radar as both a destination and newly minted ethos. The state's endless ranges and endless snow suggested endless possibilities for exploration, and my frequent photographic collaborator Henry Georgi and I were there to plumb the zeitgeist.

Bearded, boisterous, and stentorian, Henry had started his photographic career shooting rock concerts in Toronto and rafting on the Ottawa River, but his was the heart of a skier. Raised by German-speaking parents in the Toronto suburb of Downsview, he had spent his watershed ski-bumming and ski-photography season in the party-addled Austrian resort of St. Anton. We met in the early eighties through Ontario's nascent telemark scene, where I dressed in Norwegian period costume to forerun races that he'd been hired to document. Soon, I became one of Henry's models, and our photographic collaborations filtered onto the continent's newsstands. Our first real joint triumph, however, resulted from a trip to Le Massif in Quebec's Charlevoix region, a unique operation that employed school buses to ferry guided groups to the top of a 2,300-foot escarpment overlooking the St. Lawrence River where ships and whales bobbed among the ice floes. It snowed more than two feet while we were there, and Henry's photos of waist-deep powder skiing in the typically low-snow East were a sensation, forming the basis for my first-ever POWDER feature. We'd sidestepped into a career of adventuring together at the magazine's behest, as reliable to the editorial braintrust as the team of Bard and Carter that preceded us—mostly, as we would later learn, because we likewise worked cheap and would (foolishly) go anywhere.

On the "soul of skiing" mission, naturally, we were eager to embrace whatever POWDER's editors threw at us, aware of the growing gravity of our destination and that something important was brewing there. In some sense, what was burgeoning in Alaska honored the Euro "extreme" movement of big, bold, off-piste descents in the high-alpine vertical world of the otherwise human-choked Alps; in another way, this push was a typically American attempt to outmuscle that small, dedicated scene with vast wilderness, a fleet of helicopters, and a few tons of film.

Although the "idea" of Alaska was steep, deep, and unexplored, skiing was hardly new there. Hundreds of local alpine, cross-country, and ski-jumping areas had been founded in the early twentieth century by waves of immigrant miners, loggers, and fishermen. At least one legitimate destination resort drew and was owned by the Japanese. So there was more than just the loam of noisy aircraft and harebrained competitions (like the pie-in-the-sky World Extreme Ski Championships held in the Chugach Mountains outside beat-down, oil-soaked Valdez the previous year) in which to dig for soul here—there were real grass roots.

Thus, while our media peers leapt from helicopters onto massive, never-skied Alaskan faces, our first experience in the new frontier was the home hill of 1992 Olympic women's downhill silver medalist Hilary Lindh. Tiny Eaglecrest Ski Area lies outside the somnolent town of Juneau, the only U.S. state capital to which no road leads: in true Alaskan style, the island-bound town can only be reached by sea or air.

Juneau was a wild place where ravens ruled the streets and grocery-store windows advertised bear repellent and ammunition. Life was dominated by commercial fishing, gold-rush nostalgia, and tourists disgorged from ships cruising the Inside Passage. Half the population lived near the weathered toe of the Mendenhall Glacier, and the enormous, steep chutes on the face of Mt. Juneau provided the biggest urban avalanche disaster potential outside of alpine Europe (they had, in the past, released to engulf part of town).

Despite its state-capital status, Juneau was still unpretentious enough that visiting journalists might be eagerly introduced from the floor of the state legislature in the midst of a critical vote to override a governor's veto. It was a place that, long before Sarah Palin appeared on *Saturday Night Live,* reflected the fact that Alaskans didn't take themselves too seriously, where monster trucks had license plates like OVRKILL, and a woman with a voice like Irish Cream liqueur might keep your attention while Woodstock was being re-created onstage in the Alaskan Hotel, then press a napkin into your hand with a phone number and the inscription "call or die wondering."

It was an apt metaphor for the Siren call that Alaska was putting out to the ski world: go or die wondering.

IN THE RED DOG, Matt Brakel, fisherman, extreme skier, paraglider, video star, and self-professed glory hound, snapped open the lid of a large plastic bucket filled with the morning's catch of plump shrimp.

"Have one," he said.

Above him a stuffed bear slithered up a pole after a pair of human legs that dangled from the ceiling.

We barely had time to bolt down a crustacean before the bartender, standing under frontier folk hero Wyatt Earp's gun (which was mounted over an inscription that read "checked but never claimed"), informed us of the "no shrimp" rule and tossed us a bag of peanuts.

And so Henry and I sat, shelling nuts and talking cliffs, chutes, and cornices with Matt, our designated ski model, and some management-types from Eaglecrest. It was glib. It was cool. But then it got serious.

"What do you guys need?" they wanted to know, as if we were a commando team compiling a list of weaponry for some vague assault.

"Snow," I said, perhaps a little too earnestly.

"Sun," countered Henry, neatly summing our respective personal missions and perpetual conflicts.

I was writing things down on a pad that was getting blurry. Maybe I was more tired than I realized after eighteen hours of traveling, or had miscalculated the sheer volume of an Alaskan mug, but my enthusiasm was draining like a burst appendix. In the dead of night, in the rain, amid a legion of cobwebbed Alaskan kitsch, this talk suddenly seemed so business-like. This wasn't the nebulous "go hang out and see whassup" kind of assignment I was used to. Instead, the mission was clouded by specificity: find the soul of skiing, whatever that might be. But didn't I usually end up with a sense of this no matter where I skied? Did I really need to hang on every word in hopes of being struck by a lightning bolt of insight?

Probably not. As my companions' voices thinned in the barroom din, I took a deep breath, a swig of beer, and put the pad away. Before even getting started, I stopped looking for whatever it was I thought I was looking for.

RICK KAUFMAN jostled with the controls of the grooming machine as he spoke.

"I pity people who don't ski, you know? I really pity them."

He was trying not to sound elitist, I knew. And his voice carried no malice, no judgment, no scorn. Though pity came pretty close to all three.

"I mean, how do you explain sex to a virgin? You can tell them about it as much as you want, but they'll really have to experience it to relate."

His sincerity helped me ignore the fact that this analogy was the biggest cliché in the ski world, typically rendered to explain the orgasmic nature of powder skiing. But I knew what he meant. In fact, I probably knew more about what he meant than he did. It was, more or less, what you'd expect to hear from a hardcore skier. It was, more or less, what I'd heard from hundreds of diehards. Describing precisely *why* you did what you did was mechanistically impossible, because skiing is feeling versus understanding; the knowledge of experience.

It was 5 a.m., and we were trundling down Eaglecrest's front side while it snowed in that snotty coastal way that straddled the freezing point and left you guessing whether skiing was going to be pain or pleasure right up until you stepped into your bindings. By the strain on the groomer's wiper blades, I was guessing pain. But with four days of decent powder under my belt, I was more interested in Rick's musings anyway.

Rick grew up in Pontiac, Michigan, and didn't start skiing until age twenty-one. When, shortly thereafter, he moved to Alaska, he had no specific intention of getting into the ski business; as he accurately observed, few do— they just kind of back into it as a way to keep skiing. He applied for a lift operator's job at Eaglecrest in 1977. The manager at the time told him he wouldn't fit in very well,

a point of particular glee for Rick, who was now in his fif-
teenth season as operations manager.

Outside, the sky lowered and the snow glomming the
windshield thickened, wipers whining against its weight.

"It's that feeling when you hit your turns and your line
just right; you don't get winded—I mean you feel better
after the run than when you started. Communing with the
terrain. You know? God, when you have a really good day
on skis it changes your whole outlook on life. It just makes
you..."

And then together, as if rehearsed, our voices infused
with our own heavy hindsight:

"Want to go out and get shitfaced!"

CROPLEY CHUTE drops 2,300 feet from the summit of
Mt. Ben Stewart to spill onto a lake. For three days we'd
etched lines through the accumulating snow of West Bowl
(the ubiquity of ski areas naming bowls for compass points
never ceases to amaze me...) and dodged malevolent trees
above Waterfall (...nor the ubiquity of names evoking
ninety-degree plunges...), while staring up at Cropley's
gaunt face. The wide-open forty-degree expanse was as
inviting as it was scary. It hardly ever slid they said, but
when it did, it went *big*. That morning, as the ocean fog
spilling over the ridge was atomized by the rising sun, it felt
stable, and we decided to go for it.

A fair-sized gang disembarked from the top of the Hooter
Chair: patrollers, instructors, managers, and hangers-on.
Shouldering our skis, we headed up the ridge above Eagle's
Nest (...nor lofty, bird-related places...), a route that
seemed trammeled by at least half of Eaglecrest's skiers on
any given day. Men, women, children, dogs—no one here
thought twice about hiking for their turns, despite the vast
amount of terrain available from the summit chairlift. The
current train of skiers snaking up the ridge channeled the

famous grainy photo of gold prospectors crossing Alaska's Chilkoot Pass. And weren't we, after all, looking for White Gold? I watched as venerates Sigurd Olson and Lucy McPherson, two of the nicest humans I'd ever met, peeled out of line toward their own secret stashes.

Sig was born in 1923 in Ely, Minnesota, and was cross-country skiing by age four. His main interest, however, was ski jumping, which he did all over the Midwest. In 1943, he was drafted, joining the 10th Mountain Division ski troops in Colorado. His time overseas was short but eventful. After pushing through Italy's Apennine Mountains, his division was about to thread the main passes of the Alps when the Germans surrendered. Back home, he earned a master's degree in wildlife management. He and his wife visited Alaska—stop me if you've heard this before—and never left. Moving to Juneau in 1958, he began patrolling at the old Second and Third Cabin areas, which people had been hiking up to ski since the thirties. He retired in 1991 after thirty-two years of patrolling, but still maintained a serious addiction by skiing every day there was snow and writing poems about it. He passed away in 2008, and skied right up to the end.

"I hate to miss a day of skiing," he told me. "To me, that's the best incentive to get other things done."

Lucy also hated to miss a day. Born in Montana in 1931, she married out of high school and raised a family in Sand Point, Idaho. In 1963, her husband talked her into free ski lessons; immediately hooked, she began teaching soon after. Moving to Juneau, Lucy became the first instructor at Second and Third Cabins.

"Having to put your boots and skis on a pack and hike in was quite a change from Sand Point's chairlifts," she recounted.

In fact, she set a record for hiking in, always refusing a ride on the snowmobile Sig used to pull the patrol sleds.

And here they both were, years later, spouses deceased, best buddies sharing a zest for powder that knew few bounds. Five minutes with these two made you feel warm all over. With their sparkling eyes and impish grins they were, it seemed, eternally young.

Back on the hike, it took fifteen minutes to traverse the ridge. Another ten would have put us over Shit-for-Brains Chute (... and finally, it seems, every ski area must baptize several runs as an ode to the ridiculousness of skiing them), but the sun and big snow lay on the rolling parabolas below. Everyone stopped talking. Some stopped breathing. Ten pairs of eyes bored holes into 1,000 feet of cold, fresh powder. Rick looked like he just wanted to hug everyone.

We took the lines on the steeper first pitch in small groups, adrenaline chasing away any butterflies. Whoops and hollers echoed around the valley, smiles tore at our cheeks. It got even sillier when we regrouped and kicked the last pitch en masse. And the squeals of delight weren't those of jaded lifetime skiers, but those of children playing in a sandbox, splashing in a pool. Ponce de Leon should probably have been searching for the fountain of youth in the clean, fresh environs of winter mountains, not in the fetid mosquito-and-snake-infested swamps of Florida.

That was the warmup. After the usual kerfuffle of turning on and checking everyone's avalanche transceivers (an electronic beacon with both transmit and receive functions worn by all when backcountry skiing), enumerating probes and shovels (more avalanche rescue gear), and calling in a helicopter (in Alaska, an aircraft was always at the ready), we were ferried up to Cropley in two groups. In one group were Henry and Rick; in the other, me, Al the Geologist, Matt Brakel, and Nancy Peel—Eaglecrest's caretaker; ski-school director; snowboard, telemark, and cross-country instructor; off-season raft guide; powerlifter; bodybuilder, and basic human skiing machine. The summit we were dropped on was spectacular, with huge gleaming upper bowls overlooking the shimmering waters of Stephens Passage.

Matt, Al, Nancy, and I disappeared down the chute while the helicopter hovered off the face with Rick and Henry, who was bagging a few rare sunny shots. The untracked bliss got a little less blissful where the sun had been on it, and several point releases (slow-moving, wet-snow avalanches that start small and fan out) made their way down the main chute in our wakes; Matt had touched off the biggest.

Matt was getting careless, and indeed when we regrouped on a ridge he had broken away from the group, traversed the main chute, and climbed above some rock-and-tree-studded face to do God knew what. What he did was wipe out bigtime on some hidden debris before making a spectacular recovery and putting a reasonable line down into the chute.

"Goddammit," Rick groaned, peeved at this breach of collective safety. "That's why we call him 'Break-all.'"

The other side of the ecstasy coin in skiing is getting carried away when you should remain vigilant. Matt had made me antsy days before when he was pushing it in the trees and in danger of goring himself. Big jumps, unscouted landings. He knew the mountain, yeah, but . . .

It got worse. Tense as we moved downward, I was glad to reach the bottom, but nobody was behind. They were all collected above the last ridge, which on one side rolled benignly into the lower chute and on the other dropped off precipitously.

Break-all was going to jump.

It was a big drop his ski tips hung over, but at least it was onto snow. He backed out of sight and when next I saw him, he was in the air—perfect body position, legs pulled up, arms in tight. A magazine cover. It would have been a good jump.

When he hit the rock under the snow, a loud crack echoed like gunfire, and Matt somersaulted crazily in a full-body ragdoll—head, air, feet, air, head. One ski stuck in the landing above and the other javelined toward the lake; it was the kind of wince-worthy highlight a sports channel might play over and over and over.

Miraculously, he was okay. And in that moment it was hard to equate this soft-spoken, big-hearted guy whose love of skiing went back to childhood backcountry trips with his mother and included teaching tots in the Mighty Mite ski racing program, with the human cannonball taking ill-conceived risks for the camera. He was a hell of a skier, but you just wanted to slap him. Eventually, I supposed, someone—or some*thing*—would do just that. Experience had taught me that luck was never to be counted on. Skiing required the acquisition of not just physical skills, but an entire panoply of judgment circuits that, properly applied, could keep you alive.

Sadly though, Matt Brakel's luck would run out in 1999 on Mt. McGinnis near the Mendenhall Glacier, when he jumped a cornice onto a riskier route than the rest of his group was descending and was killed in a massive avalanche. "He always wanted to go big," said his girlfriend, who'd witnessed the tragedy. But was there anything essentially wrong with going big—especially when that was soon to become what Alaska was known for? "I like to squeeze fear," Matt had told me, "and I never feel more religious than when I'm skiing."

Spirituality. Soul?

SKIING CROPLEY gave me plenty to think about. That single experience comprised most of the facets of skiing: elements of ecstasy and potential disaster, group-think and prudence, individuals and thresholds. Plus a taste of the newfangled Alaskan approach: DIY heli-lifts to big, unskied faces. The Mendenhall was just one of thirty glaciers flowing from the Juneau Icefield. Lofting over it one day in Al the Geologist's homemade plane, circling spectacular vertical towers, knife-edged arêtes, and crevasses so large they could swallow the *Queen Mary,* I recognized the distinct outlines of several heli-accessed peaks from popular videos and realized how much of an impact Alaska had already had on the greater snowsports consciousness.

On that 1992 trip, it was clear that skiing's soul derived from something beyond the resort experience that went back to little other than mountains, terrain, snow, and the basic adventure of sewing these together—something that Alaska excelled at delivering. It seemed, however, that it went even farther to answer a suite of basic human desires concerned with risk. As Arnold Lunn suggested in *The Mountains of Youth,* "Ski-ing belongs to a great family of sports which owe their appeal to the primitive passion for speed. Mere speed is not enough... To secure the fine unspoiled flavor of pace you must eliminate mechanism, retain the sense of personal control, and preserve the ever-present risk of a fall."[9]

Were we *consciously* seeking such things when we skied? Maybe not. As Sig had presciently put it, "You might not know exactly what it is you're looking for when you go out for a day of skiing, but that's okay because it usually finds you."

Soul as innocence. And that, I suppose, is what I found in the new frontier.

TEN YEARS LATER, things in Alaska weren't quite as guileless. Certainly not where I stood, at the main intersection in the port of Haines, where wan afternoon light illuminated a Fellini-esque diorama of art imitating life, life imitating art, and a mongrel cast of international skiers and image makers imitating, well... themselves.

POWDER photo editor David Reddick lined up a shot of a shaggy, somnolent mutt guarding a chainsaw in the back of a pick-up; French sequence king Jean-Marc Favre caught Whistler's Pierre-Yves LeBlanc lounging beside a wooden raccoon; Austrian Ulrich Grill snapped off *Abbey Road*—like stills of another Whistlerite, Hugo Harrisson, in a crosswalk; France's Dan Ferrer captured a Warren Miller moment of countryman Guerlain Chicherit strolling the dusty street incongruously dressed in full ski wear.

Searching for the perfect representation of something vaguely categorized as "AK lifestyle" (photographers were apparently still on specific missions here), the Euro shooters were rocking pure *fromage,* which was nothing new. What *was* new were foreign interlopers interrupting the time-lapse passage of vehicles that masqueraded as traffic, creating a spectacle that had townsfolk praying for the sun to go down early. A drunk stumbled out of the Fogcutter Bar and poked Chicherit in the chest.

"Yer one of them *extreeeem* skiers, ain'cha?" he oozed contemptuously. "Well, my youngest is a *snowboarder* and he watches all the movies and *he's* gonna own these hills and your ass soon enough. So..."

But the thought, like the alcohol on his breath, had simply evaporated.

Unaware he was being challenged, or simply insulated by trademark French insouciance, Chicherit nodded politely and turned back to an even cheesier shot with a gaggle of kids and a go-kart.

"Come on, move along folks," you could imagine a cop saying as he waved the crowd away. "Nothing to see here... it's just the 2002 Red Bull Snowthrill of Alaska."

AS ALASKA'S springtime heli-ghettos of Valdez, Girdwood, Haines, and Cordova had come online over the past decade to blow up in the snowsports media, I'd returned on other assignments, marveling at the evolutionary changes barely evident on that first trip to Juneau.

By now, Alaska—location *and* notion—held a special place in the pantheon of influences on global ski culture. So much so that riders from Vermont to Austria to New Zealand to Japan referred to it simply as "AK." With a million ridable mountains and almost ridiculous snowfalls, the ski possibilities here were still endless; AK was a place of constant exploration that could never be fully tapped. The can-do businesses that opened the place up were easy to reach and relatively close to home for Americans; no wonder it became the magazine-and-video darling of the wild-and-wooly nineties. Bigtime helicopter-accessed ski and snowboard competitions had come, floundered, gone, and been reinvented. People had died, many more had been injured. Helicopter crashes had claimed some; falls and avalanches swept away others. Everybody and his brother had started a renegade heli-operation (unlike their early days, at least these now employed guides) replete with pro-skier spokesperson/co-owner(s) and Vietnam-vet rodeo pilots who would land riders atop anything. Wave upon wave of celluloid heroes had been thrown up—Kim Reichelm, Kristen Ulmer, Alison Gannet, Doug Coombs, Seth Morrison, Shane McConkey, Kent Kreitler, Gordy Peifer, and Jeremy Nobis to name a few on the ski side; Victoria Jealouse, Tex Davenport, Johan Olofsson, and Jeremy Jones as a tiny sample on the snowboard ledger. The shape skis, which were all the rage at the time of my first trip, had piled on the beef, fattening up largely with wide-turning AK skiing in mind (more on all this later).

Of course, some things hadn't changed: Alaskans still refused to wear seatbelts, and "frontier" still rang like a hollow cliché. However, when Red Bull, the always avant-garde energy-drink company announced the Snowthrill of Alaska, promising a big-mountain freeskiing competition (the new, less-extreme name for extreme-ski contests) with a twist, it was definitely time to buckle up. And the good people of Haines—fishers, loggers, and miners whose seaweed-salad days had long since disappeared into the perpetual mists of the North Pacific—could not have been more excited.

Red Bull's concept was actually brilliant: honor that which had vaulted AK to its lofty position as big-mountain Mecca by combining skiing and photography in a battle of talent, creativity, and teamwork. Twelve invited athletes and their respective shooters had a predetermined amount of heli-time and a mandate to create the world's most startling ski photography, which was to be judged online in a dozen categories, for a total cash grab of $35,000 USD. Sure, there would be a day of traditional freeskiing competition integrated into the nine-day event, but crowning a peer-judged world champ was only for shits, giggles, and some quick PR, since the photo judging wasn't to be completed until the following autumn.

Eliminating the structure around competition made the athletes more willing to step up their game. The invitational component meant they didn't have to fulfill standards to prove themselves; being chosen was proof enough. In other words, give athletes/artists their own guide, four hours of helicopter time in some of the world's most spectacular mountains, a photographer to consult and consort with, and the freedom to choose where to go, and it added up to the ultimate freeskiing session.

The event more than lived up to its billing as an historic gathering of photographic and skiing talent. And, touché cliché, it coincidentally comprised perhaps the last frontier of action sports competition in one of the last true frontiers.

Rising directly from the ocean, the peaks around Haines were impressive; Chamonix-esque spires here, B.C.-style powderfields there, and towering Himalayan-like fluting everywhere you looked. That much was obvious the first morning of the competition as the crew shuttled out to 33 Mile, the "Food, Gas, Beer"—flagged roadhouse that served as the staging area and nerve center for the event.

Like Juneau's Red Dog, the interior of 33 Mile was pure AK, with a fossilized mammoth femur, antique whiskey bottles, antlers, and portraits of dogs, cabins, and John Wayne. There were snowshoes, a turn-of-the-century broad axe, and a Palin-esque bumper sticker that said it all: "I'm Pro-Choice. I Choose to Hunt, Fish, Trap, Eat Meat, and Wear Fur."

Inside, ski gear, ropes, and harnesses were assembled amid a steady stream of regular customers unperturbed by the circus. Outside, Bruce Griggs, owner of a local heli-ski outfit was setting up central radio control and dispatch. Asked where any group was at any given time, he'd park his Camel Light for a minute, then point unerringly to some obscure alpine feature on a big topo map spread across the table.

For the first part of that day, however, only guides were flying, and all and sundry cast their eyes skyward toward a front of milky cloud trying to barge its way past three weeks of high pressure. High winds had whipped most of the snow into various solid building materials, but the guides knew a few powder zones where photographers could have their athletes pull off some one-hit wonders.

The teams were clearly anxious to get shooting, but pondered whether or not it was worth burning precious heli time only to get caught in bad weather. Each group had its own philosophy, yet watched closely to see what its competitors had in mind. To the untrained observer, *nothing* was happening, but to the delight of organizers, their concept was in full bloom: feigned laughter, intense posturing, and silent strategizing were all part of the game.

"It is better to have good light and bad snow, than bad light and good snow," said French phenom Enak Gavaggio, summing, as Descartes might have, the received sentiment about still-clear skies.

As quickly as it had invaded, the group evacuated. Half the teams decided to fly; the rest fell back on different plans—snowmobiling, heading back to town, or staging "secret" lifestyle shoots, taking advantage of less-than-ideal conditions to bag a few creative pics.

And so it went over the next several days, as teams jockeyed for position in the choppers, and storm clouds jockeyed for position along the coast. Among the logistical problems that arose: Euro and North American radios were incompatible, creating an electronic Tower of Babel in the backcountry, and pairing two teams that had different shooting objectives in one flight—for example, one team wanted big-mountain lines and the other wanted a big crevasse to jump over. When the guide nixed the jump because it would impede group movement and heli logistics, the decision sparked bitter complaint. Talk among organizers at breakfast the next day centered on the primadonna nature of this herd of artists.

"It's not that I wish the photographers were less demanding," one woman stated, pushing her bacon aside. "I just wish they were *nice*."

Perhaps the biggest rift arose in regard to the intended big-mountain contest. The excitement of five days of doing everything they wanted made putting on game faces somewhat difficult for skiers: few desired to do something that put their well-being at risk. But Red Bull, paying the freight, insisted.

The comp began on a beautiful bluebird Friday morning, when competitors were hoisted to the ridge opposite the east-facing venue to scout lines and exchange smacktalk. The men went first. LeBlanc, as usual, picked a bold, exposed line of spines and cliffs, skiing it well and throwing a few Mute grabs off large pillows until, halfway down, he crashed on a huge air. In typical understated fashion, speed-demon Harrisson tore the face apart at subsonic speed, barely registering the landings of his several jumps. Befitting his mogul-skiing background, Gavaggio hit lots of smaller airs, while countryman Chicherit also looked in control when he nonchalantly tossed a backflip off a windlip. But it was Swedish gladiator Sverre Lillequist who had by far the best run, dropping onto the face under a corniced brow and beating it senseless with steep, masterful turns and power-slides down sharp, sloughing flutes. The men were judged by the women and vice versa: Australian Andrea Binning's route was impressive as she hopped back and forth from one side to another of a prominent fin, Whistlerite Jenn Ashton's line was somewhat pedestrian by her standards, and France's Anne Catelin had a solid run of short, technical sections and modest air. American Jamie Burge kept her skis on the snow and was nuking her way to best run of the day when she blew up in the main gully. All of these heroics were accomplished on equipment that was nowhere to be found a decade ago and significantly aided the skiers' cause: super-fat (and thus super floaty and capable of higher speeds), twin-tip (upturned tails were less likely to catch on anything, making them more versatile) big-mountain skis more or less born and bred in Alaska's steep, deep snowpack. In the end, it was Lillequist, Harrisson, and Chicherit on the men's draw, and Catelin, Binning, and Ashton for the women. Despite the struggle to get these high-strung thoroughbreds out of the gates, crowning the champions went off without a hitch.

With one day of shooting left, everyone dutifully dragged themselves out to 33 Mile for one more round of filming. And though some of the riders worked hard in the hills to fill gaps in their week's body of work, the energy level had tanked after the previous day's glory. The karma bank was also running dry. LeBlanc narrowly missed turning his twenty-eighth birthday into his last when a Grade II avalanche threw him over cliffs on Tomahawk, the same peak that had taken out Jeremy Jones, Johan Olofsson, and Gordy Peifer the previous year. For organizers, it was time to call the event and declare victory.

The one-of-a-kind experimental event, never to be held again, had been a success. But it was the one-of-a-kind experimental place in which it was held—the mountain gallery that had won the heart and soul and mind of the entire global ski community—that had truly won the day. Alaska was the place where people and powder came together to reinvent a sport, the blank canvas on which much of skiing's new direction had been rendered, and the painters would return again and again to create some of the sport's greatest works of art.

WHEN IT CAME to marrying adventure, exotica, and cultural discovery to skiing, I'd set an unstoppable snowball rolling downhill. Mexico. Chile. New Zealand. Alaska. To ski was to travel, and to travel was to ski. It seems logical now that I ended up chasing skiing's considerable global diaspora more or less for a living, and that writing about these experiences was the best way to follow up on each thread of physical and psychological exploration. I was rarely looking for anything in particular on these journeys other than to experience the familiar face of ski culture in an unfamiliar setting. A lot of the things that happened along the way inspire disbelief—even in myself. But I never actually sought out what often seems like craziness of the highest order; rather, the experiences I chose offered a way for the ski world's inherent craziness to find me. I guess Sig Olson was right.

the revolution will not be televised

5 | THE MOTHERLAND

> To ski, however well or poorly, is a reminder—
> whatever one may for a long time have
> suspected—that one is alive, and that living
> is tremendous fun. There isn't any other game
> to compare with it in the world.
>
> W. JAMES RIDDELL, *MBE, after winning the*
> *1929 Kandahar Ski Club of Great Britain's Inferno*
> *downhill race in Mürren, Switzerland*

As SHOWN by their various engineering accomplishments, the Swiss are a nation of meticulous, orderly moles. Meticulous because of their attention to detail (like wrapping the handles of those little metal teapots that always scald your fingers). Orderly because everything runs on time and is neat and clean to boot. And moles because they can lay claim to the lion's share of the tunnels that riddle the Alps like so much... well, Swiss cheese. This is as solid a cultural epithet as you'll find anywhere. No need to mention that they've thrown up more lifts and built more ski areas than any other country in Europe, or that Switzerland is where Arnold Lunn and his climbing buddies turned the rural, low-octane Scandinavian pastime of skiing into both serious alpine exploration and a recreational industry—a motherland of sorts for ski mountaineering, ski holidaying, and, by association, ski journalism.

After a dozen or so visits, however, I'd learned that this image is embedded in a far more complex picture. Switzerland, in fact, is so full of clichés as to be almost a caricature of itself. Every town seems to be a surrealist abstraction of shiny, clean mountains; lace-curtained windows; clocks and cowbells; spaghetti, baguettes, chocolate, and cheese (which your orifices seem to ooze after you've been in Switzerland a while).

Located high in the *zentralschweiz*, a solidly Teutonic chunk of the ethnically fractious Swiss Alps, Engelberg (Angel Mountain) is a place of titanic terrain, massive vertical, and life-altering descents. Previously unheralded, this now-popular ski area was suddenly uploaded to global consciousness in the late nineties by roving bands of merry snowsports explorers trolling for the unknown; a place where skiing's rising new tides lapped hard against the bulwarks of obscurity and tradition.

Engelberg featured stereotypes galore: frequent, punctual train service from Lucerne and Zurich; more banks than could possibly be needed in a town of 3,500; a *Dorfstrasse* lined with neat, wooden-shuttered hotels; and a chunk of medieval history in the form of a large Benedictine monastery founded in 1120—but it was also a place that challenged convention. For instance, contrary to popular opinion, Swiss Germans apparently *did* have a sense of humor. Otherwise, why would they have installed Rotair, the world's only revolving tram, over the Titlis Glacier so that British punters (and plenty of the Queen's hand-picked whiners could be found here) already reeling from altitude, dizzying views of yawning crevasses, and lunch-time schnapps, would have yet another excuse to throw up all over their (usually) mauve one-piece suits?

Unfortunately there were no doughy, green-gilled Manchester nurses to take the piss out of in the tram that photographer Paul Morrison and I took aloft one morning in February 2004. Exiting, we schussed down cold, dry snow on the Buckelpiste—one of only a handful of named, groomed runs in an area the size of Rhode Island (the Swiss tend to name mostly landmarks at their resorts)—rode a T-bar across a lakebed, and hopped on a short chairlift to Jochpass. Although it had snowed sixteen inches two days before, there appeared to be nothing unskied left—no matter how far beyond the pistes we gazed. I was stunned at the thoroughness with which this massive place seemed tracked out. It wasn't at all as I remembered. I did know one spot, however, where constant wind refilling could deliver at least some sweet powder even days after a storm. We traversed under a soaring cliffband and around the corner to this series of usually reliable slopes but were shocked to discover the entire stash had also been pounded into oblivion.

A lot had changed in Engelberg. And fast.

ON MY FIRST trip here, a *POWDER* assignment in 1996, I'd met Geny Hess, whose family's eponymous hotel had been a landmark in the village since 1884. He'd greeted us warmly, emerging in his chef's uniform from the kitchen of his five-star Tudor Stübli, and promised to guide us on some off-piste skiing. Finding someone who knew the ropes in terrain as vast and dangerous as Engelberg was important, and getting a package deal with the guy who cooked your food and kept your room clean was a major bonus.

The next day we'd rendezvoused at the Stern Bar—a circular, clear-sided circus tent on snow—overlooking the sickeningly steep Titlis Glacier on which a guide and client had just inked improbable first tracks down 4,000 feet of vertical. Geny stared at these etchings in a familiar and unnerving way.

"Uh, that's like, a waterfall of ice," I said.

"Yes. Beautiful, no? Maybe we go..."

Incredibly, there were but five skiers besides us on the precipitous glacier. Geny guided us carefully between seracs and over staircase drops through untracked, knee-deep snow—but not without incident. At one point Geny stopped to extract a clueless snowboarder from a small crevasse, and, concerned by a small avalanche we kicked off, he dug an elephant-sized snow pit at the top of one of the steeper pitches to check on conditions. As we looked at the horizontal layers revealed in the pit walls, the profile showed consolidated flakes adhering to a scary base layer of fifty-thousand-year-old blue ice. Apparently things would be fine as long as the ice stayed put. When we reached the bottom, Geny had glanced up at the sun.

"Now," he'd said with great solemnity, "it is time we make the Laub."

A 1935 BRITISH book entitled *The Ski-runs of Switzerland,* by James Riddell, contains a black-and-white frontispiece depicting a monstrous face with a shallow central gully. Shadowplay infers the slope's sustained thirty-five to forty degrees, and there's enough scale to do justice to the 4,250-foot vertical. Easily the book's most drool-icious photo, it demonstrates that skiers back in the day salivated over the same things we do today. The entry on the list of illustrations reads simply "Laub, Engelberg."

Getting to the Laub had been surprisingly easy for an off-piste descent—two chairlifts then a short cat-track schuss to a gate hung with the usual warnings: "Death, Dismemberment, No Rescue." A couple of thrusts with our poles along a traverse and the whole face spread before us:

untracked and sweetly steep, it was a mega-ramp of deep blow-in perfectly preserved on a northeastern exposure. We'd pushed off, ripping down 300 vertical feet before pulling up at a rock. There, while he dug another snow pit, Geny related his most memorable ride down the Laub. Skiing alone (foolishly, he admits), he'd dropped in and kept right, usually the safer route. Three turns in, the slope had busted loose and in seconds he was traveling sixty miles per hour in a billowing powder storm that went 3,200 feet down the face. Relieved of his rucksack and skis along the way (avalanches are surprisingly adroit at undressing their victims), Geny had popped up at the bottom buried to the chest, barely alive but a whole lot wiser.

The Angel had spared him.

Our new snow pit indeed revealed a buried weak layer of faceted sugar snow, but cohesion in the upper snowpack suggested there would be no problem unless bigtime warming occurred in the next few minutes. We dove in.

Skiing the Laub was like an exhausting dream in which you're drawn from scene to scene at ridiculous speed with no idea how spent you are until you stop. It's a run like no other, and in powder, it's mind-altering. No heli-operation outside of Alaska would even think of cutting clients loose on a descent that long and steep, and if such a slope lay adjacent to a North American ski area, it would have been shredded long ago. As a reminder of how far we'd descended, the snow at the bottom morphed to crust over an abundance of avalanche debris. We picked our way through the rubble toward the rustic warmth of Restaurant Ritz, a traditional stop after making the Laub. Geny ordered up the requisite concoction of weak coffee and schnapps while we stared out the window at his precipitous backyard.

We spent most of that evening in Geny's renowned three-hundred-bottle vintage wine cellar. Much laughter, numerous bottles, and many red-eyed snapshots later we staggered up from cobwebbed catacombs hung with hunting trophies and photos of legendary Swiss ski racer Erica Hess (no relation), for whom Geny had been personal mentor. A loud, sloppy evening filled with excellent *nouvelle cuisine* shattered yet another fondue illusion about Swiss cooking, and before we tottered off to bed we'd made plans to meet Geny for another guided tour.

"This one," he intoned, more solemnly than usual, "is *very* special."

THE GELTYBERG was a stunningly blank sea of rolling, consolidated waves. The 6,000-vertical-foot run started on that undulating ocean of snow, hourglassed into a rock canyon, then doglegged over a series of hanging terraces toward the valley. Dropping in was like sliding down the throat of the Alps. The massive glacier's sunlit tongue rolled slowly into the shadows of a dizzying gorge, and our lone tracks rolled with it.

Geny was nonplussed by the absence of humans, whereas American freeski queen Kristen Ulmer and I were finding it all a little unbelievable. Ulmer had rolled into town to join the *POWDER* photo shoot during the night and appeared at breakfast in her usual Eveready-bunny mode, a set of well-sharpened nails on the chalkboard of our collective hangovers and all a bit much for the hotel's proper Swiss staff. Geny had raised one inscrutable eyebrow when she started spewing about fist-fighting with the police during a film shoot at an Italian resort, but after he saw her ski, she commanded his full respect.

As he had on the Titlis and the Laub, Geny pit-stopped at all the traditional safe points on the descent, explaining the route and its hazards: a narrow ridge above a gaping plunge that had to be sideslipped down to a traverse, a series of sketchy ramps beneath massive, rock-shedding cliffs. Geny was in his element, and at several points the usually reserved hotelier whooped and hollered like the brash North Americans accompanying him. His old-school, legs-locked-together style appeared as smooth as butter whether he was in powder or crust, so following behind him I was surprised several times by changing snow conditions. Fortunately, I avoided tripping up in any of the frequent fall-you-die zones. At most stops, Geny grinned like a Cheshire cat, but at one he gazed contemplatively across the landscape.

"My friends and I were the first to ski the Geltyberg," he said in a hushed voice. "It was June 5, 1965. We started in powder at the top and ended in mushy spring snow right around here. Then we had to walk a fair way."

He'd stared downvalley with a muted smile. What, exactly, resided there—satisfaction, reverence, respect?

A fair way indeed, for it was another half-hour of glades, hidden haylofts, and bushwhacking before we'd skied across a bridge on the valley floor to the Fürenalp rail station, another of the Angel's massive vertical stashes under our bewildered belts.

FOR MOST North American skiers, weaned on the instant gratification of shortish, lift-served, in-bounds slopes buffered by intimidatingly unpopulated wilderness, this was the element missing in our education: ski over a mountain range, into a different valley, find another village, take the train home; descend into a neighboring country for lunch and ride *their* lifts back; make a several-day tour across the roof of the world, bunking in improbably massive refuges; spend all day exploring a single magnificent run; next day walk up a mountain to rattle cowbells while you cheer on your country at the spectacle of an international downhill race. This—Europe's more catholic model of skiing—was what drew me back time and again to the Motherland.

My first trip to Engelberg had offered a true, generational connection rooted in both a traditional mountain

culture and a newfound global thirst for Europe's gloriously
unmanaged terrain. Engelberg had a comfortable free-for-all
attitude without the French do-or-die ethos of the piste-
free Aiguille du Midi in Chamonix or La Mieje in La Grave.
Not that otherwise-coddled North Americans like me didn't
appreciate the ballsy brio of the latter, where lifts shot skiers
aloft many thousands of feet and deposited us in unmarked
alpine arenas to fight our way down through glaciers, couloirs, and vast expanses of forest, inviting us at every turn
to get into as much trouble as we wanted. If we didn't show
up at the bottom, well, *c'est la vie*—we were on our own.

"How's the skiing?" I remember asking a purse-lipped
clerk at La Grave's ticket window the morning the *téléphéri-
que* lift finally opened after being shuttered by a ferocious
three-day storm.

"Good," replied the grizzled matron, glancing up at the
plumes being fired off the mountain by hurricane winds
and snatching the euros from my hand all in one motion, "*if*
you're a good skier."

Although there were many hallmarks of ski-area modernity in Engelberg, they had blended seamlessly into the
otherwise historic milieu of one of Switzerland's oldest
winter resorts, a place central to the history of skiing.

In 1883, both the famous monks of St. Bernard in their
eponymous high-mountain pass and a certain Dr. Otto
Herwig-Hold in Arosa, a tiny community in the remote
mountains south of Chur, began experimenting with newfangled Norwegian-made wooden skis. In the same year,
skis and sealskins (attached to the bottom of skis to provide traction while climbing) were brought to nearby Davos.
Then things moved fast: the first ski club in central Europe
was founded in Munich in 1891; Switzerland's first club
was at Glarus in 1893, the same year that a group crossed
the Jochpass from Meiringen to Engelberg.

German Wilhelm Ritter von Arlt had brought a pair of skis from Sweden in 1885 and made the first ski ascent of a 9,800-foot Swiss peak in 1894, both defining and becoming the de facto father of ski mountaineering. The first actual alpine tour (extended travel on skis above treeline) recorded in the Alps took place the same year, when the Branger brothers teamed up with Sir Arthur Conan Doyle (yes, the Sherlock Holmes creator) for a traverse from Davos to Arosa. This feat sparked much interest and, by 1897, German ski pioneer Wilhelm Paulcke made a partial traverse of the Bernese Oberland with Mssrs. Beauclair, Lohmüller, Ehlert, and Monnichs (the latter pair were subsequently killed in an avalanche on Susten Pass in January 1899—the first fatal skiing accident ever recorded). In 1898, Paulcke skied to 13,780 feet on the Swiss–Italian border of the Monte Rosa massif with the well-known Swiss pioneer Robert Helbing. In February 1903, Helbing was the first to complete an important section of the now-famed Haute Route alpine tour from Chamonix, France, to Zermatt, Switzerland. Dr. Hermann Seiler, president of the Monte Rosa section of the Swiss Alpine Club and co-proprietor of the Seiler Hotels Zermatt, organized Switzerland's first ski-training course in January 1902. The twelve capable students ascended another Swiss–Italian peak, Cima di Jazzi, on their fourth day.

Paulcke's traverse of the Oberland glaciers had kicked off the first Golden Age of ski-mountaineering exploration, which lasted twenty years and ended with Arnold Lunn's first ski ascent of the highest peak wholly within Switzerland—the 14,770-foot Dom de Mischabel.

By the time Morrison and I were skiing there in 2004, the venerable Engelberg Ski Club was celebrating its centennial, having incorporated in the year that the first skiers descended from the summit of Titlis, at that time believed to be the highest mountain in Europe (either an illusion or the effect of too much schnapps). The entire village was in on the party: the bakery sold a special anniversary bread, shops crafted window displays featuring nostalgic iconography, restaurants decorated their interiors in early-twentieth-century style. A costumed ski race took place on the Klostermatte and was judged according to attire and skiing style—as wooly as possible on both counts—followed by a great anniversary ball at the town's *belle-époque* culture and meeting center, the Kursaal.

Had the large itinerant population of skiers and snowboarders in town had any say in the affair, however, it's quite likely the official language of this venerable Swiss organization's centennial would have been... Swedish.

Engelberg's popularity had soared since my visit eight years before, and although I shouldered some responsibility for its increased profile after penning a rather large exposé in *POWDER,* it was widely acknowledged that by 2004, a turbo-diaspora of hard-charging, vertically starved, AK-addled Swedish freeriders had turned the Alps into the "Shralps." When I'd first visited, there were two Swedish ski bums; now there were over fifty. The Vikings, however, weren't the only burgeoning foreign incursion.

IN LESS THAN a decade, Engelberg had become so popular that Morrison and I had barely exited the train before we ran into a couple of Whistler friends: photographer Damian Cromwell and popular coverboy Dan Treadway were skiing with big-mountain champ Jen Ashton and an international posse just returned from a freeski boondoggle in Bulgaria. Our exchange was typically, and comically, devoid of any hint of surprise.

"Hey, how's it goin'?"

"Great. You guys?"

"Good. How's the skiing?"

"Pretty beat 'til yesterday's snow. Now it's blower over marble."

"Cool."

"Yeah. See you in the bar?"

Later, the Eden Bar, its door plastered in freeride-related stickers, was indeed the place to be. Not only did we find Treadway, Cromwell, and Ashton lapping up the daily two-for-one beer special, but also renowned photographer Mattias Fredriksson and a crew from the infamous Swedish film company Free Radicals (only Swedes command English well enough to pull off such an erudite double entendre). In another corner, with his wife and too-cute child, sat legendary Swedish big-mountain slayer Per Huss (né Gustafsson), practically a Swiss citizen after basing himself in Engelberg for several winters. There was another acquaintance, Daniel Friedli, who ran the international hub then known as the Snowboard & Telemark Shop in the town's Hotel Bellevue, and was the partner of a Whistlerite living in Engelberg. The ski world, as always, proved infinitely small, even—or perhaps especially—in places as large and seemingly obscure as Engelberg, a mountainous kingdom in which you could disappear in an instant. A task that we hoped to accomplish.

As with previous visits, the folks we met proved key to sorting out the good, the bad, and the truly awful after a nasty spell of weather. The previous week, a *foehn* (the infamous warm wind from the Mediterranean) had blown through, melting and messing with the snow. This thaw was followed by a hard freeze, and then sixteen inches of angel dust. Another daily four to eight inches on top of that had sweetened things considerably, but the rock-hard base layer persisted.

After our disappointing morning on the talus cones, Morrison and I re-created my long-ago descent with Geny of the showpiece Titlis Glacier. Unlike that occasion, however, this time saw traffic aplenty; we actually had to *wait* at several points while flummoxed skiers picked their way down through ice tongues, seracs, and moraine debris. And despite the glacier's vastness, it failed to deliver the powder stashes I'd remembered. Chastened, we'd opted to finish the day on the Laub. But, lo and behold, this had also been shralped—not a single unblemished line to be had.

Throughout the week, Morrison and I had elbowed aside floundering Brits to retrace our earlier run down the stunning Titlis, maneuvered over to the Jochpass and its long, untouched aprons, and worked through trees under a set of large cliffs in an obscure part of the resort, cycling on an eight-person "bucket" lift that looked like it had lifted ore from a mine. However, it was our final morning on Angel Mountain that was truly heaven-sent. Squeezing in a last run before catching a noon train to Zurich airport, we found two feet of the lightest, driest powder imaginable up top, the kind you just pointed downward in, arms out front on the steering wheel, and hoped for the best as you burrowed through like some high-speed tunneling machine—something the Swiss could appreciate.

As we exited the tram, salivating at the thought of hitting the slope directly below, we were shocked to find no less than three film crews, several photographers, and a glut of ski and snowboard pros. Legions jostling for position outfitted, like us, in the international uniform of ski-bum freeriders: super-fat twin-tips, stickered helmets, and slimline backpacks stuffed with shovels and probes.

God damn Alaska.

IN MOUNTAIN towns, free thinking goes hand in hand with alpine liberation, attracting not only sport-minded folk but also those looking to escape the insanity of a modern world that refuses them respite. That such places often lead individuals to cook up their own particular brand of insanity—cleverly disguised as eccentricity—is moot. You meet all sorts of freaks in mountain towns, and the bigger the town, the bigger the supply. In Engelberg, this included Herr Hoedl, the proprietor of a small sandwich shop. A fifty-year-old Austrian inventor who drove what he called an "autoplane" (and what you and I would call a parade float) that he'd built by fusing the guts of a Volkswagen bus to the body of a World War II fighter jet, he'd overheard that Morrison and I were from Canada and rushed over one day as we were eating.

"Do you know anyone at Bombardier? I've been trying to get them to look at my mechanical horse idea for *years*," he whined, rolling his eyes upward and throwing his hands in the air.

It turned out that he had a crazy-ass notion for a spring-loaded, sit-astride, low-emission all-terrain vehicle. He also had plans for a sit-down snowboard (WTF?)—which he drew on a napkin with no prompting—and, perhaps more bizarrely, a deep knowledge of and abiding admiration for then–Canadian Member of Parliament Belinda Stronach.

How a man of his strange genius also happened to make the best baguette sandwiches in Switzerland was just another happy coincidence of ski-town gestalt. Herr Hoedl, however, came by his eccentricity and inventive nature honestly, as his home and native land was actually known for weirdos fond of similar frontline tinkering and fastidiousness. And when it came to Austrian mountain mavens, none was weirder or more eccentric than Mathias Zdarsky. Historian John Allen explains how this nineteenth-century Renaissance man earned the weightiest title in all of skiing:

If modern skiing owes its development to one extraordinary individual, a singular pioneer, it is Austria's Mathias Zdarsky. Painter, sculptor, teacher, philosopher and health guru, Zdarsky was also an eccentric inventor who developed the steel binding—the first to hold the foot in a stable position, the basis of all ski bindings today. His step-by-step ski instruction method with the introduction of a stem turn, his founding of a mountain *Torlauf* (gate race) in 1905, and most of all his insistence that skiing could and should be enjoyed in the mountains—as opposed to merely foothills—all attest to his right to be called the "Father of Alpine Skiing."[10]

Born in German-speaking Moravia in 1856, the talented youngest of ten children was self-taught in all of his endeavors. He saw his first pair of skis in a traveling show in 1872 and almost sixty years later could still recite their dimensions. However, it would take fifteen years and the popularization wrought by Norwegian Fridtjof Nansen's heroic 1888 crossing of Greenland before Zdarsky paid much attention to these implements. In the 1890s, when Austrians started to emulate the Norwegians working and studying in their country by skiing with primitive bindings and making telemark turns, Zdarsky ordered a pair of Norwegian skis. He analyzed them carefully, declared more or less that they sucked, and proceeded to invent his own ski and binding. His gear and a carefully thought-out methodology utilizing a single balancing pole caught on quickly in Austria, and he went on to teach an estimated twenty thousand people how to ski.

Zdarsky instructed at international conferences, where he passed on knowledge to Austrian, Belgian, Brazilian (?!), German, Polish, and Czech skiers. He trained the Austrian army, whose officers went on to train everyone from the American to the Japanese military. Although Arnold Lunn (not a fan of the single pole) would declare that Zdarsky "taught a bad style," he would give the man kudos for the interest he generated in the sport and the advancements he made in equipment and sensibilities. Clearly, with his assertion that skiing need not be confined to the gentle foothills, where it was preferentially practiced, but could also be accomplished on the steepest and most challenging alpine slopes, the "Newton of Alpine Skiing" also has at least honorary importance to today's generation of big-mountain acolytes.

We, of course, had no clue about this connection, and probably just as well; Zdarsky would roll in his grave at the sight of what is happening to the virgin snow on his favorite slopes. As I'd discovered in Switzerland, things were changing in the Alps. Even in places where nothing *ever* changed. Like Austria.

THEY WERE Hemingway's Humps. The ones Ernest himself toured over with a few adventurous friends in the 1920s when skiing was mad and daring and new, when he was first exploring the region eventually made famous in his stories. Like most Austrian pistes I'd sampled, they were fast and fun, the ground beneath unsculpted by machinery. As a result, they were also damningly and endearingly off-camber.

However, being repeatedly shot sideways at high speed wasn't enough to scuttle another stunning day in the Alps. The previous week's snow was well spread around in Silvretta-Hochjoch, one of several ski resorts lodged high in western Austria's Montafon region, and it sat atop a deep base that encased most of the rocky fins currently poking up in other areas of the Alps. That meant lots of leftover cliff drops and big-mountain lines of all sizes for the young athletes gathered for the Nissan Freeride World Tour event the next day—and more powder for myself and the rest of those content to simply watch the event.

The venerable resort was buzzing in February 2007, its restaurants and bars packed; it seemed alive with the kind of purpose and vibe often missing from Austria's time-burnished resorts, where, despite citizens learning to ski before they can walk, the focus had long been on regimented racing and piste-bound technical skiing—the combination for which this country could claim complementary Motherland status with its neighbor Switzerland. I was happily swept along in a flood of contemporary energy.

In the Darwinian squeeze of a lift line (unlike in North America, where entry lanes funnel skiers into relatively self-regulating mazes, European lines are sink-or-swim corrals where the strong move quickly ahead at the expense of the weak), I merged with an old guy and we loaded onto an old double chair. He said something in German, and I told him, *nicht sprichst Deutsch. Ruski,* he asked? No. But *parlez-vous français,* I wondered? *Nein.* What about Italian? No. I asked if he spoke Spanish. No. We were at a total impasse and yet somehow over the next ten minutes, with *mots* from each language, he found out I was a Canadian from Whistler traveling the alpine intersection of Switzerland, Liechtenstein, and Austria. He thought it *loco* that a Canadian was visiting Europe when everyone wanted to go to Canada, *ja?* He thought my *grossen* skis were better suited to Canadian *poudre* because Austrian *pulverschnee* was maybe not so *bellissimo.* He was six and five fingers old. He had been to Philadelphia. He had a *nouveau* titanium (knocked on knee) that worked *bueno* (the old one was *kaput*) and was pretty happy with his *wenden* (wiggled his hand to simulate turns). At the top, we wished each other a nice day in the same Berlitz mash-up, then skied off toward different countries.

This, I realized, was how Europe worked. The Austrian Alps were also undergoing a renaissance—and venerable

Montafon was a happening and fresh region—but some things still happily pushed back time.

KARIN WEINBERGER represented an Austrian youth-marketing company that worked with local resorts. She met me the next day at Hochjoch's mid-station, where a glut of gondolas, trams, chairs, and various other mechanical nightmares converged on a plaza of sprawling restaurants, outdoor bars, and a fun-park packed with puffy, multi-hued suits dragging skis, snowboards, sleds—and attitude. It seemed like a full-scale party was underway, but it was just business as usual at Hochjoch.

Karin turned out to be a kindred *pulverhund,* so we headed directly over to the north-facing side of the mountain to ski a short wind-loaded face known to avalanche frequently but hold powder for weeks. Dropping down into the trees, we illegally plumbed sweet bowling lanes between towering conifers. The skiing was so good that we made the one-time poach six times, simply strolling back along a road to where an ancient double chairlift that Karin had ridden up from Silbertal, where she lived, intersected with the ultramodern eight-person chair we were currently cycling.

After the last round we downloaded to Silbertal on the creaking, antique double, at one time the world's first chairlift to feature a cover that riders could lower to escape the elements. A strangely squared-off aluminum contraption straight out of a retro space movie, it effectively sealed riders into a tin-can with a window. The maddeningly long ride down gave Karin time to explain the upheaval rattling the region's long-entrenched, race-minded ski culture.

Energizing the youth scene at Hochjoch had apparently been as simple as building more terrain parks, the clarion call for teenagers who had come to have the most say in choosing a holiday destination for the family. Karin's company also worked to organize local and international events on the mountain (like the Nissan Freeride World Tour), bringing in filmmakers, photographers, print- and online-magazine journalists who would ultimately reach the young mobile professionals who formed the new wave of moneyed ski and snowboard tourists. This strategy was obviously working. An important European snowboard film company had rented an apartment in the valley for the entire season, and the previous year more than fifty different media outlets had visited the nearby Silvretta-Nova ski area alone.

At the bottom of the mountain is a parking lot with room for maybe ten cars, wrapped around a barn into which the old chairlift winds in and out. Beside it sits a retired school bus gilded in wood. Inside the bus are a stand-up bar and several seats fashioned from tree stumps. When Karin and I arrived, the world's smallest après-ski hangout hosted a couple of wrinkled instructors, their faces resembling the woodcuts lining the bus's interior, who were smoking and complaining about the lack of snow in the valley and, as always, the influx of foreigners. Though we were still at the same resort, we'd apparently passed through the modern vibe of the Hochjoch galaxy and descended into a time warp on one of its outer edges.

We ordered tea *mit* schnapps, and soon the old bus was crammed to its maximum capacity: thirty crazed humans— all locals—engulfed in smoke and singing and drinking to their day like a small country would celebrate its independence. A Republic of Skiing—spontaneous and timeless in the same instant. More things that never changed.

ALTHOUGH IT WAS a mere twenty-six miles long, Austrians had still seen fit to stuff eleven ski areas into the

Montafon Valley. Much as I would like to have sampled them all, I knew I'd learn more than enough by visiting the three that Karin was involved with. In general, I was told, the focus was on park freeriding at Nova and on off-piste freeriding at Hochjoch. I wasn't sure what Gargellen was about, though sightseeing was definitely in the running: a series of wide alps straddling a ridge flowing off an impressive peak, the views from Gargellen's summit to the greater Alps were spectacular.

There was still powder to be had, too, so I traversed a small lake into a shadowed valley below the stark rocky chutes of 9,100-foot Madrisa Peak. The valley soon filled with alpine ski–tourers bent on milking lines that were much steeper than they looked from across the valley, but at that early hour it was all mine. From the bottom I contoured around onto another steep flank—the Madriss Steilhang—and rode untracked magic down to the gondola base. Returning to the top, I hiked a twisted ridge and dropped over the back, turning in the exquisitely deep snow that lurked between the large iron fences placed on hillsides everywhere to prevent avalanches from thundering down onto pistes, roads, and villages.

An entirely different side of the resort lay beyond the highest lift, and I found more fresh snow—not to mention hundreds of dedicated tourers straining toward a low saddle and the south-facing terrain that dropped off St. Antönier Joch into Switzerland. Heading down the other way, anachronistic clusters of open-sided stables, musty barns, and sagging restaurants (none of which accepted, nor had even heard of, credit cards) recalled the medieval winterscape of Brueghel's *The Hunters in the Snow,* a feeling reinforced by the frequent smell of manure.

Montafon's intersection of occasional modernity and coddled posterity was clear that night, one that began by poaching wireless Internet at the Hotel Montafoner Hof in Tschagguns, then eating across the street in Gasthof Löwen, where Hemingway had often dined. Pictures of Papa H. adorned the walls, but then there were pictures of many things, as well as coats of arms dating to the 1630s. H.'s passage was but a tiny blip in an historic timeline for an establishment that had run continuously since 1500. The simple country fare was as timeless as it was in H.'s day, when he likely sat there marveling over that very continuity. These days the wood-paneling and historic aura is contradicted by the youthful nature of a contemporary crowd that sips flavored schnapps martinis, laughing and drinking like it's a London nightclub.

It seemed I'd fallen further into H.'s footsteps in the tidy town of Schruns when I checked into Hotel Taube, where H. spent the winters of 1924–25 and 1925–26. His wife and child had joined him from Paris, but, naturally, he also had a mistress a short train-ride up the valley—a journalist he eventually married.

The Taube's desk clerk, Pepsi, was a fountain of local knowledge, and though his recall appeared genuine, he was but a baby when H. stayed there. Doubtless he was aided by his parents' stories and a scrapbook full of cracked, sepia photos of H. walking Pepsi's dog or sitting outside the hotel, smoking and drinking with his buddies as their weighty hickory skis with dangling leather bindings leaned against the wall.

Pepsi hobbled on a bum leg, an ancient, undisclosed ski injury. Hitching through corridors, he cycled from parlor to front desk to the family's warren of rooms hidden in the back—like the small dining area where a painting of the church next door by an American friend of H.'s hung on an aquamarine wall, and where H. had played illegal poker with Pepsi's father and the police chief (who knew precisely when the constable on duty would be making his rounds).

I imagined H. bowed over the table in the smoke-filled room, cards to his chest, bluffing his way to a win while stealing glances at the snowflakes illuminated in the gas-lights outside, anticipating another powder day on the mountain.

Unlike much of the new Montafon, Hotel Taube was little changed from those days: halfmoon doorways and old brass locks intact, porcelain sinks and oddly sculpted urinals unaltered. Walking through the hotel felt like traveling not only through a building but through time, history, lives. In my passage, I aimed for quiet, but the Taube's ghosts were having none of it—floorboards creaked out short, unpunctuated sentences as I tiptoed toward the bathroom, the sounds of another loud party rising up the stairs from the hotel's bar.

THE FOLLOWING morning I set out to explore the largest and most popular resort in the area. Although the Montafon Valley held many secrets, Nova wasn't one of them. The mountain was busy given that it was Sunday and the start of the Dutch and German school holidays, but the world's steepest, longest, fastest (and only slightly scary) gondola delivered us into another gargantuan wonderland. From the summit, I looked out over mind-boggling "freeride zones" (Euros loved this phrase), off-piste areas the size of Monaco hemmed by a handful of super-buff pistes that would soon host a crowded homage to Austrian inventiveness: hard-boot snowboarders, short-ski slalom racers, and blue-jeaned Bigfoot (the original "snowblade"—a wide, super-short ski that would have drawn the scorn of both Lunn and Zdarsky) aficionados all *feeling ze carve* together and, more than occasionally, feeling each other at insanely high, out-of-control speeds. Collisions were legion.

Unlike in North America, however, if you get hurt on the hill in Austria you have to pay to have yourself *removed* from the mountain and delivered into the embrace of Austria's *free* health care system—a nice touch that shows how far ahead Euros are in the personal responsibility game, why lift tickets are half the price they are in North America (a much-reduced liability load), and why way more people ski and board per capita there. But, as I'd seen, they remained happily stuck in the past on key cultural fronts.

We were looking forward to that evening's pagan spring celebration called Funken, in which seventy-foot-tall firewood cones topped by a green Christmas tree and a witch stuffed with gunpowder were ignited and danced around by a largely drunken gentry downing schnapps tea, and chewing and choking on various large *wursts*. These pyres took days to assemble and were placed in highly visible locations to build anticipation.

"It's always good when someone else does all the work and then you get to burn it all down," an Austrian freeskier summarized in describing Funken's distinct appeal.

It was night and the fun was about to start. With ten cones sprinkled around the valley and its hillsides, Karin and I decided to station ourselves at the highest one in Bartholomäberg so we could look down on the others. Sure enough, everyone was drunk before the first flame had licked pine; by the time our cone was lit, so was the crowd. Organizers started with a massive, mill-sized pinwheel of burning brooms before sparking the tower. People dressed in the post-medieval outfits of early valley dwellers muddled around the burning structures with pitchforks and hoes. Our cone burned fast, flaming up in seconds and blowing the witch off her perch before most of the wood was even crackling.

From our high vantage, the valley looked like it was full of oil-well fires. When there was naught but smoldering ashes left, we headed off to dinner at another ancient alpen eatery that boasted its own trout pond. On the walk, stray snowflakes wended their way through the interstices between clouds of condensing laughter, the way they had ever since skiing had found its way to this womb.

Modern skiing's Motherlands were changing with the times, but by morning new snow would have given Montafon the only kind of makeover that really mattered.

6 | A SCATTERING IN A COLD WIND

All the other skiers vanished. No sound,
nothing—they just disappeared. I felt as if I
was spinning around. I stopped and yelled but
there was only the noise of the wind. It was
like being dropped in a bowl of milk. As I stood
there ... I saw an amazing sight—a huge boulder
came hurtling up the hill past me.
ANONYMOUS, quoted by Hilary Parke,
Scottish Skiing Handbook, 1989

SNOWBOARDING swept the global winter landscape in the early nineties.
Like a motorcycle gang pulling into a sleepy Nebraska town,
the sudden arrival in the mountains of this high-energy
youth culture led to panic in some quarters and guarded
embrace in others. In Europe, blockheaded ski manufacturers desperately added comical bells and whistles—and a
strange surfeit of letters and numbers—to each new crop
of boards to stave off extinction (then threw in the towel
and started selling snowboards), whereas in North America,
resort owners attempted to contain the mayhem in snowboard ghettos known as "terrain parks" without scaring

off their ski customers (it proved a brilliant move). Alaska, however, was new enough and big enough to serve as a blueprint of exploration and innovation for both sports, and snowsports media rushed to magazine racks, video stores, and the nascent Internet with images of the burgeoning revolution. Skiers and snowboarders represented two highly independent markets, and the sudden need for high volumes of interesting and/or quirky content kicked off a turbo-charged scramble to mine the culture of the world's new and/or unusual snow destinations. The quiet, long-existent brotherhood among these places, which had dwelt in relative obscurity, suddenly became a hyper-connected and globally understood commodity. It was even given a name: The White Planet.

My new *job,* as a full-time writer and editor at POWDER, was to out-think and out-experience others in my position at rival magazines. Which is how I'd found myself in Corner Brook, Newfoundland, the first stop on a tour of several North Atlantic islands. Not only were these wave-lapped outposts little-known ski destinations, but I wanted to know what, if anything, the sport had in common across the iceberg belt.

A hop, skip, and great big jump down Humber Arm fjord from Marble Mountain—the local hill where, I kid you not, skiers were frequently decked out in full sou'westers—the Blomidon Mountains were a windswept jumble of bowls, chutes, buttes, and gorges that featured mostly bare-ass peaks. West winds off the icy North Atlantic hemorrhaged snow onto these promontories, a deluge of fat flakes that blew across tabletops of bright orange peridotite—a heavy-metal-heavy eruption of the Earth's mantle so toxic it couldn't support vegetation—to pile deeply in leeward bowls and create high-alpine conditions at a mere 3,000 feet above sea level. And when the region's frequent fog was on holiday, views to the uncommonly azure waters surrounding the Bay of Islands were enough to make even the staunchest landlubber weep into his mitts. What I'd discovered on my first of several trips here wasn't just powder skiing with the only snowcat operation (skiers are transported up a mountain in a modified, bench-filled grooming machine perched atop a set of tank-like caterpillar tracks) east of the Rocky Mountains, but true adventure skiing on some pretty outrageous terrain. Who knew?

Well, Glenn Noel for one. The affable, soft-spoken powderhound who owned and (occasionally) operated Blomidon Cat Skiing was trying to show fellow Newfies and the rest of the northeastern ski community that Corner Brook was more than just fun-hog heaven for summertime fishing, mountain biking, sea kayaking, and hiking. Come winter, this place had it going on like nowhere else in the snow-starved east: amazing cross-country and alpine skiing, spectacular touring in spectacular mountains, and terrain and snowfall that conspired to allow something as condition-dependent as cat-skiing. Did it matter that Noel had only taken up skiing at age twenty-eight? That he had never driven a cat or even skied from one? That he had no idea how to make a business of it? That he was telling this to journalists who would repeat it to everyone? Well, only if you were keeping track (pun intended).

Noel had actually started cat-skiing as a hobby with friends after purchasing a funky "ski-dozer" that the local telephone company once employed to reach winter repair jobs along its frequently downed lines. Not surprisingly, the lure of easily accessed powder had hooked Noel deep. Like a savvy drug dealer, he'd quickly figured out that selling powder was the best way to keep himself in it.

It wasn't quite a Newfie joke, but there'd been humor aplenty in getting Blomidon Cats up and running. The

Trials of Glenn included the financial hurdles of broken-down cats (mechanical versions are more finicky than real felines), attracting customers to a remote corner of a remote island, winning over the usual gamut of local nay-sayers who apparently preferred the cycle of fishing and government-assisted poverty followed by no fishing and more poverty (someone even sabotaged a bridge Noel had built over a creek on one of his access roads), plus weathering a freak winter drought in the company's inaugural season. However, Noel had persisted, turning his dream into a unique reality for adventure-hungry eastern skiers with few other choices. The nearby province of Quebec boasts La Traversée de Charlevoix, a sixty-five-mile trek through the taiga and tundra landscapes of Parc des Grands-Jardins, as well as the similarly subarctic Chic Choc Mountains of the central Gaspé Peninsula. Both of these areas are back-country-touring ranges where skiers can encounter sensitive caribou herds wandering the high plateaus and must be wholly self-sufficient because there's no commercial mechanized transport. (A onetime heli-op in the Chic Chocs shuttered after its first season due to the almost constant inclement weather.) Thus, a seaside snow dump like Corner Brook, where you could fly in from any city in the east and head directly into the backcountry in a weather-proof cat had considerable potential.

Unlike a savvy drug dealer, however, Noel rarely made money, sometimes broke even, and profited only in keeping his habit sated. (Years later, Noel's father would win a multimillion-dollar lottery prize, putting an end to any bottom-line considerations; Blomidon was then free to run as the hobby snow farm it was at heart.)

Though the name "Blomidon" dated to Newfoundland's early explorers (you could almost hear Captain James Cook sailing into Corner Brook harbor in 1767, growling, "Aye mateys, them there's the Blow-me-downs...”), it was now newly apt. No one who went “down below” with Noel came back anything but blown away by the combination of what passed underfoot and in front of their eyes. I was likewise impressed.

On the day we skied Charlie's Bottom, a wide-smiling glacial cirque, our crew comprised Noel, guide Mark Sang and his brother Steven, freeloading Marble Mountain marketing director Mark Sexton, a couple of giggly local girls of uncertain affinity, me, and chain-smoking Jake, a happy-go-lucky oil-stained mechanic, cat driver in training, and all-around gopher. (Note: *all* cat operations feature a Jake.) After descending several appetizing but bony couloirs that morning, we'd ended up white-caning various other bottoms in low visibility, skiing creamy butter over well-baked toast. Then we headed higher and dropped down a line paralleling a strangely straight-running creek.

“You're skiing on a fault doncha know,” insisted Noel. “The Nort' American plate is here,” he said, pointing at blank snow, “and sometin' else is over dere. Whatever 'tis.”

He wiggled a finger toward some burnt orange peels that might have been a rock outcrop.

It was a weird sort of geology lesson but effective in that most of the group immediately treated the fault as if it were about to split open, staying on the ridge. Which left the gully open for Steven and me to drop into. It quickly became scary free-fall steep, then very, very deep, before following a mellower trough into the valley where we promptly collapsed on shaking legs.

“What the hell was that?” asked Steven.

“You just skied a fifty-foot waterfall,” Noel informed us.

I wasn't surprised. Unlike the liability-conscious shepherding found at most cat-ski operations in the west, Blomidon had all the hallmarks of Alaska's early heli-ops:

rogue pilots, ad hoc guides, and a free-for-all atmosphere that encouraged you to ski where you wanted and take as much air as you wished. Plus ever-present flasks of rum and the occasional joint. Giddy up.

At lunch we babbled about moosegers, salt turbot, fatback, cod tongues, scrunchins, seal-flipper pie, screech, and swish—all apparently food or drink, and all apparently consumed by us over the previous few days.

Later we cat-climbed through bonsai conifers to the summit plateau, skied across the top, scrambled up over some wind-scoured peridotite, and dropped into Charlie's Bottom. Mark Sang expected bulletproof, but I'd assessed the wind marks on the summit from across the valley and bet on p-o-w-d-e-r. I won. Or rather, we both did.

It was kind of exquisite and there, thigh-deep in the lightest of North Atlantic chowders, Sexton had an epiphany; he'd never experienced a run like that and was clearly astonished to be doing so in his backyard. And here was a guy who'd grown up in Corner Brook and skied the well-powdered slopes of Marble all his life.

As it did hourly, weather threatened after lunch, and visibility wandered farther south, but that didn't stop us from clawing our way back across the summit toward a brace of short, fifty-degree couloirs. A ferocious wind and full whiteout prevailed when we finally gained the peridotite sentinels marking the entrance to an unskied drop which, in another ode to AK-like daily discovery, we named Grip Me.

It was all that new.

The Sangs and I leapfrogged down the throat, reaching open talus below, where we leaned back with satisfaction and let our skis run straight at top speed in the fluff, mirroring old black-and-white photos of ski pioneers who looked like they were having fun but were probably just afraid to turn their huge planks in anything over their ankles. Then it was back to the chugging cat and the warmth of Corner Brook, where I waited out the latest storm in the comfort of Strawberry Hill, a converted turn-of-the-century manor overlooking the salmon pools of the Humber River, where even the Queen had once pulled up her skirt. A pair of brothers named McCarthy claimed to have taken good care of me that night, though I have my doubts: I awoke face down on the floor with my clothes on, drool on the floor, and a faint hint of cod on my lips. Had I been "screeched-in," the ritual rum-consumption and fish-kissing Newfies loved to foist on those "from away"? I'd never know and no one would ever say, but it was telling that several other writers I sent this way had identical experiences.

My final day saw a mad dash to squeeze in some last-minute runs. Noel turned the cat up through a maze of black spruce and larch toward The Terraces, a series of rollicking, gladed benches adjoining the previous day's playground. The sun flickered through a thick curtain of flurries billowing in off the ocean, occasionally revealing a sky of glorious blue. I ripped line after powdery line with more giggling female freeloaders and Jonathan, yet another sibling Sang had dragged out.

Skiing was magic again, though changeable conditions made fat skis a must. I wondered whether or not such an operation would have been viable before the advent of AK-bred fatties, or whether local powderhounds would have been confined to Marble, where black-diamond runs were rated "Moose Difficult."

Viability be damned, skiing in Newfoundland was likely older than anyone thought. The Vikings, the world's first traveling ski team, were there some five hundred years before Columbus and his boys infected the Caribbean with smallpox, syphilis, and, ironically, the rum-running that would sustain the once independent nation of Newfoundland (it had only reluctantly joined Canada in 1949).

To this day, no one is sure why the wind-battered island that everyone calls The Rock was labeled Vinland by Viking seafarer Leif Ericsson, but it makes perfect sense to me: when you spend most of your life bobbing around in a wooden ship surrounded by icebergs, even a verdant splash of lichen might cast a place like Newfoundland as a thickly vegetated paradise. Especially if, like Leif, you'd spent your formative years under Greenland's towering icecap... or were born amid the stark volcanic rubble of a place called Iceland.

MARGRÉT HARPA HANNESDÓTTIR, winner of the 1990 Reykjanes Peninsula beauty contest, gnawed on the knot of dried fish hanging from her mouth and rubbed handfuls of viscous white mud on my shoulders while expounding on the curative powers of the Bláa Iónið (Blue Lagoon). She insisted that the silicate-rich water pooling in the vaporous shadows of a futuristic-looking geothermal-heating plant in a lava-field on the peninsula had wrought no end of miracles for the afflicted who frequented this public spa.

Floating on my back, I stared up through the mists enveloping the pool—one second they were descending shrouds, the next a swirling tempest indistinguishable from the bruised clouds scudding overhead—and wondered whether a global switch to geothermal power might likewise eventually keep the hounds and jackals of climate change at bay. As if in mute answer, snowflakes materialized from the fog to alight like cold, wet kisses. At least that much was pleasant. Otherwise, the air stank of sulfur (again), and we were surrounded to every horizon (again) by a chaotic jumble of the Earth's guts turned inside out and left to dry. Fair symmetry given that atop the basaltic rubble stood miles of wooden racks hung with fish, also turned inside out and left to dry.

The whole scene looked and felt like a movie set.

ICELAND MAY HAVE inhereited its phantasmagorical landscapes from a rip in the bottom of the ocean, but this island nation's cultural heritage could be traced directly to Norway. Since the latter was the birthplace of skiing, Iceland had long-embraced the sport in kind. Although its tiny population supported only a handful of tiny ski hills, there were mountains and icecaps aplenty and no shortage of backcountry bravado to make use of them. Photographer Henry Georgi and I hoped to tap into a few of these efforts.

Leaving the Blue Lagoon's opalescent waters behind, we followed a tortured coastline north of the capital, Reykjavík, battling squalls of every conceivable form of precipitation. By the time we hit the south shore of Snæfellsnes Peninsula, a fierce blizzard bearing down from Greenland had turned the universe into a one-dimensional wall of wind and snow. We tiptoed across Frodarheidi Pass through deepening drifts, dropping down to a north coast that truly felt like the end of the Earth: the blizzard thickened and the ocean raged, tossing ice floes onto the road and fear into our hearts.

The whiteout was so severe that we were halfway through Ólafsvík—a tough-as-nails fishing village known for its, natch, malicious weather—before we knew we were in it, and Guesthouse Höfdi seemed a mirage we half-expected to vanish. But it was real, as was the welcome by Arnljótur "Arri" Arnarson, who gathered us in with his hot soup and soft voice.

Arri's dream was to build a year-round ski area on Snæfellsjökull, the massive glacier covering the Snæfells Volcano that, apparently, loomed above Ólafsvík. He shared that dream with many, including a quiet, lanky snowmobiler named Søvar who flew through the door like *Seinfeld's* Kramer, followed by what was left of the blizzard. Søvar nodded greeting, sat down, and yanked out a pile of maps, charts, and photos taken on the volcano, the latter revealing strange shapes and peculiar, unnaturally hued light. Were the photos even real? Søvar and Arri handled them like religious icons, speaking of the mountain in reverential tones.

"When the weather clears," said Søvar, "I will take you up the volcano."

Snæfells was no run-of-the-mill lava furnace. Writer Jules Verne had set the beginning of *Journey to the Centre of the Earth* here, his protagonists descending into the crater to start their trek. An award-winning film, *Under the Glacier* (people from Snæfellsnes often uttered the peculiarity "I was born under the glacier"), based on the one-of-a-kind masterpiece by Nobel laureate Halldór Laxness, addressed the weird and mystifying occurrences in the surrounding countryside. However, knowledge of the mountain's pervasive power—which explained Arri's and Søvar's demure behavior—went back even farther in time. Nostradamus (1503–66), French master of the apocalyptic prediction, is said to have cryptically foretold the Ronald Reagan–Mikhail Gorbachev summit meetings of the early eighties in Reykjavík based on the location of this peak. Ancient power lines drawn from Egyptian pyramids also sliced through the Reykjanes Peninsula to converge on Snæfells, and the volcano featured prominently in several Icelandic Sagas, the great oral traditions chronicling Norse discovery and occupation of the island. It was all pretty heavy juju for a potential ski area. Maybe too heavy.

It was windy that night, and fishing boats chugged carefully into the harbor. Arri's cook stuffed us with an excellent flounder in pastry and spherical, bright-yellow potatoes washed down with fifteen-dollar bottles of Viking beer.

"Tomorrow," Arri assured us, "the wind will shift and we will see Snæfells."

I sure hoped so; we couldn't afford to sit around drinking beer.

The weather was indeed clearing the next evening, save for a lingering mushroom hanging over the volcano. After dinner, the call came from Søvar, and Henry and I scrambled like firefighters to join him, his sister, and two powerful snowmobiles on the Snæfellsjökull road. Following undulating valleys upward, we broke out under a jagged peak where it met the broad expanse of the volcano's northwest flank and the base of the glacier. The mountain was enormous, the cloud deck now a donut below the peak. At forty miles per hour, we reached the cloud soon enough, and after ten minutes of featureless fog, beheld two gargoyle-like spires of boiling rime rising three hundred feet above.

It was then that Snæfells seized me, as it had countless others, with a strange, overpowering sensation, like being granted audience with some supreme being. Looking over the sea, I saw that the sun and moon hung at the same height, throwing dreamlike colors across the landscape. The face below the summit spires was an intimidating forty-five degrees with a noticeable bergschrund (a crevasse that commonly occurs where a glacier abuts a steep face) running across its base, but we were able to descend the grippy, rimed surface and cross the 'shrund safely to ski down to Søvar and his sister. They delivered us back to the saddle and then left, the snowmobiles becoming specks as they disappeared into the valley, their persistent whine reduced to a sound like buzzing flies.

Our denouement was cranking long, high-speed turns down the glacier in the glow of a rapidly lapsing sun. It took a full twenty minutes to reach the snow machines where they waited among Stonehenge-like ice formations thrust up, according to Søvar, by volcanic eruptions beneath the glacier. What? As if Snæfells' weather weren't enough, apparently these guys wanted to build a ski area atop cracking glaciers and an exploding volcano.

WITH ANOTHER blizzard blackening the northern sky in the morning, we retreated south to Reykjavík, reveling in the many sights that had been obscured during our drive in. Vast moonscapes left us slack-jawed, and the size and diversity of lava flows was mesmerizing; the land was truly suffused with magic.

It was also, like Laxness's novels, suffused with weirdness. On the capital's trim streets, where the air was achingly fresh and the women all had yogurt complexions, we were chased by a demonic young girl brandishing a spear made from a bread knife lashed to a broomstick. The look in her eye suggested evil gnome (why not?—surveys find that 75 percent of Icelanders believe in troll-like beings known as Huldufólk, or "hidden people"). She actually tried to stab us, then smiled sweetly. In retrospect, the absurdity said a lot about Björk's music and the zombie whine of bands like Sigur Rós.

Fortunately, Ingi Ingersson showed up at Hótel Leifur Eiríksson the next morning to rescue us in his very cool monster truck. We shared his ultra-sophisticated four-wheel drive and several similar units—all of them equipped with enormous tires, extra gas tanks, dual crankshafts, fore and aft winches, air pumps, roll and pitch gyroscopes, altimeters, radios, cellular phones (before cell phones were even known), and satellite navigation systems—with a

British tour group. Supposedly we were going skiing, but it felt more like we were going to sail around the world.

This time we followed the coast south from Reykjavík, crossing the broad delta of the White River before ascending a plain of tephra (volcanic fragments) regurgitated by nearby Hekla, Iceland's largest volcano, which had most recently suffered indigestion the previous year. On the ride, Catherine, a well-informed Brit, kept us spellbound with quasi-believable stories. Her trove of local yarns included a traditional bedtime saga about the outlaws Evinder and Hatla, who spent twenty years on the run for sheep stealing and were in the habit of tossing their children into waterfalls when the youngsters got too big or troublesome. In a lilting voice, Catherine sang the lullaby Hatla offered her children to explain why she was dumping them. It was beautiful, haunting, and... kinda freaky.

Icecaps were visible on the horizon in several directions as we climbed onto the country's interior plateau, where we left the road and spent the afternoon being pulled, water-ski style, behind the trucks through a snowbound desert that could have been the cover of a Pink Floyd album. Finally, we bounced over a pass and onto the plain below Landmannalaugar, a weighty name framed by some weighty geology. Ingi and I immediately climbed several hundred feet up one of many spurs flowing from an ancient volcano and had a whooping turning duel down its flank in another phenomenal wash of low-angle Arctic light.

At the foot of the ridge, abutted by a tumult of lava, the Landmannalaugar Hut was surrounded by fourteen snowmobiles, replete with fluorescent flags, all parked helter-skelter. Though people drove into the area to mess around in their 4WDs or, like us, do some ski touring, it was also a popular stop for snowmobile safaris. A group of French adventurers was soaking in the hot springs of a lava flow at the foot of a multicolored mountain of rhyolite, chugging whiskey and smoking stinky Gitanes.

More odd colors floated around them in the hot springs, where mats of sulfur-metabolizing blue-green algae ruled. You had to watch where you sat: marauding blasts of scalding water could poach you in a flash, and if you dug your fingers even an inch into the sandy bottom, they would burn. The hot springs, however, afforded the best view of the area's dazzling display of ochre, fuchsia, and otherworldly brown mountains. Nearby, a white cornice overhung a burgundy hillside where acrid vapors sputtered from sulfur-rimmed fumaroles; it was like hell veneered in snow.

Ingi outdid himself at dinner, preparing smoked salmon and a savory leg of lamb cooked on hot lava, which we appreciated after days of consuming and being nauseated by whale blubber and putrid three-month-old shark meat, chased with these delicacies' mutual antidote: the gasoline-like, anise-laced schnapps known as Brennivín (Black Death). We didn't want to know the etymology of the name.

In the morning, Ingi, Henry, and I spent several satisfying hours under unusually clear weather skiing the perfectly corned face of a large hill downvalley from the hut, leaving tight tracks on the wide-open 1,000-foot slope. Though we'd jettisoned the rest of the group, our activities remained surreal; like the previous day, when Ingi had blasted Pavarotti from the truck stereo as he towed us across the desert, our descents were accompanied by music. Strains of Tchaikovsky and "The Ride of the Valkyries" from Wagner's Ring Cycle rose from the valley floor. The incongruous ballet continued at the bottom, where a possessed Ingi swept through leaning lava towers clutching an invisible partner to the lilting strings of "The Blue Danube" waltz. While the sun blazed on cold, crisp snow and steam rose from smoldering vents, Ingi spun one final time, let out an ecstatic cry, dropped to his knees, and raised his hands to the plunging ridges across the valley.

"These mountains lie in the sun like a beautiful woman," he cried, "and I must make love to them!"

Even *skiing* in Iceland looked and felt like a movie set.

MY NORTH ATLANTIC tour felt like a drinking binge, so it only made sense to go someplace where consuming too much alcohol was unavoidable. Scotland turned out to be one of the strangest places Henry and I would ever put plank to snow—and not just because the snow wouldn't stay put or the eternally fogged-in mountains were only there in theory, but more because circumnavigation of its handful of ski areas followed another well-worn route, the Malt Whisky Trail.

The immediate comparisons that sprang to mind on first(ish) sight of the Scottish Highlands—New Zealand's South Island and Chilean Patagonia—were largely due to the a) profusion of sheep and paucity of humans, b) abundance of trout and salmon rivers, c) brown-hilled, cardboard landscapes, d) heinous peaks veiled by mist and scary weather, and e) banshee winds and changeable snow. The latter would rule the trip, but frequent stops for distillery tours would make it tolerable.

Winter weather in the Scottish hills was uniformly miserable. The country was battered by both oceanic and continental storms—sometimes on the same day—resulting in wild fluctuations in freezing level, precipitation type, and visibility. At our first stop, CairnGorm Mountain near Aviemore, we narrowly missed colliding with startled reindeer that materialized on the slopes with regularity from thick fog. Some kind of precipitation was falling sideways (a feature of most storms here) and although it *was* crystallized water, it wasn't snow. I'd never seen anything like it: it was neither sleet nor true ice pellet, but lighter, irregularly shaped masses, the size and consistency of Styrofoam packing that, in the driving wind, felt like hairbrush bristles being bounced off your face. This was my introduction to graupel. In the maelstrom, it was hard to tell which way was up, down, or sideways and impossible to maintain balance while standing still on any low-angled ground. Though skiing blind quickly became art out of necessity, it was almost a godsend to find ourselves atop a fifty-degree chute named, appropriately, Flypaper, where gravity took care of our orientation.

According to Hilary Parke's somewhat tongue-in-cheek *Scottish Skiing Handbook,* unrealistic expectations about learning curves and weather were the main cause of people dropping out of the sport. But five minutes at a Scottish ski field—where snow was farmed with myriad crisscrossing fences to corral it for at least those five minutes—and your expectations were so low that anything short of a full gale was considered pleasant.

Perhaps this explains why Scottish skiers are the most ardent enthusiasts on the planet. Their tolerance—indeed enjoyment—of every conceivable misery is unsurpassed in the annals of sport. Even at Glenshee, the nation's largest ski area, located just south of Braemar, herds of soggy skiers lunched in their vehicles, marooned and anonymous in an endless car park, windows steamed and ski boots tucked under the running boards. This seemed strange until we saw the queue that wound from a pitiful café out into the driving rain. On the pistes we joined skiers and boarders wearing balaclavas and dressed head-to-toe in Gore-Tex, battling on against the elements, turning aimlessly down heather-laced, sheet-ice hills they couldn't even see, hoping always for the grail of a sunny day. Clearly, the Scots' credo fit the old bumper-sticker saw: The Worst Day of Skiing Is Better Than the Best Day at Work.

In the Spittal of Glenshee, a popular watering hole where medieval travelers once gathered and formed armed groups to cross the mountains (worried about wolves—both human and canine), the owner had lamented the theft of a precious Urinal Rock (I'd been strangely pleased to know there were such things) inscribed with "Prince Charles Pissed Here," as if it were a family heirloom or one of the Crown Jewels. Perhaps it now was. American extreme skiers Scot Schmidt and Glen Plake were heroes here as well, as cinematographer Greg Stump's *Blizzard of Aahhhs* (the 1988 film that kicked off the global extreme-ski revolution) cycled endlessly on the VCR. The Scots eyed the powder scenes like they were lunar landings, and the expressions of lust on their faces confirmed that the oft-cited sexual lure of deep powder was predictably exacerbated for those permanently deprived of it.

After skiing at Scotland's first commercial ski area, Glencoe near Fort William (since shuttered), we ducked into the Clachaig Inn, where talk around the woodstove by bushy-browed men was of mushy gullies and insipid climbing; heaps of rope, crampons, and ice axes were piled by the door. Everyone wore gaiters, and the bar proudly boasted every single malt in Scotland: among the bottles hung ice screws and carabiners for sale. The walls were papered with photos of Hamish MacInnes, doyen of Scottish mountaineering, and fiddles wailed in the background. Climbers and ski mountaineers staggering in on the edge of death could find all means of resuscitation here—whisky, ale, tea, and portions of food large enough to choke Nessie: tables bristled with platters of haggis, neeps, and tatties; pints of ale, Guinness, and shots of single malt with names like Sheep Dip. Consequently, staggering seemed more intense among those leaving.

By the time we reached the upper plateau of Nevis Range/Aonoch Mor—Scotland's newest ski area, and the one on which we made our final, somewhat drunken turns—we were expecting the usual boilerplate. Instead we found cold, dryish snow that actually provided great turning with views of Scotland's highest peak, Ben Nevis, in the background. For the first time in days, Henry and I weren't *druchit* (soaked) and so, eyeing a conga line of skiers, telemarkers, and kilted snowboarders (I'm not making this up) hiking toward a run that plunged to the valley floor, "we'd caught them up" (caught up with them) by pushing hard with our sticks (poles) and joined the procession. This motley crew dropped en masse into a large *corrie* (cirque) and "bashed around" (rode) until they were all "knackered" (tired, broken), confirming for me that whatever else the Scottish mountain scene was all about, its snow sports all lived side by side in peace and misery.

The Scots' ability to accommodate in the mountains went beyond the typical British stiff upper lip. Perhaps it harked back to earlier incursions along the Scottish coast, let's say during the ninth century or so, by a group of indefatigable North Sea warriors that had thrown up settlements around the modern country's northern reaches and archipelagos and claimed the arc of supersized islands to the north and west that petered out at the North American plate. Perhaps, in a flash of low-angled maritime light, it could even be seen as positively Scandinavian.

WHERE ICELAND'S edges had proved somewhat green, Greenland's were proving decidedly icy. This was interesting only in that we'd just run aground on a rock in the Arctic Ocean with ice floes thudding off the metal hull of the SS *Coffin,* in whose lower bunk I was pretending not to be panicking. We'd eventually float off the rock on a rising tide, but it was the kind of thing that happened with alarming regularity in the wild environs of Greenland, the last stop on my North Atlantic tour.

Even if the Viking ski team hadn't been muttering "Greenland's icy, Iceland's green" through frozen beards and chattering teeth as they rowed their sea-monster long-boats between the two islands—mantras not exactly being part of the pagan way—the phrase rang true enough to represent the biggest paradox in the North Atlantic. But here was another: Iceland, with its violently erupting land-scapes, lava deserts, and lack of significant elevation, actu-ally had a few ski areas and a whole lot of skiers; Greenland, with mountains galore, glacial tongues lolling off its cen-tral icecap to the ocean at every turn, and a winter season that lasted, uh... forever... had no real skiing to speak of. I wanted to know why.

WELL, ALMOST NO skiing. Greenland did have Larseraq Skifte, Apussuit ski camp, and a whole lot of hope.

A striking man raised traditional Inuit in the West Greenland outpost of Maniitsoq, Larseraq was fortunate enough to have been schooled in Fairbanks, Alaska, and in Dartmouth, New Hampshire, where he learned English, the ways of the outside world, and a sport he'd never seen—skiing. Returning to Maniitsoq in the late seventies, he was full of ideas, a passion for skiing, and a belief that outdoor recreation and tourism were essential both to delivering the global we're-all-in-this-together humanitarian mes-sage and to preserving Inuit culture.

It took a few years for people to listen, but eventually Larseraq and his newly formed ski club forged ahead with plans for a ski camp at Apussuit ("big snow"), a domed glacier twenty miles across open water from Maniitsoq. Greenland's Home Rule government kicked in for huts, snowmobiles, and even a grooming machine. Some day,

Larseraq hoped, ski teams from abroad would visit Apussuit for summer training, providing a crucial exchange with the outside world for citizens, and a glimpse for outsiders of the recreational potential of his native Kalaallit Nunaat—Land of the People.

Although it seems strange that the skiing diaspora of Scandinavian and European alpine countries that accompanied the great pre— and post—World War II emigrations and settled over most of the globe between the 1920s and 1940s landed so late in a place so ripe for germination—80 percent of the landmass is icecap, 15 percent is mountains, and snow falls in every month of the year—there were important reasons why. Pancake-flat Denmark, which has controlled Greenland for hundreds of years, isn't exactly a skiing hotbed, and the Greenlandic Inuit, whose lives revolve around hunting and fishing, have always been focused on the sea. In that environment, wooden planks couldn't hold a candle to dogsleds, the preferred mode of transportation. In fact, natives thought explorer Fridt-jof Nansen's landmark 1888 ski crossing of Greenland—the well-reported journey that sparked much of Europe's nascent interest in the sport, including the likes of Mathias Zdarsky—to be complete and utter madness. The idea of being out on skis away from safety in the cold and dark of winter seemed a huge gamble. It all added up to passive disinterest. Until Larseraq.

Skifte's dream had crept closer to reality after a fortuitous meeting with Paul Freemont-Smith, Jr., a wealthy trustee at the Carrabassett Valley Academy, a ski and snowboard training school in Sugarloaf, Maine. Their association led to the first American ski racers sampling Apussuit's pistes and to an exchange program where, like Larseraq, a few fortunate Inuit skied and were schooled in the States.

In the early nineties, Freemont-Smith led an expedition to Greenland that included a film crew, POWDER's Steve Casimiro, and several pro skiers and snowboarders. The resulting article and TV show were supposed to boost Apussuit's aspirations to create a destination ski area and help stimulate tourism in Maniitsoq, which, like North Atlantic towns from Corner Brook to Reykjavík, was reeling from depleted fish stocks.

Although the snow and skiing on 3,000-foot Apussuit were very good, it was largely uninteresting terrain, so that first crew of adventurers spent more time exploring by helicopter—particularly the nearby block of ragged, steep-peaked glacial geology known as Hamborgerland, one of the most spectacular sights along the west coast. The surrounding archipelago was peppered with historical sites like Ikamiut, a haunting abandoned village destroyed by a tidal wave and now populated only by weathered skulls propped on open crypts. Canadian ski legend Trevor Petersen, who had been on that first trip, developed a deep-felt kinship with the stunning land and its generous people. After he perished in a 1996 avalanche in Chamonix, a memorial in his honor was erected near the Ikamiut burial grounds, and a few ashes scattered.

I felt a similarly powerful connection. In Ikamiut, hardscrabble cultures had flourished for three thousand years, fearless hunters plying freezing ocean in skittish boats of wood, whalebone, ivory, sinew, and sealskin, maintaining balance with a narrow paddle while accurately throwing harpoons to wrestle up life-giving animals that weighed several tons. The combinations were intricate but efficient. A dance of skill with natural forces. Like skiing.

Traveling largely by boat (remember the ss *Coffin?*) with Larseraq and another American-schooled Inuit named Fredrik, we scoured the coastline for likely looking slopes, climbing hundreds of feet above the ocean under hanging glaciers and leaden skies to explore unnamed peaks for the first time. Navigating crevasse-riddled glaciers and dealing with the ever-present risk of avalanches, each ski run involved a seeming season's worth of snow conditions starting in the powdery high alpine and ending in mush at the edge of a shimmering copper fjord, the smell of the sea in our nostrils, whales breaching on the horizon. Each descent was more transformative, even those around the more urban environs of Sisimiut.

Located along a mountainous section of the west coast, Sisimiut is the country's northernmost ice-free port. It also sits astride rich whaling grounds and marks the southernmost extent of walrus habitat. Fishing runs the economy there: nearly ten thousand tons of shrimp are processed annually in a plant next to the bright, colorful harbor, but the spectacular mountain backdrop gives the town an almost alpine feel. Indeed a nearby glacier, like Apussuit to the south, was developed as a ski area for the local ski club—yet another initiative of the ubiquitous Larseraq.

The town is also home to Larseraq's biggest triumph, the wildly successful Arctic Circle Race, an international cross-country loppet that attracts hundreds of Euro and North American racers every spring. This event, more than any other, ultimately put Greenlandic skiing on the map, despite a three-day course over terrain so difficult that people have been lost to avalanches and heart attacks. With rival local factions of dogsledders and snowmobilers cooperating as support teams, the initiative has inspired many kids to take up cross-country skiing and other sports, activities that, as Larseraq had predicted, have played a beneficial role in the future of the country's social fabric.

Despite this success, Larseraq's dream of a ski camp at Apussuit was put on hold while Freemont-Smith ran a heli-ski operation out of Maniitsoq for a season. As it had in other North Atlantic locales, however, downtime due to poor weather and sky-high costs eventually killed that idea. (Alaskan heli-ops are also notorious for vast stretches of downtime, but that place is easier and less costly to reach than anywhere in the North Atlantic.) Eventually there was a resurgence of interest in developing Apussuit as more than just an adventurous place to go ski touring. Ski-lift lines have been surveyed, and someday the ski clubs of Maniitsoq might have their own little paradox rising above the glistening waters of the world's largest island: a ski area accessible only by boats that would jostle with whales for parking space in the fjords—just as the Vikings did.

I DIDN'T EXACTLY have carte blanche, but there was money to spend at magazines in those days and few of my wilder travel ideas went unconsidered. Building on the foreign baptisms of Chile and Mexico, a concatenation of magazine articles, obscure books, rumor, and innuendo drove the wanderlust behind my tour of the White Planet. This desire wasn't about ticking countries off a mental world map—that was just gravy cooked up by geopolitical boundaries. For me, much of skiing's intrigue lay in how the planet's long-term forces combined with the momentary tantrums of the atmosphere in different places—geology, in all its multifarious forms, meeting meteorology, in all its angry outbursts—and how this crucible intersected with the cultures inhabiting them.

The North Atlantic's litany of stepping-stone islands and quasi-connected bedrock had delivered a few lessons, but I had another water body in my sights: the Mediterranean. Oddly, skiing actually had serious beachheads in most of the countries ringing this warm sea, each quite distinct. These places would certainly be different than those of the North Atlantic, providing ready comparison: New World versus Old; cold versus warm; Nordic and colonizing sensibilities versus timeless mountain cultures. The bigger questions, however, were the same. Who were the people in these places? How had they come to this sport (or it to them) and whither its direction there? I would soon find out.

7 | A SCATTERING IN A WARM WIND

I didn't talk to anyone much; I just skied and
traveled. Everything was like cut-glass crystal:
sharp, fine, pure... Maybe I had just forgotten
what life was really like.

BOB JAMIESON, "Me and Truck," *Skiing*, 1972

A FALAFEL SANDWICH is built around
deep-fried balls of ground chickpeas
and spices folded up in a pita with tomatoes, greens, and
garlic sauce. For North Americans, a falafel is *the* icon of
Lebanese cuisine. Back in the day, when Henry Georgi and I
got together to discuss article ideas for the upcoming winter, we met for falafels at El-Basha, a hole-in-the-wall operation on Toronto's Bloor Street that catered to artists and
writers.

The walls were hung with faded tourism posters from
the halcyon days when Beirut was a jet-set jewel, Paris of
the Mediterranean. Some featured beach scenes; others,
ancient ruins; and still others, soaring alpine backdrops
and glistening white slopes interrupted by the squat symmetry of snow-clad Lebanese cedars. It seemed about as
exotic as winter could get.

"Think of the skiing," I'd say wistfully, knowing that the prevailing political and military dangers of the time would keep all but the most foolhardy from poking around those slopes.

"Yeah," Henry would enthuse, garlic sauce clinging to his beard as he held the remainder of his lunch aloft like a torch, "and think of the falafels!"

Our glib exchanges belied reality. For as long as I could remember, nightly newscasts had provided armchair views to the slow destruction through war of Beirut, one of the world's great cities, and my friends and I had long since passed from questioning the horror to making nervous jokes about hijackings, suicide bombings, and the short life expectancies of a string of Lebanese prime ministers.

The situation wasn't funny, of course, but Lebanon's woes had become meaningless. Beirut was war, and war was Beirut. Fantasizing about skiing there made great lunchtime conversation, but it was a pipe dream of the highest order... until the civil war suddenly ended and I had a fortuitous encounter on the windswept peak of New Hampshire's Mt. Washington with Lebanese-American Rich Elias.

Climber, poet, philosopher, dreamer, and orphaned native son, Rich had spearheaded the 1993 International Peace Ski, in which he'd led a platoon of thirteen adventurers from ten countries to Lebanon to climb, ski, and work in a medical clinic. Peace Ski was a bold initiative. Like Larseraq Skifte, Rich's previous climbing and skiing adventures had taught him the worth of the outdoor experience for crossing cultural and language barriers. Peace Ski had reunited Rich with his birthplace and furthered the cause of amity and cooperation in the process. Non-military foreigners weren't common in Lebanon at the time, and Peace Ski had ignited a sense of hope for renewal and a brighter future. And now he was planning a return trip. Was I interested, he wondered?

LANDING AT BEIRUT airport was predictably strange. The plane swooped down over burned-out hangars onto a dangerously cratered runway. Inside the skeletal terminal, where police and military outnumbered travelers, the fierce display of weaponry that would accompany our days began. Large, shot-up billboards featuring grim-faced ayatollahs rose along the garbage-strewn highway into town, appearing to say "Welcome in our Destructed Country!"

East Beirut, where the fifteen-year war had raged fiercest, was a monument to survival. The exterior of any building still standing was constellated with bullet holes and the gaping wounds of rocket attacks. And yet, people were cooking on small fires in the rubble, hanging out the wash in wall-less apartments, picking up the pieces of perpetually shattered lives. The city, located where cities had stood for three thousand years and civilizations had come and gone so many times that historians couldn't agree on how many, was again in transition. Bulldozers and cranes were cleaning, demolishing, renovating, building. With everything half-wrecked or half-finished, it was hard to see where the destruction ended and the resurrection began. But the city was alive with purpose and so was I.

Two days later, I stood atop The Cedars, a ski area in the high alpine an hour northeast of Beirut that was named for the last enclave of the gargantuan trees found there and nowhere else in the world. Giant cedars weren't the only thing that grew there: it was also the place where Lebanon's first ski seed had landed and blossomed. After an enthusiastic engineering student brought the sport back from Switzerland and generated interest in the early thirties, the French Army set up a ski-warfare school at The Cedars to train soldiers in mountain-patrol techniques. The program also produced the country's first expert skiers and a nascent ski area. In 1942, James Riddell—the man who often shared the title of Father of Modern Ski Journalism with Arnold Lunn—had lodged here, administering the Middle East Ski and Mountaineering School for the Australian 9th Army (I know...). Gazing over the open terrain, I could see what had made the area so attractive for these endeavors. It had snowed overnight, the sun was shining, and below stretched expanses of invitingly untracked powder. No more than fifty people were skiing on a handful of lifts operating at the mercy of the country's sporadic power supply. From the summit ridge, you could gaze west over the shimmering Mediterranean, then descend almost 4,000 vertical feet to a vast basin drained by a rock-cut canyon so enormous it defied description—though Khalil Gibran, born on its edge, and author of *The Prophet,* had tried.

Dropping onto that slope was as close to realizing a vision as skiing Mexico's dirty volcanoes; the exotic scenery, unexpected late-March powder, and the turns I lost track of after a hundred amounted to the best skiing I'd had all season—not to mention reproducing the poster from El-Basha.

Unfortunately, Henry had become unavailable, so I'd joined Rich, photographer and ski-bum extraordinaire Nolen Oayda, who was born in Australia to Lebanese immigrants, and, for comic relief, snowboarder Shane Gould. Shane was improbably headquartered in South Carolina, where he designed for his own snow/skate/surf streetwear company. We had sketchy plans to complete a four-day traverse of the Lebanon Mountains from The Cedars in the north to the larger Faraya-Mzaar resort in the south.

The next morning, we set out to climb Qornet es Saouda (The Black Corner), Lebanon's highest peak at 10,135 feet.

Rich, Nolen, and I skimmed over the rocky terrain like hares, while in the distance Shane wallowed on snowshoes like an overloaded tortoise for what would prove to be a four-hour death march to nowhere. Our escorts, the enthusiastic, twin-costumed Lebanese Army guides we'd nicknamed Fric and Frac, doffed their flimsy cross-country skis and were wisely kicking steps up the vertical halfpipe of a couloir, followed by Shane, who now put both his snowboard and snowshoes on his back. The rest of us zigzagged upward on skins, a warmup for the next day's planned traverse. Unfortunately, we weren't really sure where we were going—we didn't have a map. When a dense fog descended, we stopped to consider whether or not to continue. While we sipped water and scarfed a snack, Fric and Frac, who carried no such supplies, suddenly whipped army-issue 9mm pistols from their waistbands and began firing. Not realizing this was recreational, Nolen and I hit the snow with hands over our heads, while Shane hung calmly in the background. After emptying a clip, a smiling Fric offered me the gun. Horrified, I declined. Nolen, too. Not Southern Man Shane.

"Sure, I *love* guns," he enthused, blowing off a clip in the direction of the nearest Syrian encampment.

It might have been an echo, but I was pretty sure I heard shots being returned. Either way, we decided that proceeding without a map in such conditions was folly.

Locating topographic maps of Lebanon had been problematic. An agency that could supply them—maybe—quoted an astronomical $2,400 USD, and our efforts in London en route also turned up nothing with enough detail to navigate by. The next day, in the Lebanese Army's barracks at The Cedars, I discovered why. These high-mountain plateaus were of great strategic importance, and *only* the military had maps. When I finally saw one in the office of the corporal who ran the barracks, the 1:20,000 rendition that showed even the most minute undulations took up half the room. We'd thought the traverse would follow an obvious route, but poring over this wallpaper cartography revealed a lot of up and down to Faraya, and though we could bear generally southward, without a map we'd waste valuable time taking indirect valleys. And what were those *thousands* of tiny tick marks layered over our proposed ski route?

"Oh," said the corporal, "those are land mines. But not to worry my friend, they are covered in snow... perhaps."

And that was the end of any attempt to make an off-piste traverse.

Nolen had seen a military map as well. Demonstrating how small the global ski-adventuring community is—or at least the supply of easily accessible adventures—a group led by Australian guide John Falkiner, Italian ski-touring doyen Giorgio Daidola, and Norwegian telemark guru Morten Aass had preceded us in Lebanon, and Nolen had joined them before he met us.

That group's experience had proved much different than ours. Hot, sunny weather, no new snow, and even a three-day traverse—albeit in the opposite, unmined direction from the one we'd planned. Departing from The Cedars, their first stop had also been to summit Qornet es Saouda... maybe. Like us, they couldn't tell from the borrowed French military map whether they'd actually done so. Unsure of their position, they'd holed up in a shepherd's cave after skiing long, luxurious slopes peppered with dwarf, mushroom-shaped conifers. But next day, they'd somehow navigated their way to the deserted hamlet of Marj Hine, where they slept on a rock-slab rooftop. The trip finished in Baalbek, where they were mobbed by people who'd *never* seen foreigners and awakened by an Israeli air raid near their hotel. Nolen had taken it all in stride; compared to attempts by his aunts in Tripoli to marry him off to Lebanese women, an air raid was small falafels.

I'd first met Nolen at the 1993 Telemark World Championships, and we'd hit it off. After only days in Lebanon, his childhood Arabic had come flooding back, keeping us out of trouble when Rich wasn't around. Together we'd climbed and skied outrageously long faces at The Cedars, crawled down the throat of storms and sniffed out powder stashes at Faraya, attacking with abandon and joy. Locals were fascinated; we were the only people skiing off-piste, the only on pins (telemarking hadn't been one of Lebanon's many revolutions), and, bonus, Nolen was Lebanese, affording him special status.

At Faraya, we'd all bunked in the funky Euro-style Auberge Suisse and promptly been marooned by a raging three-day storm of pernicious wind and horizontal hail, graupel, and snow. Most unnerving were the constant lightning flashes that provided momentary luminescence during the darkened, powerless days. The accompanying volleys of rocket-strike thunder made it feel like we were being shelled. Eventually, enforced confinement got to us, and on the morning of the third day we ventured downvalley to a privately operated platter lift (the resort's lifts were closed). Pulling down the spring-loaded bar and putting the platter between our legs, we rode up in an ill-defined universe, followed by a fine run in uncut meringue. Visibility, vertigo, and balance were a problem, but, as always, the handicap made for more challenge. The odd lightning strike appeared quite distant. Shane was concerned, but the crusty lift operator insisted any errant bolt would be drawn to nearby microwave towers, and besides, Nolen and I—steeped in a wisdom befitting our greater ages and experience—insisted that if such a thing were said by a knowledgeable local, then it must be so. We all got on the lift again.

Shane disappeared into the cloud, grappling with a platter that had jerked from his crotch and now threatened to tear his arm off. Somewhere behind, Nolen and I rode calmly through the seamless fog. Shane dismounted at the top and knelt to check his bindings. Nolen stepped off the lift after him and moved several feet to the side. I let go of the bar and was halfway through my first step when the world lit up like a searchlight in a shoebox. Welder-torch sparks from the lift tower showered over Shane as we all flew through the air. The lift-cable glowed orange as the lightning blazed down it, grounding out through the motor at the base and stopping the lift. Shane looked at us like we'd just tried to kill him.

Of course, Shane also had some positive experiences, hammering 3,000-vertical-foot natural halfpipes and surfing the windlips overhanging small bowls. He ingratiated himself to the burgeoning local snowboard community and befriended mysterious Mr. Khalife, the benevolent seventy-year-old owner of Auberge Suisse who'd showed us much hospitality. Shane helped Mr. Khalife adjust his new snowboard properly and took him out for some pointers. In moments like this, sharing fun in the snow, the country's recently abrogated hostilities seemed distant; other moments, however, could swiftly bring them all back.

THE PHOTO ON the wall in Enfe showed happier times, the family standing together on the beach. Now one brother was dead in a terrorist action and the rest were scattered across two continents: Rich, his brother, and sister in America; his mother and father in the apartment they'd owned for thirty-five years. On our way to Faraya, we'd stopped in this coastal town to visit Rich's parents. The room we slept in had once been shelled; it had been tastefully redecorated with a large wardrobe and two beds, but the tapestry hung over the repair work did not quite cover the circular re-mortaring job that seemed like a bull's-eye.

When Rich arrived, there were tears, smiles, kisses, laughter, and much embracing. A steady stream of people flowed into the apartment; it was hard to tell relatives from neighbors, but perhaps they'd become one and the same in a war-torn existence where everyone looked out for each other. The table was piled high with hummus, tabbouleh, lubneh, falafel, and shish taouk, and we were urged through much hand-gesturing to dig in. Afterward, the warmth was palpable as we sat drinking Turkish-style coffee, nodding politely at the Arabic banter, and answering the few English or French questions we could. It had been two years since Rich visited with Peace Ski, only then, with the war just ended, things were tenser, the battle-hardened gentry not yet believing hostilities would not erupt again. Before that, Rich had not been in Lebanon in twelve years.

The past, however, wasn't on anyone's mind as we rode a chair at Faraya with Rich's childhood friend, Wahlid, a sporting-goods retailer in Enfe. As we surveyed the terrain below, Rich was just another ski bum with his tongue hanging out. The snow that had fallen while we were at The Cedars lay untouched beside the groomed pistes, and we aimed to give Wahlid his first out-of-bounds experience. Pausing briefly at the top of Mzaar Peak, Rich pointed out Mt. Sannine, a lording spire about which he'd written poems and dreamed endlessly. From where we stood, it looked like the summit could be accessed with maybe an hour of touring, at which point you could ride a 4,500-foot couloir down to the valley floor. It looked inviting, although the laser sun at these latitudes was working the couloir, and a fair amount of avalanche debris plugged its lower reaches.

"Forget it," said Rich, "there are Syrians up there."

"So? We've stopped at a dozen Syrian checkpoints," I countered.

The Syrian Army occupied the northern part of the country, while the Israeli Army held the south, both groups sharing law and order duties with the beleaguered Lebanese Army.

"Yeah, well they've been cooped up in a small hut all winter, probably out of communication during the storm, and if they see you approaching with a backpack, they're not going to wait until you get there to ask who you are."

"Oh."

Instead we skied along a sweeping north–south ridge, keeping an eye on the rocky, windbare slopes to the west, and the enormous cornices flanking us on the east. Just outside the area's boundary, I dropped a few feet off a cornice onto the upper face of a large bowl; Rich and Wahlid cautiously cut in below. It was perfect spring skiing: six inches of unconsolidated powder straight down the fall line to a small valley. While Rich and I salivated, sudden concern overcame Wahlid's usually easy features.

"How will we get out of the valley?" he asked.

"We climb," I said, "maybe fifteen minutes."

"You mean take your skis *off?*"

Wahlid was perplexed. Rich chuckled in the background.

"Why not ski over here toward the lift?" Wahlid added, pointing toward the piste.

"You get *more powder* this way," I said, lighting into my first turn, "and that's all that matters."

Wahlid shrugged and followed, whooping and hollering like the first-timer he was. Sweating furiously on the short slog out, Wahlid wasn't quite ready to become evangelical about virgin snow, but I suspected we'd left behind a convert, another contribution to the Peace Ski spirit. And with all the hardware still in people's hands, they needed all the pacifism they could get.

GUNS GENERALLY make me nervous, but after you've had enough of them shoved in your face, it gets funny.

One day, we piled into a battered Renault, its chintzy roof-rack crammed with skis, to return to the army barracks. The air smelled of flowers, a foot of fresh snow glistened, and tottering, bullet-pocked columns in the nearby ruins of a Roman temple added a surrealistic air (a theme in most of these adventures; had Fellini or Dalí skied?). At the gate, a pubescent guard thrust a cocked AK-47 into the cheek of driver François—a French-Lebanese man whose father had helped develop The Cedars—while another guard checked under the hood, presumably for explosives. Incensed at the intrusion and naïveté of these child-soldiers, François crammed his burning cigarette into the barrel of the gun and shoved his door open, bowling over the frightened kid and screaming Arabic invectives. We were terrified.

"You *idiot*," François spat at the prone kid, "do you really think *five* people would be driving a car bomb?"

Given such scenes, I was barely fazed when I was skiing knee-deep fluff during a strawberry sunset as the big storm cleared off Faraya, and a man on a balcony holding a bottle of wine in one hand waved at me with a silver .45 gripped in the other. At home this would be the semiotic of a madman on a shooting spree; there, it was an invitation for a drink.

The previous day, skiing a higher slope during a whiteout, I'd been confronted by two guys shouting and pointing their AK-47s, potentially bringing a whole new meaning to the term face-shots. It turned out they were only trying to warn me of a ten-foot-deep anti-aircraft placement in the snow ahead, into which I would surely have tumbled had they not intercepted.

Rich had gun stories galore, but the comic ones were all overshadowed by one tragedy. As we walked the hills above Enfe, syrupy almond blossoms on the air, Rich had calmly told me about the wedding where a friend was firing a sub—machine-gun into the air while sitting at a reception table. Too drunk to hold the weapon steady, he'd put a bullet through the head of another of Rich's friends. Guns were part of life here, but their proliferation still seemed at odds with the feelings of personal safety necessary for humans to get along. And getting along has never been especially easy in the Middle East. To admit you had no clue what was going on in Lebanon was to take the first essential step in understanding. I thought I'd understood once, as an idealistic college student playing the coffeehouse circuit with my band, when we'd penned an ode entitled "The Ashes of Lebanon." But seeing things on the ground now rendered those facile attempts at political awareness embarrassing. Not knowing that Lebanon would descend into chaos several times in the coming decade, it seemed those ashes were finally being blown away by the winds of change and optimism. Hope was replacing darkness with light and we were helping—the language of outdoor experience did cross barriers, and skiing was its most international dialect.

Our final day in Lebanon, skiing a foot-and-a-half of new powder in brilliant sunshine, I met Mr. Khalife's son, Chafik, who'd driven up from Beirut that morning. He'd mentioned the day before that he wouldn't be skiing because he had work to do, so I expressed surprise.

"Ah," he began, "this is always a difficult question: to ski or to work? But on such a day, my friend, the answer is easy."

THE RENAULT incident in Lebanon would be one reason you haven't seen too many "Ski the Mediterranean" pamphlets at your local travel agent.

That and simmering tensions in almost every place with a ski area or two: Cyprus (Greeks vs. Turks), Corsica (French vs. Spanish Basques), Sardinia and Sicily (The Mafia), Morocco (Islamic fundamentalists vs. all), and the Golan Heights (don't even ask) are enough to scare off even the most entrepreneurial ski-tour operator bent on marrying sun, snow, and cultural experience. It's a sad reality because, as the French and British military contingents that discovered and built these ski areas had known, these all boasted good skiing and plenty more. Neighboring Turkey and Greece—despite historic ethnic acrimony of their own—were now comparatively civil, which might explain why they supported genuine domestic ski industries, and why Greece was the next stop on my own tour.

There were many similarities between the Greek and Lebanese ski scenes—like breakfasts of olives, hummus and pita, fresh fruit, and ouzo (it was *arak* in Lebanon). Plus sunny, wide-open, above-treeline skiing and the pervasive aura of the past so lacking in North America.

History was everywhere in Greece, as underfoot as the ever-present litter. In a Mercedes dealership on the highway out of Athens, the showroom floor surrounded the roof of an excavated tenth-century Byzantine chapel. Beneath that lay a marble edifice from one of a half-dozen civilizations to precede the ultimately malignant Christian invasion. This archeological casserole explained why construction of a new subway for the 2004 Summer Olympics in Athens was, in 1999, still proceeding at a snail's pace: workers had been reduced to digging with toothpicks and analyzing every grain of soil to see if Zeus, Hercules, or some other god might have peed there. Which probably wasn't a bad thing. Ancient history influences a people's thought and behavior in a way that modern society can't, engendering a certain philosophical bent that makes learning about the different outlooks of the people you meet the real prize of a ski adventure.

I'd already logged a handful of sunny, blissful days of climbing and touring at the Parnassos ski area above the Temple of Apollo, where the oracle had been received at Delphi, plumbing dizzying couloirs and hanging snowfields, when the Warren Miller film crew and other pros I was accompanying suspended their shooting because of weather. Waiting for a blizzard to clear off the peak, we descended to the coast through the world's largest olive grove (nine *million* trees, the oldest over 2,000 years) and spent the afternoon swilling pine-tar-tinged *retsina* wine at a seaside restaurant overrun with feral cats. At the next table, a stout, jovial, well-spoken man and self-declared skier chatted us up about the improbably good sliding we'd been enjoying on Parnassos, with its views to the ocean and Mt. Olympus, distant home of the Greek gods. Tom Nestor had eventually invited us to his house on the hill, where we enjoyed a strange mixture of nautical motif, *Playboy* magazines, and a pounding disco beat. We downed coffee and Tom's traditional candied orange peels while scanning the pictures on his wall—Tom with Lyndon Johnson, Tom with former friend Aristotle Onassis.

"I split with Ari because he and Jackie *never* should have married," he said. "JFK was my idol."

One photo was an old black-and-white of his mother and sisters sitting beside the very wall that now encircled his garden. Tom snapped it just after World War II with a camera his American uncle had sent him, his first-ever picture. The family had no money and few possessions then, their only food olives, bread, and a small jug of wine.

"We had nothing, but we were happy," recalled Tom. "That's why I call this photo Miserable Happiness."

Now, with two grown daughters in Athens, Tom had retired to his childhood home. To ski. It was simple. He offered us fresh blood oranges and grapefruit from trees he'd planted himself and smiled as we commented on their fragrance and taste.

"Life is a gift from God," he summarized, fingering a pair of well-worn skis leaned in a corner, "but good living is a gift of wisdom."

Yes, of course. And there was certainly wisdom in adventure. Which is what made François and the Renault seem more like a fond memory and kept alive an itch for the stark juxtapositions of skiing that landed you in places like Greece.

And what could be starker than circling back to where the warm soul of the Mediterranean met the cold heart of the North Atlantic?

CHIPY COULDN'T believe his considerably bloodshot eyes. Lounging outside El Snowbar on the main plaza of southern Spain's Sierra Nevada ski area—a daily ritual for the small contingent of local ski bums—Chipy had shattered the afternoon torpor by suddenly leaping to his feet. Hemorrhaging smoke from the latest in an endless series of hash joints, he pointed excitedly, eyes akimbo and barely able to contain his flailing hand, and turned to his friends.

"*Mira chicos!* Freeskiers... *como nosotros!*"

Chipy's tight-knit cabal had no choice but to follow his finger toward a knot of strangers exiting the gondola station. Although they were somewhat obscured by thick, descending snow, there was no mistaking the source of Chipy's excitement: four dudes in their baggy, New School clothing, helmets, and fat skis plastered with stickers.

"We *must* meet them," Chipy exclaimed, as the gang nodded slow, bewildered ascent.

Those dudes were us.

COMBINING VISIONS of sun-soaked spring skiing and early-season beach-bumming, I'd caught a flight to Madrid with some Whistler buddies: photographer Eric Berger and pro skiers Shawn "Smiley" Nesbitt and Richie Schley. It was a four-hour haul south to Sierra Nevada, the unlikely crown jewel of Spanish skiing and godfather range to a world of similarly named cordilleras in Nevada, California, and elsewhere. After Chile and Mexico, you might call it a pilgrimage of sorts.

The monotonous drive across plains flatter than any North American prairie was interrupted only by incongruous three-story billboards of a giant black bull in silhouette. When the land finally wrinkled, folded, and thrust up where the plate of a nascent African continent had first introduced itself to Europe, canyons yawned, mountains loomed, and sunny hillsides sprouted an olive pelage that, like Greece, ran to every horizon. The smell of freshly pressed olive oil hung thick in the air, and emerald pyramids of local "estate" bottlings rose in every gas station.

Teased by lines of rocky peaks dusted in new snow, we dropped into the basin of the ancient city of Granada. Above it hovered the impressive 11,410-foot Sierra Nevada massif, highest range on the Iberian Peninsula. To reach the ski area, we followed the usual zigzagging road upward through tiny villages, orchards, roadside honey concessions, and textbook vegetation zones—thick vinery, dry scrub, open forest. It finally petered out in a ridgetop smattering of dwarf pine, dominated, fittingly, by one last three-story bull. These giant bovids—one-time liquor-ads that had gained cachet as cultural icons—were only slightly

more bizarre than the live bulls kicking through the roadside snow, looking for something to eat that wouldn't give
them a Slurpee headache.

The community of Sierra Nevada clung to the mountainside like the more medieval villages lower down the
mountain, but any similarity ended there. Clusters of soaring concrete, resembling the modern mountain blight that
is the purpose-built Euro ski resort of the sixties and seventies, climbed the hillsides. It was clear, however, from
its low profile and ad hoc architecture, that our chosen
bunkhouse, the Hotel Telecabine, had been around longer.
Indeed, it was the village's original hotel, a labyrinth of
dusty rooms and dustier photos.

Suddenly our plan seemed well conceived: fresh snow
lay in glabrous mounds under a blazing sun, and the mix of
Spaniards, Portuguese, Argentines, Moroccans, and Brits
crowding the resort's surfeit of deck space confirmed it was
also game on in the après-ski department. We could see
across the Mediterranean's steely waters to the shores of
Morocco and its own ski territory of the high Atlas Mountains. Gilbraltar's eponymous rock hovered in the haze to
the west, guarding the gates to the Atlantic.

We wasted no time charging the gondola into the alpine,
then riding chairs up a series of low-angled pistes. The lift
layout was typically cluttered and illogical but nevertheless
dense with riders. We wanted to get as high as possible to
take advantage of the new snow in an adjacent valley where
lift service had been suspended for the season, but we
proved no match for a speedy cloudbank racing in from the
Strait of Gilbraltar. Stepping off the final T-bar, we skied
into the kind of featureless, high-alpine milk bowl that
Europe was famous for drowning jetlagged victims in.

Beating a hasty retreat back to the base as snow began
to fall, Papa Berger (so-named for his organizational
and herding skills on trips) bumped into Tincho, a local

snowboarder he'd once photographed in the small resort of Chapelco near San Martín de los Andes in Argentina. A brief but animated conversation ensued, and we arranged to meet him at a local café for beers. Tincho had shown up with a posse of wide-eyed locals marching in parade-step, and the usual Tower of Babel cracked open in Spanish, French, and English. It was quickly apparent that Tincho's *gente* were dedicated souls weaned on North American ski videos who spent as much time as possible where most Spaniards dared not—*afuera* (outside) the heavily choked *pistas*. The problem for iconoclasts in outposts like this was that there was less opportunity for the kind of cross-pollination and camaraderie taken for granted in more mainstream resorts. No constant stream of like-minded folk—which is why we stood out.

"*Estamos,* uh—*cómo se dice?* We are—freeskiers," asserted a short, easy-going Argentinian named Mauricio whose searchlight smile beamed from the most savage tan imaginable.

"This is true," added a larger guy named Chappa, who was brooding over a freshly broken ski, "and we have a video, too."

Of course they did.

Hoping that we represented the long-awaited Freeski Mothership come to rescue them from Planeta Pista, their leader, who'd been listening, stepped forward with offers of guiding assistance, crazy descents, and local secrets. Satisfied that we'd come in peace—or at least to take pictures— and in lieu of any direct communication, he pulled out a chunk of hash the size of a tennis ball.

And that was how we met Chipy.

EDUARDO CHICHERO Xaffon was the figurative mayor of Sierra Nevada (there was one in every ski town, usually of far more political import than any elected representative).

He spoke the most English of the group, but his more salient qualifications included being a long-time local guide, ski instructor, bon vivant, guaranteed last man standing at any fiesta (and likely first on the slopes), plus co-owner of a popular summer nightclub on the Malaga coast. On the hill, he kept busy greeting coaches, instructors, and groomers—many of whom were one and the same—but it was in the nightclubs that he was truly king: bartenders, DJs, managers, and patrons cycled endlessly wherever he held court, his constant laughter and bobbing page-boy haircut an anchor in the stormy, strobe-lit sea of humanity.

His posse was equally effusive and comprised the Argentinians—little Mauri and his smile, plus big, clownlike Chappa—and Ingrid, a beautiful, soft-spoken girl of Moroccan, Spanish, and French descent, goddess-mother to the bunch. Their enthusiasm was both contagious and overwhelming. As a well-known ski photographer, Berger had experienced "savior" syndrome in snow ghettos as far-flung as China and Iran, but couldn't recall any other place where people had been so glad to see him. The feeling was mutual: Chipy and company were Sierra intimates who wanted to share their high-altitude kingdom with us.

They also had a sense of humor. Mauri riffed on the intersection of the "Xtreme" craze in commercial marketing and the group's ski aspirations when he jerked his head toward his *amigos*.

"We call them Chip-X and Chap-X," he deadpanned.

NEXT MORNING the sky cleared, revealing six inches of dense, wind-hammered snow, unremarkable for an alpine environment save that it was *pink*. Low-pressure systems parked off the West African coast often blew red sand across the Mediterranean from the Sahara, tinging the snow. The phenomenon was frequent enough to have its own name, *kalima*.

Our first up-close look at the broad resort revealed ridgelines dominated by weird buildings: a double-turreted observatory and an enormous, ten-story, Dr. Evil–like satellite dish graced the highest point between the Alps and Africa's Mt. Kilimanjaro. We took the lift up and, after bagging a few mediocre runs on low-angled pistes, dropped over the backside of the mountain to ski chutes filled with creamy kalima. The frosting cut away in tectonic slabs, but they were manageable enough to consider another attempt at reaching the next valley. Before that thought coalesced into action, however, it socked in again and started snowing in earnest.

It was almost noon and our expected rendezvous with Team Chip-X had yet to materialize; naturally, we found them at the bottom, lounging outside El Snowbar.

"We just arrive, and now look," spat Chipy, waving his hand at the snow in disgust and sinking back into his chair. "But is OK, because tonight is big party."

There were, in fact, *big* plans on the horizon. It was Friday, and people were streaming into town for a massive end-of-season snowboard contest. We were excited for a little cultural incursion but getting on the Spanish party program proved challenging. Nobody ate dinner before 11 p.m., and the restaurants remained packed until 1 a.m., when clubs opened their doors; the clubs in turn were ghost towns until two. Then... insta-fiesta!

Thus, it wasn't until 2:30 a.m. that, barely awake, we finally joined Chipy & Co. at Sticky Fingers Bar, where an over-pierced DJ mixed trance house beneath psychedelic murals of Jimi Hendrix and Bob Marley. The bar harked back to the sixties in other ways, too, as its dark, sofa-strewn balcony was pretty much reserved for hash smoking.

A product of proximity to both deeply rooted Moroccan tradition and the crazy, world-party capital of Ibiza, the
sickly sweet pungence of hash was omnipresent on lifts and
decks, in lounges and bars. No one seemed to mind the full-
on public consumption that was as inescapable as cigarette
smoke. Which is why, when things got really murky for
me around 5 a.m., I blamed the not-insignificant effects of
secondhand smoke. The haze was so thick that our blood-
THC levels were probably high enough (pun intended) to
make Olympic snowboarder Ross Rebagliati's drug test in
Nagano look like he'd been breathing pure oxygen.

When we struggled awake several hours later, more than
a foot of wet snow had blanketed everything. Word came
that the snow gods were scheduled to unload all day, and
that nothing would open on the hill. With this news, we
rounded up the gang and headed for the coast.

On the hour-long drive to Motril, we were besieged by
sheets of heavy rain and torrents pouring off rocky cliffs
and running across the pavement. The coast was equally
miserable, but it *was* the Mediterranean, where palm trees
ruled and hibiscus were in bloom.

We strolled the beach past a forlorn pub that Ingrid
insisted you couldn't get within a mile of in the summer, and instigated a stone-skipping session less focused
on the number of dabs than how close to Africa you could
stretch your throw. Chipy herded us down a road, through
a hedge, and in the back door of the most prestigious restaurant on the strand. The waiters called him by name and
within minutes, we were seated at a long oak table, drinking wine, eating olives, and feasting on calamari so fresh it
swam down your throat. The courses kept coming: garlic
shrimp, snapper, and every size and shape of bait-fish that
we could chow down—head, bones, and all. Hours later, our
bellies full, we headed back into the maelstrom toward historic Granada.

Centuries ago Jews, Moors, and Catholics lived in peace in this part of Spain; like Tangiers across the water in Morocco, Granada once had French, Spanish, Jewish, and Arab quarters. It was a prosperous, bustling city where the filigreed masonry of classic Moorish design fused with the buttressed arches of soaring cathedrals. Then came the Crusades and all hell broke loose in the name of heaven.

Today, Granada's ancient Arab and Christian sections contrast in endlessly fascinating ways. We found ourselves stepping off a winding cobblestoned alleyway of teahouses, arches, and mosaic facades to be suddenly confronted by a lofty Baroque cathedral of incredible architectural detail laden with massive statues, glowering gargoyles, three-story doors, and a spacious, pigeon-filled square focused around elaborate iron fountains.

In the dimly lit recesses of a Moroccan teahouse, we eagerly sank into pillows and ritual rounds of mint tea poured expertly by Chip-X from an intricately worked brass urn while he waxed excitedly about the epic skiing the storm was no doubt delivering above. Revitalized at the prospect, we dove out into the downpour for the drive back to Sierra Nevada. Chipy suggested we take an alternate route. Looking up the precipitous canyon of his proposed detour at the blackness obscuring the massif, we naturally wondered aloud over its condition.

"*No problemo*," insisted Chipy, whose ode to wishful thinking had accelerated into chain-smoking hash joints.

As any seasoned traveler knows, those words, in any language, are the kiss of death.

What ensued was the most heinous drive up to a ski area in any of our group's long and storied careers of heinous drives up to ski areas. Chipy's road was the quintessential "back way," a single-lane, hairpin stepladder climbing 3,000 feet from the bottom of a gorge up a wall so sheer you could parachute from every corner. Our tiny, jam-packed rental cars whined like weed wackers as they fumbled on the slick, pebbled surface—and that was before we hit snowline. Soon enough, as the light faded, a familiar sheen gripped the pavement, and we were laying terrifying tracks in fresh *nieve*. We spun through enormous drifts, barely able to see through the raging blizzard. By the time we slid onto the main highway, it was choked with two feet of snow in various states of consolidation. The last few miles were a nightmare of fishtails, near misses, and skidding buses. Lost, snow-covered bulls occasionally staggered from the darkened shoulders onto the road.

Once we were safely back in Sierra Nevada, Chipy remained annoyingly sanguine.

"See? *No problemo,* right?"

Killing him would have hurt our chances in the clubs, and we needed until at least 5 a.m. to unwind.

THE UNPRECEDENTED storm lasted another two days, and while the biggest snowfall of the season continued—actually one of the biggest *ever,* burying cars to the point of being unrecognizable—we kept busy throwing tricks off urban features, hanging in the clubs, and, eventually commandeering a big-screen TV to watch *los argentinos'* video. Onscreen, at their home area of San Carlos de Bariloche, they ripped through everything in sight, posting legitimate claim to a freeski heritage. Chipy's flailing Euro-carves, filmed at Sierra Nevada on short parabolic skis with tiny poles (because you leaned so far over in the carve you were too close to the ground for real poles) replete with touchdown hand protectors, raised serious questions and a fair amount of laughter.

At last, on our final day, the snow had ceased, but pea-soup fog continued. We went up the lift early anyway and started working a series of cliffs under the satellite dish.

Because the snow was super deep, the boys were happy to go super huge off the cliffs, Mauri impressing with his compact style and Smiley with a willingness to plumb the deepest craters left by the others. Powder lines were everywhere, and when the fog started to lift, we bolted to the top, bent on finally touring the adjacent valley. From the end of the T-bar, we bootpacked ten minutes to the summit, where we hung our tips into space over a backside slope that fell 3,000 feet into a huge valley. The face was wind-scoured, with huge swaths of old kalima exposed under a latticework of drifts from the more recent storm. We skied a few chutes before the fog returned and sent us scurrying back to the resort, where we found a broad, unclaimed slope under the observatory. It took us twenty minutes of wading through waist-deep drifts to reach the run, but it was worth it in the end, if only to watch the hapless Chip-X cartwheel in the deep snow and come up smiling.

All too soon, we had to leave Sierra Nevada in the same rush in which we arrived, and it was surprisingly hard to say good-bye.

At the beach it had poured, and on the mountain it had snowed so hard we couldn't ski, but Chipy, Mauri, Chappa, and Ingrid had bent over backward for complete strangers without expecting anything in return. They had made a whim worthwhile. As was the case in all the countries I'd visited, people had proven to be the gems of southern Spain's mountain culture—the true treasure of Sierra Nevada.

OCEANIC OUTPOSTS, however, weren't the only thing off the skiing public's radar: entire trends were struggling through growing pains and major evolutionary shifts in relative obscurity. One of these was the discipline of telemarking that I'd taken to with such alacrity back in the day.

I was exclusively a freeheel-skier until the mid-nineties, but out of professional necessity I had parted ways in the late eighties with grassroots tele-racing. Naturally, when a journalistic opportunity to revisit the race scene presented itself, I jumped, interested to see how it had morphed in my absence.

It was an eye-opener.

8 | LAST SALAMI, LAST PILGRIM

Free the heel and the mind will follow.
POPULAR TELEMARKER'S CREDO

Free the heel and the face will follow.
POPULAR ALPINE SKIER'S REJOINDER

MONTE BIANCO'S frozen facades glistened in the sun like wet ravioli. A tumble of massive ice blocks offset by heart-stopping cliffs and impossibly tall spires loomed constantly in the periphery, never seeming quite real. That ski runs poured over these improbable steeps wherever someone had festooned the rock with a lift seemed even less real. Stranger still, a high-speed Super G (Super Giant Slalom) course spilled some 1,250 feet down Rampa Nera, traveled by speeding figures in body suits and helmets, genuflecting over skinny skis. The course was so icy that gatekeepers wore crampons to keep a grip on the slope. Perhaps most bizarre of all was that I stood, bladder aflutter, listening to a twenty-second countdown in the start gate.

I'd traveled to the 1993 Telemark World Championships in Courmayeur, Italy, as a journalist, returning to the familiar milieu of tele-racing as an observer on assignment.

But before even unpacking, I'd run into a couple of Canadian national team members locked in discussion in the hallway of the Hotel Centrale. Another teammate hadn't shown up.

"How sharp are your skis?" they asked, before we'd even managed hellos.

If the locals hadn't been aware what was about to descend upon them that spring, there was no mistaking the boisterous horde of competitors from fifteen countries parading through the narrow streets with their horns blaring and songs rattling windows. Fortunately, Italians have a great sense of humor. Even the old ladies leaning in doorways laughed when their heads were almost blown off by cherry bombs thrown by an aged squad of Austrians sporting vast acres of bald scalp. The Japanese bowed, the French blew kisses, and the lone Andorran clutched his banner with mercenary zeal. The Swedes were nattily dressed, the Canucks *au sportif,* the Brits wore kilts, and the Norwegians were decked head to toe in sweat-inducing woolen tradition. True to form, the earthily attired Yanks surreptitiously sucked on beers as they strolled, waving at maidens hanging from balconies like it was a post-war liberation parade, swiping bottles of wine at the reception in the village square, their hands snaking furtively under tables while the crowd swarmed mounds of cheese, salami, and salt pork. Speeches were made, hands were shaken, and a drunken international cabal played hacky-sack beneath the setting sun.

It all seemed pretty casual, but of course, it wasn't: in the bowels of the Hotel Centrale, the Norwegian team's shockingly extensive crew secretly pored over videos, surreptitiously remounted bindings, and continued the never-ending task of tuning a never-ending supply of skis for their never-ending supply of world champions.

THE DROP-KNEE TURNING technique for freeheel equipment was invented and perfected in the nineteenth century in Norway's Telemark region by ski-master Sondre Norheim, then lost in blustery enthusiasm for the increased security and power of fixed-heel bindings and new turning techniques popularized under the tutelage of titans like Zdarsky and Lunn. But after fifty years off the radar, the telemark turn had been revived in the mid-seventies by backcountry skiers in the American West who were seeking greater freedom on lighter gear. Although these experiments began with flimsy cross-country skis, wire-bail bindings, and floppy leather boots, a new generation of telemarkers rapidly evolved and diversified the sport and its equipment; by the mid-eighties, a litany of specialized, better-engineered bindings, skis, and boots had appeared. Telemarking was still largely portrayed as a backcountry pursuit—indeed, soft snow was where freeheel gear and techniques retained weight and mobility advantages—but any good all-around freeheel skier was also well versed in alpine techniques which could (and quite often had to) be performed on freeheel boards for the sake of safety and speed control.

In a classic full-circle scenario, beefed-up gear led telemarkers into the more difficult, changeable snow conditions found both in the high-alpine backcountry and at the busy ski areas from which they had fled. And if you were going to be hanging out with your buddies on a piste, the most natural thing in the world, as Lunn and company had shown, was to organize a race. The fun and rush of trying to edge out a rival in a head-to-head format using tremulous technique and skittery gear that was never intended to handle high speeds had also helped drive product enhancement and modification by manufacturers—though never fast enough to keep up with demand. Necessity was indeed the mother of invention in telemarking's Brave New World; when I first started racing, top competitors were cutting up stiff, white-plastic restaurant buckets and bolting these pieces to the backs of their leather boots to provide more leverage in the gates.

In the early years of telemarking's modern renaissance, the official haters were largely change-resistant alpine skiers (the same ranks who would soon bristle at snowboarding's rise). For example, many resort operators at the time wanted to banish freeheel skiers to the backcountry "where they belonged." However, ski-tech pundit Tim Petrick, in a column he frequently penned in POWDER, accurately perceived the existence of something uglier and more persistent: a division in the telemark community between purists and moderates. It didn't matter that thousands were finding new life and challenge in the backcountry, on groomed slopes, and in gates, or that it wasn't for everyone and never would be. Some zealots just got plain righteous about it. Especially in racing, where boatloads of misconception, much idealism, and unhealthy delusions of grandeur quickly led to philosophical divisions over equipment and technique that instantly mired the sport in puritan politics. Most equipment issues—ski width, height above the snow of the binding mount, leather versus plastic boots— were meliorated by standardization, but in 1993, the chasm between the liberal and dynamic American model of turning and the more narrow European interpretation remained.

To oversimplify, Americans argued that if skiers made a telemark turn at every gate (dropped rear knee, space visible between both legs as defined in the rules) then it didn't matter what they did in between, and anything that increased speed and control—such as adopting a parallel alpine stance, derisively labeled "norpine"—was within the spirit of racing and represented a legitimate evolution of the overall technique. The Scandinavians railed against this approach as if it were a breach of faith, insisting that racers move smoothly from one telemark position to the next with no hesitation. (Ironically, my own scholarly investigations with Chris Hart had found that old Norwegian instruction books—as biblical as you could get—advocated returning to a parallel stance *between* telemark turns.)

There were, naturally, some purist-minded Americans who favored the European ideal. Already in 1981, when freeheeling had been out of the closet for only a few years, tele-guru Steve Barnett wrote in *Cross-Country* magazine: "The telemark revolution has gone too far. The equipment has become too similar to alpine... with high boots of the alpine type and with big telemark competitions which have become more and more like slalom competitions with parallel turns."[11]

Rejecting the new equipment, however, was like telling tennis players that graphite racquets and nylon strings were *too* good and should be abandoned in favor of traditional wood and catgut. If racing's mandate was to go as quickly, efficiently, and safely (i.e., in control) as possible under a given set of conditions—in this case negotiating gates at high speeds with freeheel bindings—then it was only natural that equipment should evolve to meet those demands. Editorials were written, scathing rebuttals returned. It was all pretty funny. For a while.

ALTHOUGH I TELEMARKED plenty and had many race victories under my belt, I hadn't chased a gate in two years, and I immediately declined the invitation from my compatriots. It was hard to imagine casually stepping back into racing at a World Championship. However, celebrated sportswriter George Plimpton had always been one of my heroes because of his shocking disregard for personal safety in the name of climbing into the belly of any story's beast. And so I ended up in the starting blocks, hesitant and helmeted, gravity about to have its evil way. It wasn't until the start lights flashed that I fully accepted there was no way out.

There had never been a Super G—the high-speed hybrid between Giant Slalom and Downhill—at a telemark championship before, where Giant Slalom and Dual Slalom races predominated, and so this one wasn't even part of the official competition. Nevertheless, most racers were excited about the prospect of higher speeds than usual. Skiing out of 106th spot, I'd had plenty of time to stand around the lower course and watch racers blow past with the sound of skaters carving the corner of a speed track. It was unnerving.

But the first thing I noticed after leaving the start gate was the absence of ruts; the wide-open course meant you could *really* ski. It all came back as I sank into my first turn: lead with the inside hand, exaggerate the hip, drive the outside foot around for the carve, then get off the edge and into the next turn in one smooth up-down motion. No matter that I didn't exactly follow this blueprint every turn (there may, actually, have been some "norpining") or that I braked above certain fall-away gates. Fear had fled, and it was a relaxing, albeit speedy, ride to the finish.

Norwegians took nine of the top eleven men's spots, with Swedes in second and eighth. The top five women included four Norwegians and a Canadian in third place. That wasn't how I remembered the pervasive American domination of my own racing career.

The next unofficial event, the head-to-head Dual Slalom was once the exclusive domain of America and it too saw a Scandinavian sweep. To their credit, seven American men qualified among the thirty-two finalists, but only one made it to the second round before being bounced by the Nordic juggernaut. Even Artie Burrows—always strong in the event he practically invented and a man I'd raced against for years—was a first-round victim of the eventual winner. The only American woman to qualify was knocked out by a Norwegian in the second round.

What was going on? The American fall from grace in tele-racing seemed complete, and the Norwegians were all over the sport like hyenas on a carcass, tossing scraps to a few Swedes and Finns. Had the success of Norwegian wunderkinds Hans Gunleiksrud and Olav Bjarne Lysklett in the late eighties actually represented the vanguard of a second telemark revolution? Not only did these guys dethrone those who'd smugly laid squatter's claim to their historic turn, but they also managed to change the sport's momentum by inculcating elements of "traditional" style into the international rules. Add government-sponsored development programs and strong leadership (Gundleiksrud would soon become Norwegian national coach), and you had a Scandinavian stranglehold that wouldn't soon be relinquished; some of their top skiers were *still teenagers.*

The problem was obvious. Russ Tuckerman, a longtime racer from Bozeman, Montana, saw tele-racing's future in the U.S. as dismal.

"There are too many older racers ready to move on and no new ones to take their place," he stated flatly.

"Is that because of the popularity of snowboarding?" I wondered.

"Well... how many twelve-year-old telemarkers do you know?"

Tuckerman had a good point. Ned Ryerson, however, a passionate but nerdy "organizer dude" (in popular parlance) from Aspen, Colorado, would point to that town's forward-thinking school system, which had purchased tele gear for student hut-to-hut trips, to Dynastar's recent development of a children's powder ski and boot, and to citizen's tele races in Aspen that attracted plenty of young folk. This begged the question of whether the demise of tele-racing might sound the death knell of telemarking in North America. Ryerson thought so.

"Racing isn't really what telemarking is all about," he said, "but how else do you expose lots of people [to the sport] at the same time?"

But if that was the case, then why was it that almost all names an American skiing public would associate with telemarking—adventurers like Steve Barnett, Ned Gillette, Tom Carter, Alan Bard—had absolutely nothing to do with racing?

Aficionados who'd never pondered this question got the opportunity when a panel discussion on the future of telemarking commenced in Courmayeur's civic center one night during the championships. The participants told the tale: Giorgio Daidola, editor, professor, explorer, and patron saint of Italian telemarking; Pat Morrow, Canadian seven-summiteer and all-around telemark poster boy; John Falkiner, Switzerland-based Australian adventurer, stuntman, student, convert, and teacher; Morten Aass, Norwegian televangelist turned Italian hero, and a trio of his local disciples; several backcountry equipment designers; and Grunleiksrud, the only obvious racer. A local journalist offered an historical perspective, suggesting that current telemarking fundamentalism in Italy was partial penance for the country's significant role in vanquishing freeheel equipment from the Alps when alpine skiing was developing in the thirties. Daidola had confirmed this bizarre sentiment during a chairlift conversation.

"We must correct this mistake," he'd said, as if he were referring to a genocide.

Perhaps befitting the nebulous topic, the discussion that night seemed particularly unfocused. It was hard to follow;

people made contradictory remarks and ended up agreeing with each other. Among the more annoying concepts promulgated was the notion that the telemark "was not just another turn." I thought it ludicrous to ascribe divine status to a physical maneuver; it *was* just another turn, and not recognizing that was the problem. Young skiers would be well advised to learn fixed *and* freeheeled techniques concurrently, opening themselves to the entire alpine and nordic realms. Clearly, emphasis on overall skill played a huge role in Norway, where skiers handled all terrain, all conditions, and all courses with equal panache. The country also had a huge pool of skiers to choose from; in those days up to 50 percent of skiers at Norwegian alpine areas were telemarking. However, none of Norway's current crop of pros was in the room to address the point—they were all back in the Hotel Centrale wax room.

Overall ability was clearly the future of competitive telemarking, and it was obvious during the official Giant Slalom and Classic races. The Classic, which combined uphill, downhill, and jumping, was always grueling; however, the Italian course was brutal. Many racers had problems with a set of camel humps below the landing of a big jump. While stretchers carted others away, Norwegians sailed over the jumps in textbook fashion, landing long, sick airs with ease. Canadians fared particularly badly; at one point, Canucks were being peeled off the course faster than they could be shoved through the starting gate. Add two serious cases of compressed vertebrae to the litany of twisted limbs, and the course suddenly looked like a meat grinder. It could, however, be skied properly with the right approach, even by those who rarely saw such steeplechases. Burrows flashed over the jump in a perfect egg, legs drawn up, hands low, landing sweetly, far below the minimum distance line. He blasted through the gate, pre-jumped the second drop perfectly, and absorbed each compression in turn. Still, Ryerson remained skeptical.

"Do we really want a race that only 10 percent of skiers can finish?" he opined. "Besides, it costs a bloody *fortune* to put on a Classic!"

So there it was. The North American–European axis of disagreement also involved the structure that a competition should take, but this was no surprise. Although the camaraderie and heady goodwill of the opening ceremonies had made me think the politics plaguing the sport had subsided, I was wrong. During the Super G, I'd overheard condemnation of gate judges, seeding, and equipment restrictions. Indeed, International Telemark Commission meetings were still dominated not by plans for the future, but by the usual sniping over rule-change proposals. The Swedes lobbied against jury rules; binding lift-blocks of certain dimensions were approved (spawning a spate of drilling and mounting in the Norwegian pits); and the American-sponsored proposal for wider skis was again squashed (this may have been the stupidest outcome of all given the soon-to-occur fat-ski explosion). The Canadians pretended to be polite while squabbling about everything— penalties, seedings, DNFs, and their own internal political rifts.

"The skiing has improved incredibly, but almost everything else is the same as ten years ago," Burrows confided, adding, "it's still a silly sport."

Silly enough that I canceled my own resurrection and spent the rest of my time skiing Courmayeur's catalogue of steep chutes and bowls. For all intents and purposes, they were empty. Was I the jaded racer who'd outgrown a sport that refused to grow up? Perhaps, but I wasn't alone.

Between the unofficial and official races, the Italians hosted a polenta-fest at the Maison Vieille, an ancient stone hut half-buried by snow. It was a great party with an impressive theatrical demonstration of the history of skiing, choreographed and performed with consummate accuracy by the indefatigable Norwegians. At some point it started snowing, and by midday there was over a foot. I snuck off with Nolen Oayda, Morrow, and Daidola to snake untracked lines from the big upper bowls down into a mantle of plunging slopes covered in naked tamarack under the hanging glacial teeth of Monte Bianco. Daidola's easygoing disposition was a stark contrast to the charged atmosphere at the top of the race courses. He'd telemarked on every continent and in every conceivable situation, including 26,000-foot peaks, and yet his skiing was so relaxed as to resemble chocolate syrup flowing determinedly over ice cream. His angular profile and classic arms-spread-wide stance cut an impressive figure as he sifted effortlessly through knee-deep snow—the textbook telemarking Chris Hart had introduced me to—making it all the more contradictory that racing would be the vehicle used to sell it. Yet, perhaps the contradiction was more perceived than real— after all, you always had a choice.

Diving into a copse of trees, we heard loud laughter bending around falling flakes from behind. Turning to see who might be following, we fittingly found John Falkiner and the rest of Team Clambin hard on our freeheels.

OVER THE COURSE of the eighties, a nondescript cluster of cabins set on an ancient alp known as Clambin, south of Verbier, Switzerland, had quietly become the center of the international adventure-ski universe. It was home to Falkiner, American ski model/photographer Ace Kvale, and his mentor, Canadian ski photographer Mark "Marko" Shapiro, who by documenting their exotic adventures and eclectic skiing, had inspired an entire generation of skiers and photographers, including my frequent collaborators Eric Berger, Henry Georgi, Scott Markewitz, Paul Morrison, and Nolen Oayda. And it was a place where a revolving door of ski bums, mountaineers, journalists, pro skiers, models, and wannabes gathered to pay their respects, exchange stories, and plan adventures.

Along with intrepid adventurers Alan Bard and Tom Carter, the exploits of Team Clambin (whose name jokingly referenced Aspen's famously stiff Team Russell photographers, John Kelly and John Russell) that appeared in POWDER throughout the eighties opened many skiers' eyes not only to the depth, breadth, and potential of skiing, but to the big ol' world in general. That skiing could take you to distant lands was a revelation that had changed many lives, including my own.

The photography emanating from Clambin diverged from the usual stifled European and North American fare in both style and content; it featured big in-your-face action, bold lines, wild air, exploding powder, jaw-dropping vistas of high-alpine ski touring, and the cultural exotica of mountain adventure in places as far-flung as Russia, New Zealand, and India. It translated to an entirely new ski dimension at a time when many were still squinting past the sunset of the seventies' freestyle era for skiing's next horizon.

Telemarking happened to be that next big thing, a new commodity successfully marketed by the unwitting fun hogs of Team Clambin. Inspired by Pat Morrow and his crew, who had cruised through Verbier with the Karhu demo ski team's famous Freedom of the Heels tour in the early eighties, Falkiner, Kvale, and Shapiro took to the nascent sport with a vengeance. In no time they'd dragged their telemark setups to the four corners of the Earth, photographing them in every conceivable terrain—and some that was previously inconceivable.

Although their travel, adventure, and freeskiing renaissance had started on the back of Marko's groundbreaking action photos, it also spilled into the industry at large: Team Clambin broke new ground in contracting ski models, hiring assistants, obtaining samples from manufacturers, organizing photographic retainers from companies, and just generally treating ski photography and adventuring as a business. A 1988 *POWDER* story by Lito Tejada-Flores entitled "The Clambin Kids of Verbier" basically showed that "the dream" was attainable: it was possible to get paid to ski and work in a hypnotically beautiful, radical, and distant place. This revelation had profound effects on skiing in North America.

And so it was with an almost mythical reverence that former *POWDER* editor Steve Casimiro and I visited the neatly shuttered wooden chalets of Clambin on April Fools Day, 1994, just as the infamous trio was winding down their business empire. Like so many other acolytes before us, we spent a heady night around a communal table swapping stories with these unlikely, low-key heroes.

In town the next day, we found that the tiny Clambin Productions office was still very much a focus of the Verbier scene. It was tucked up under an old hotel at the back of a small shopping complex, and though there were no windows to let in the inspiration of the Alps, there was the timeless ambience of hand-hewn logs and sagging doorways. The walls were covered in not just familiar, but downright famous, photos. Light tables, computers, fax machines, and film-editing equipment cluttered countertops alongside messy desks and bulging files. In the back was a gear bunker in which all the clothing and equipment used for models on shoots was stored. It was like glimpsing the inner workings of some long-since decommissioned behemoth—the engine room of the original SS *Freeski*.

By this point, Marko and his wife, Francesca, had moved to the neighboring alp of Les Esserts, and though the rest of the crew still clung to the forested mountainside in Clambin proper—John and his wife, D'arcy, in their high-ceilinged traditional cabin; Ace and Anne next door in their little hobbit abode with the funky sunken kitchen—things in general had slowed considerably. All of them had young kids and less time for frolicsome adventure. John was also locked in the long, all-consuming trudge toward becoming a professional Swiss Mountain Guide (he would become the first foreigner to do so). And when Ace finally moved home to Ophir, Colorado, several weeks after our visit, it officially closed a chapter in ski history.

That night, as if by design, it started snowing. And snowing. As a result, Casimiro and I eventually skied some of the best Verbier had to offer, lines immortalized in countless Clambin photos passing magically underfoot. We left with a storm out of the North Sea still raging in the rearview while our heads spun with epic tales, warm laughter, and ever more possibilities for adventure.

A fitting denouement for the last pilgrims to Clambin.

THE CLAMBIN LEGACY in telemarking, however, was in scarce supply back in Courmayeur. Norwegians swept both the Giant Slalom and Classic, thoroughly vanquishing the Americans and reclaiming their birthright turn for good. All that was left was the wrap-up blowout. The Italians had been incredible hosts, serving excellent food to throngs of indiscriminate diners at every well-stocked party. The finale likewise featured an incomparable feast. Much *vino* was consumed and, naturally, things got silly. The last thing I remember was a drunken Norwegian watching as a cherry-faced Tuckerman stuffed a five-pound wheel of cheese into his jacket then headed for the door. The Norwegian paused for a moment, seemingly intent in thought, then staggered toward the serving table, clutching a bottle of wine in one hand, the other outstretched, his bloodshot eyes riveted on the last unsliced roll of salami. He was going to get it and win the party, too. Just as well, as it may have been his last hurrah.

The Clambin crew—who'd never run a gate on tele skis—had arrived at this global gathering to find that the tele-tribe had long ago splintered. They would, however, find themselves on the right side of that wishbone: serious racing events would fall to the wayside over the next few years and be replaced with large, eclectic international telemark festivals more focused on fun, frolic, and pinhead camaraderie and led by a dedicated (and possibly penitent) group of Italians. Telemarking would largely soldier on as a backcountry, big-mountain pursuit, logically throwing in with bigger trends like fat skis and freeski contests, twin-tips and terrain parks. Leather and pins would be left far behind for the safety and power of high-cuffed, alpine-style boots and beefy, releasable bindings. Yet despite the efforts of several filmmakers and even a dedicated magazine, telemarking would remain on the margins, little more than an uncannily high-tech echo that, like skiing's geographic outposts and storied old-world past, was largely off the radar.

However, every once in a while, there would be a grandiose attempt to portray telemarking to the skiing public as charmingly embedded in the greater glisse-sport canon. But it didn't help anyone's cause when these attempts were inglorious disasters.

the
revolution
may be
televised
after all

9 | ICECAPADES

From the time we first put him on skis at the
age of three, I started to worry. I've never had
one peaceful day in my life.

NINA CHRZANOWSKI, *on her son Peter*

FOR THE thousandth time that day, Chris
Scott wondered what the hell he'd got
himself into. Wondered because twelve hours after reluctantly parting company with the other members of Team
Coast, he'd failed in his bid to crawl back to civilization.
His neck was sunburned beyond recognition. His knees
ached like an arthritic octogenarian, patellas grinding
unnaturally over the now-pitted surface of each cartilage,
the result of carrying a heavy pack and teetering in isothermal snow on one-and-a-half snowshoes.

Scott had never been on a backcountry trip before. For
that matter, he'd never even worn snowshoes, and these
ones—a weird, solid-metal configuration that had survived
an expedition to K2—couldn't handle British Columbia's
Callaghan Valley, where he wandered aimlessly behind
three people he didn't know but who he trusted to deliver
him from this nightmare.

He was silent because there was little to say while his ersatz saviors argued over the contradictory information from altimeters, compasses, maps, and their own intuition. Ultimately, they admitted they were lost. Lost, because they'd missed the exit road after following a grizzly trail too low into the drainage, where bear tracks now criss-crossed in every direction. They'd decided to bivouac on a river island that was connected to the forest by a delicate snow bridge, which they presumed would collapse in early warning if a hungry grizzly arrived in the night.

It was a night that pressed down slowly on the fuchsia sunset pooling behind the Powder Mountain Icecap to the west, while a honey-colored full moon rose over the peaks in the east. The moon illuminated Bruce Edgerly's naked body, bent at the waist, his hands spreading his butt cheeks to the breeze in an attempt to aerate two days' worth of chafing.

"Now *that's* extreme!" Frank Salter and I simultaneously exclaimed, looking up from freeze-dried blueberry cobbler that tasted more like flavored sawdust. It was a mocking reference the organizer of this event would have understood; Peter Chrzanowski had once muttered those same words while being rescued—with a severe concussion and minus his ski boots and socks—from a crevasse in the Peruvian Andes.

Which got Scott wondering, for the thousand and first time, what the hell he'd got himself into.

IF NOTHING ELSE, filmmaker and evangelist of the extreme Chrzanowski was respected for the sheer audacity of his frequently wild-ass ideas. Given that multi-day back-country team events (think of the original Eco-Challenge) weren't exactly a new concept, at first blush his proposed Multiglisse Traverse seemed almost pedestrian. In fact, it displayed hallmarks of brilliance. First, the idea was both timely and unique. Modeled after European "Raid" (pronounced rad) events, the traverse's basic premise had teams of five racing a three-day course across high-alpine wilderness. Unlike the strictly alpine-touring Euro version, however, it would celebrate both the current fascination with backcountry travel and the eclectic modern-day milieu of so-called *glisse* sports (from the French word for sliding): teams would thus include at least one woman, one man, one alpine tourer, one telemarker, and one snowboarder. Second, there would be none of the Alps' quaint overnight shelters/restaurants en route—competitors would carry everything they needed for three days of survival in the mountains.

Third, staging the race over the ice-capped jumble of B.C.'s rugged Coast Range, more-or-less adjacent to the Whistler-Blackcomb resort colossus, would make it aesthetically attractive to potential competitors and wanna-be-cool New York–based ski magazines that might eventually rank it "North America's number one multi-glisse event according to some of our readers." Fourth, timing the event on the full moon—a wistful Chrzanowski-ism aimed at securing favorable weather—was yet another point in the plus column. Lastly, the simultaneous Mountainfest, which would feature an adventure-sports bazaar, exhibitions, handicrafts, food, beer, music, and a giant portable screen on which festival-goers could monitor the progress of the first multidisciplinary race in the alpine world (transmitted live from the Pemberton Icecap by a squadron of satellite-wired cameramen riding shotgun on snowmobile support vehicles), seemed even more promising, if slightly ambitious.

Yes, a multimedia, multiglisse circus was the perfect vehicle to deliver backcountry to the masses, figured Chrzanowski, bringing core mountain culture the long-overdue attention it deserved and selling the lifestyle to an apparently clamoring North American public—along with its attendant gear and clothing, of course. Or such would be the view of any potential sponsor. At its most fundamental, however, the traverse was conceived as an opportunity for people to both celebrate and learn from the mountains while making a statement about the potentially unifying nature of the alpine experience.

Lured by such glossy noblesse, partipants trickled north to Whistler, forsaking the springtime warmth of Los Angeles, Boulder, Seattle, and Vancouver in favor of glacial ice. By noon on Friday, thirty-one people on eight teams were scattered along the southwestern flank of Brandywine Mountain, broiling under a May sun that played hide-and-seek with the tail end of a three-day rainstorm. The staggered start had been delayed three hours because of difficulty in ferrying participants and their everything-but-the-kitchen-sink baggage to the departure point. Spirits were high despite ominous signs at the racer's meeting the previous evening—many no-shows, lowered entrance fees, reduced mandatory team size (from five to three), overlooked race safety and equipment checks, squabbling snowmobile support volunteers and organizers, an unspecified race route over an overwhelming distance rumored at between thirty-seven and sixty miles.

"Uh... we're figuring that out right now," was the hesitant answer offered by organizers to every direct question posed.

However, a paucity of concrete information didn't seem to matter once we were on the move in the mountains. Nor did it seem to matter that in an hour of casual shuffling, Salter, Edgerly, and I had passed or caught up to almost everyone who'd started ahead, save a few super-charged, ganja-fueled locals (Team Dirtbag's Troy Jungen and Ptor Spricenieks, who later recorded the first descent of Mt. Robson's infamously unskiable North Face and cited Chrzanowski as their inspiration). This said less about our touring prowess than others' lack thereof; we were there to report on the possible Next Big Thing in glisse competition, *they* were supposed to be racing.

Thick, wet snow slowed everyone, but especially dogs and snowboarders, who respectively found that paws and snowshoes sucked equally in such conditions. By late afternoon, many people's private doubts about the event morphed to audible worries; no race officials or checkpoints had been seen, and the map showed that the distance to the proposed Camp One wasn't shrinking all that quickly. Hours behind us, we'd find out later, backcountry guru Paul Ramer was worriedly shepherding members of a local women's unit, Team Femme, whom he'd had to teach en route how to climb on the alpine-touring gear he'd loaned them. The uphill slogging was relentless, and finally, on the col below the summit of Brandywine, came the first opportunity to rip the climbing skins off for a long downhill into the basin below the Powder Mountain Icecap. However, truly awful snow turned the descent into a trial, and it took a half-hour to reach the human specks we'd spied from the summit. Arriving at the small knot of skiers clustered beside a heavily littered avalanche path, we discovered that what we'd prayed was a checkpoint was actually a forlorn Chrzanowski sitting in the snow with a broken leg and a dead radio.

WITH HIS BOUNDLESS enthusiasm but jaded reputation as an alpine accident looking for a place to happen, Peter Chrzanowski was the traverse's biggest asset and largest liability from the get-go. Case in point was this latest in a litany of personal disasters that included paraglide crashes, a well-publicized debacle on Mt. Robson, ski-mountain-eering accidents in which companions were killed while he remained miraculously unscathed, and the infamous crevasse fall in Peru. And then here, being pulled behind a powerful snowmobile, Chrzanowski had clipped the tow rope onto the waistband of his climbing harness to leave his hands free for filming. He'd foundered in the difficult snow and torqued his leg against his boot cuff after being dragged helplessly behind the machine. Shaking off the injury, he'd continued touring and filming for hours before admitting to a major problem. When we arrived, he was still claim-ing he'd only "tweaked his ankle," though it was obvious to anyone who had seen such things before that he'd snapped his fibula.

And with that, Chrzanowski became the first and most significant victim of a severe lack of safety contingency suddenly exposed by a series of events over which he had little control. He couldn't be evacuated by snowmobile because snow conditions had reduced the promised sup-port fleet to a handful of high-horsepower machines, and even these could barely get up the larger bowls with only a driver. Without a radio, he had to wait until one of the sleds returned to Whistler and called in a rescue chop-per. (He was eventually plucked from the basin just before sunset.)

After ensuring he wouldn't die, we'd left Chrzanowski to his misery and returned to our own. By this point, I was suffering nerve damage caused by the foolish combination of a forward-leaning boot and a cable telemark binding (the cable attached at the front of the binding and was cinched around the heel of the boot), both of which increased for-ward pressure whenever I flexed: the ball of my foot was on fire with every step. *Everyone* was flagging, and the only thing that got many of us to resume our metronomic slog was Chrzanowski's pronouncement that it was only an hour more to Camp One.

In fact, it was over four hours later that we spied smoke rising from the trees at the base of Ridge Mountain and staggered into a hastily erected *alternate* Camp One, which was still hours from the originally intended site. We joined Team Dirtbag, Team Coast, and a handful of others, including bewildered volunteer Androo Mitchell, a wool-hatted acolyte of the ever-optimistic Chrzanowski.

"Androo, did anyone rescue Chrzanowski yet?"

"Dunno, my radio is dead."

"Where are the snowmobiles? What if someone here needs to get out?"

"Someone will show up... eventually."

The lack of communication and the fact that we'd covered less than a third of the route forced those of us who'd made it to Camp One to seriously reconsider our options.

In the morning, Team Dirtbag chose to continue, as did Team Coast (with the addition of photographer Carl Skoog but without Chris Scott, their snowboarder). Scott, the only snowboard entrant to make Camp One, was suffering and chose to exit the race with Salter, Edgerly, and me. For our part, we weren't just hurting but livid at the lack of foresight evidenced in the outrageous distance and faltering safety net. We figured that stomping down to Whistler via a logging road in the Callaghan Valley to kick Chrzanowski's miserable butt was the preferred alternative to being stuck on an icecap when our flights home left Vancouver. Thus, it was irrational anger that caused us to think we could follow a grizzly bear just out of hibernation to the logging road below.

While we wandered the Callaghan Valley, Team Ramer plus several stragglers finally arrived in Camp One on Saturday afternoon after having slept in a high pass overnight.

After reaching Chrzanowski, they'd traveled for hours across the Powder Mountain Icecap, stopping around 11 p.m. In the windy pass, Paul Ramer had dug a pit with snowblock walls for his two-person tent, into which he squeezed with his daughter, Kris, and a Team Femme member. Chad, Team Ramer's snowboarder, and Jeremy, a snowboarding race volunteer who'd somehow come to be wandering the mountains in cotton pants with no gloves, dragging his snowboard and carrying a cowboys-and-Indians K-mart sleeping bag in a green garbage bag, had dug a coffin-like pit to sleep in, overtop of which they lay their snowboards.

On Saturday, they'd all broken camp late and traveled several hours to a deserted Camp One. Soon the remainder of Team Femme appeared. With nobody around and no idea what was going on, Ramer felt they should stay put. Some women wanted to continue, not realizing the consequences, and Jeremy, wanting his photo to appear in a snowboard magazine and make him famous, struck off in the direction of the icecap by himself, sheepishly returning minutes later.

"And he would have been famous, too," said Ramer, recalling the incident, "as the first idiot to die on the Pemberton Icecap dragging a snowboard."

Later that night, wandering alone on Powder Mountain, Jeremy was plucked up by a plane that spotted him by chance as it returned from a fuel drop. At some point during the day, the three men and two dogs of Team Seeing Colors had also been airlifted out. When snowmobiles sweeping the course for missing people arrived at Camp One around 6 p.m. with this news, Team Ramer and Team Femme decided not to move. Team Dirtbag, which had previously been leading the race, bailed via the Rutherford Creek drainage after finding themselves off-course and facing scary avalanche conditions on Mt. Callaghan. (They also had no food because the majority of their supplies had been with their long-departed snowboarder.)

On Sunday, everyone finally came to their senses. After our forced bivouac, we stumbled out of the bush before noon and were picked up by a jeep containing none other than Chrzanowski, his bandaged leg propped on the backseat. While Team Coast continued its slog toward Meager Creek, Teams Ramer and Femme followed our errant tracks out the Callaghan Valley, trusting our direction-finding in the same foolish manner we'd trusted the grizzly. Of course, we wouldn't find any of this out until we were back in Whistler.

Although it took three punishing days to cover the eventual distance of forty-seven miles, Team Coast proved that the traverse was doable by the prepared and dedicated. *Coast Magazine* editor Steven Threndyle, whose Bataan death face on the first day labeled him "most likely to be evacuated," rallied from near exhaustion to finish. Robbin McKinney snapped a ski on the first day but went thirty-seven miles farther on his duct-taped board. Greg Stoltmann had helped carry Chris Scott's snowboard before Scott had bailed with us. Besides pushing themselves hard, Team Coast had carried proper maps, plotted strategic route alterations, and adopted the right attitude.

"We were on our own now," Carl Skoog had figured after the first camp, "and we weren't going to see anybody until the end."

Still, he'd been fully prepared to continue because he was actually having a good time. After the first half day, the traverse had evolved from a competition to a friendly group tour, which is what backcountry skiing is really all about.

On Sunday, the final and supposedly easy day, the team had started early with a long gradual climb across the remainder of the icecap to its northern edge, then a descent over a series of 1,600-foot drops linked by short climbs over downward-sloping shoulders on their way to Meager Creek. But they weren't perfect: they missed a massive clear-cut that would have allowed them to ski right out instead of becoming bogged down in ultra-steep forest all the way to the valley floor. They arrived at the hot springs around 6:30 p.m., soaked their battered corpses, and proceeded to the Pemberton Hotel to collect their prize.

Somehow Chrzanowski's continued eagerness and the fact that he actually *was* looking for lost people defused our need to kill him, although Edgerly still managed to burp out a few harsh words between gulps of the sponsor-donated sport drink that Chrzanowski, ever the promoter, had immediately handed us. But it was when Chrzanowski started whining that Threndyle had torn into him—he'd visited Team Coast on the icecap with a film crew—that I understood the wretched truth: Chrzanowski may have been pathologically incapable of understanding human thought or emotion, but he was right. What had Threndyle expected? What had I? What had anyone for that matter? We'd all willingly entered a sketchily planned, first-time event that carried a huge risk factor, solely for fun. Hell, the fine print on the entry form was *six pages long*. Who had read it all thoroughly? Who'd actually brought all the equipment required? Whose responsibility was it to be prepared for any eventuality in the backcountry?

We'd complained about the impossible-to-navigate-by 1:1,000,000 maps issued by organizers, but few of us had taken advantage of the opportunity to buy proper maps when they were offered. We'd criticized the length of the race, but few of us had actually trained to travel fifteen-plus miles a day with a heavy pack in the mountains. And, as the feeling returned to my toes around September, it was also obvious that some people hadn't thought too hard about their equipment.

In reality, Chrzanowski could be faulted for little more than overestimating competitors' abilities and preparedness, and for clinging tenaciously to his rose-colored vision despite the mounting litany of disaster. He'd faced some last-minute problems of his own: the British Columbia Ministry of Lands suddenly got cold feet about liability issues and washed its hands of the traverse (some minion had even faxed an "Illegal Land Use" warning to Chrzanowski's Vancouver office just to be on the safe side); the day before the event, a snowcat and advance team of snowmobiles were unable to negotiate rotting snow above treeline and failed to deliver a badly needed cache of snowmobile fuel onto the route (which meant no preset camps or checkpoints and no extra fuel for safety-support vehicles); BC Tel Mobility suddenly pulled its cellular phone sponsorship, worried over negative publicity from Pemberton locals whose area wasn't serviced by the company, leaving organizers to cover a 116-square-mile area with radios whose batteries couldn't be recharged on the icecap. It certainly wasn't Chrzanowski's fault that we'd been lulled into stupidity by our assumption that everything he said would happen, would. After all, these *were* the mountains.

ALMOST IMMEDIATELY, questions raised by the "Reverse Traverse" went from blame-seeking for the myriad screwups to how best to operate such an event and what level of personal responsibility competitors should assume. There were questions about the lack of support for a grassroots event by Whistler, a resort many felt was bloated by its own success; about why B.C. Parks had not approved the originally planned and easier Spearhead Traverse route in Garibaldi Park, excluding a low-impact mountaineering event from the land despite allowing commercial heli-skiing to operate there; about whether competition—long before anything like the Red Bull Snowthrill of Alaska was conceived—of *any* type should be held in the backcountry; and, perhaps most intriguing, about why, if the course was *so* impossible, a handful of people had finished it?

The answer to the last question was that it *was* possible for the prepared and dedicated, a fact that ultimately accounted for the strange dramatic arc of most entrants. During the boatloads of thinking time we had while the race was underway, we'd all largely forgotten about embracing the concept of a dreamy spring party for the ski-mountaineering fraternity and obsessed about two key things: the overlooked traverse promotional poster promising "A Difficult Race across High Mountains" and Boy Scout doyen Baden Powell's motto, "Be Prepared." Between these thoughts hovered fleeting images from an absurdist play: repetitive slogging through montane Kabuki, moments of paralytic exhaustion, transcendent pain, hopelessness, surrender, and fits of violent anger. Yet despite these personal ordeals, we would all eventually absolve the organizers and take ownership of our choices, pronounce the experience wonderful, harbor no regrets, and express an inexplicable desire to return, somehow vicariously adopting Chrzanowski's own dichotomous gluttony for adventure and punishment. Which, if one were cynical enough, might even have been the plan.

In order to give the race both life and afterlife, Chrzanowski had hoped to live-broadcast certain portions (presumably the mountainous beginning and end since it was hard to imagine anything duller than exhausted people shuffling over a pancake-flat icecap for hours on end) and edit the footage into a follow-up movie. Thus, cinematographers buzzed the course for awhile in aircraft and on snowmobiles. Unfortunately, many of these people (including Chrzanowski himself) were less prepared than the competitors: a camera crew composed of a skier and snowboarder was dropped on the icecap on Saturday, but the skier had no climbing skins and the snowboarder no snowshoes, stranding them in place for two nights. When the snowboarder fainted from heat exhaustion on Monday, the skier left him to get help; the abandoned boarder, an arts student, kept busy recording morose on-camera monologues about fear, loneliness, hunger, and making it back alive.

After a chopper retrieved the delirious kid, Chrzanowski deemed the dramatic footage the perfect opener for a film, unwittingly ensuring that all hundred or so people who eventually watched *The Multiglisse Traverse* might find the concept intriguing but never, *ever* want to participate in anything remotely similar. It was like opening a ski-racing broadcast with footage of horrible crashes complete with unconscious, ragdolling bodies, visibly twisted limbs, gut-wrenching audio, and heli-evacuations of torn-up racers, when what you really hoped to engender among viewers was more than a fleeting interest in the sport. But wait... didn't ABC's *Wide World of Sports* do just that for, uh, twenty or so years?

10 | JUST SAY CHEESE

In a game of milliseconds, once you've
controlled for course conditions with skis and
wax and training, the difference between first
and second can lie in the athletes' creativity—
and this is art, not in the visual or audio sense,
but expression from within nonetheless.

DR. ANDREAS RAUCH

VAIL WAS bleak that evening in February
1999. In every corner of the venerable
resort, snowless trees begged the redemption of a winter
frock, straining harder than usual toward the gray, mocking sky. But when you entered the Lodge at Vail—official
headquarters for the Alpine World Ski Championships—
the ambiance improved. You'd stepped into the bosom of
the international ski-racing fraternity, a dozen languages
competing for airtime in the wooden-beamed synod.

Tanned, broad-smiling Euros chatted happily while
grim-faced Americans and Canadians, cell phones and
walkie-talkies to their ears, conducted post-mortems on
the latest casualty: North American ski racing. Yet despite
an absence of homegrown heroes, these guys should really
have been pleased. With a mixture of western hospitality,

exemplary volunteerism, and unparalleled efficiency, Vail—as it had during a previous World Championships in 1989—was showing the world that it could indeed throw a sporting event like no other. Not to mention party like it was 1999. And this success could only be good for racing on this side of the pond.

There was more at stake this time. The 1989 event was slick but poorly attended, with low TV ratings, and the FIS (Fédération Internationale de Ski), racing's governing body, had insisted that any encore do better. Ten years later, Vail rallied, with over twenty broadcast hours between NBC and ESPN plus a European network's staggering three hundred hours of coverage. In the sponsorship department, time-tested Euro icons—manufacturers of cheese, chocolate, pasta, beer, ski clothing, fine cars, and precision-engineered timing devices—were all represented.

"Unfortunately," one wag later put it, "it added up to a European TV event conveniently airlifted into America's most pseudo-European ski village."

The exposure was certain to help Vail's flagging fortunes as a toothless mountain in an age of extreme, but given our continent's proclivity for selling short-term hoopla and heroes over the pursuits themselves, could it actually elevate interest in ski racing here? The show was variously billed as "The Last Great Party of The Twentieth Century" and "The Last Great Race of the Millennium," titles that reeked of ephemerality in a sport desperately seeking a path to longevity. With the big-mountain and park-and-pipe freeski revolutions now in full swing, however, the 1999 Alpine World Ski Championships were also, for all intents and purposes, The Last Great Chance to Sell Ski Racing in North America.

I'd seen up close that selling backcountry solitude through televised multiglisse events was about as likely to succeed as selling the soulful telemark turn through big international race meets held far off skiing's traditional grid. But at least the latter model borrowed from the only mass-appeal marketing machinery that had *ever* worked in skiing: alpine racing. That the broader allure of high-level racing as an entry point to skiing only really captured the Formula One—addled minds of Europeans, however, had never stopped passionate folks on this side of the ocean from occasionally crossing their fingers and hoping for the best—despite little chance of success. After all, even the most fortuitous sales tools had failed to deliver in the past.

ONE MINUTE, 45 and 59/100ths of a second. That's how much time it took American Bill Johnson to win the men's Downhill on February 16, 1984, in Sarajevo, Yugoslavia. It was the first gold medal ever won by an American male in an Olympic alpine event and the first medal period for an American male in any World Cup Downhill.

"This course was designed for me," Johnson had famously asserted to an Austrian TV news team immediately following his first training run in Sarajevo, "and everyone else is here to fight for second place."

It was quite a prediction, and nobody took it seriously.

But he *had* won, and the media made great hay of this brash young man and his cocksure prescience. What the hacks failed to note, however, was that the man largely responsible for Johnson's victory had taken on the job of coaching the U.S. men's ski team in 1980 with a verbal guarantee that he'd deliver a Downhill winner within four years. Given the dismal history of American performance in the discipline and the infinitesimally small probability of prediction afforded by a sport where the top ten finishes were often spread over less than a second, his was indeed the more outrageous statement.

Outrageous to all but the slight twenty-eight-year-old Austrian who'd made it. Dr. Andreas Rauch had complete confidence not only in his ability to identify the type of talent and creativity required in a potential ski-racing champion (he did, in fact, pick Johnson for the Downhill squad over the protestations of U.S. Ski Team brass), but also in his ability to judiciously apply the necessary science and psychology to place that athlete on the podium.

In June 1992, I'd traveled to Quebec City, where Rauch lived with his Canadian wife, Sofie, to interview him for an in-depth profile in *POWDER*. I was mesmerized by his insight, candidness, and counterintuitive approach to racing, something that, like the majority of my skiing peers, I occasionally watched but cared little about.

Born in Schlins, Austria, in 1952 and on skis from age two, Rauch raced seriously until he was fifteen, then decided to focus on academics. While studying physical education and mathematics at the University of Innsbruck, he also became a National-Certified Ski Instructor and Ski Guide of Austria, a National-Certified Ski Coach, and physical education coach for the Austrian National Development Team.

Rauch's ability to think about ski racing in the long-term became obvious between 1976 and 1980 when he was head coach of physical education for the Men's Alpine National Team of Austria and coach of the Downhill Team. Despite being the same age as the men he was coaching, Andy (as his charges called him) managed to gain their respect and saw Franz Klammer crowned as World Cup Downhill champion, Josef "Sepp" Walcher win the World Championships at Garmisch, and Leonhard Stock and Peter Wirnsberger collect Downhill gold and silver respectively at the Lake Placid Olympics in 1980.

In line with his appetite for new challenges, Andy took on the men's coaching job for the U.S. Alpine Team that summer, under contractual promise of complete control over team choice, training, and scheduling. An eventual violation of this agreement led him to quit before the 1984 Olympics, but not until he'd tackled Johnson's potentially virulent moxie and redirected at least some of it. In the interim, he'd seen Phil Mahre become World Cup overall champion three years running (1981–83) and Steve Mahre win the World Championship in 1982.

"How will I find the right talents to fulfill my promise in such a huge, diverse country with so many people?" Rauch remembers thinking on the plane flying over.

At the time he was working on some hypotheses and had queried coaches in the field to see how certain kids were doing, not just in skiing, but in baseball, gymnastics, tennis, and soccer.

"My questions were designed to find good *skiers* as opposed to *ski racers*," he'd told me. "*Those* I definitely didn't want."

In fact, Andy's experience had convinced him that what he really wanted were talented, all-around athletes who learned fast. You could, he believed, teach a gifted athlete the techniques of ski racing. You could not, however, teach someone whose brain was wired with technique how to be a talented athlete. As the Norwegians had asserted at the telemark roundtable in Courmayeur and had shown repeatedly, a good skier was someone who skied everything well—bumps, powder, steeps, slow, fast—while a racer was simply able to use a specific technique in gates.

During his selection process, Andy immediately eliminated kids who, from ages six to twelve, were race-training in clubs, following coaches down the hill all day and running gates that didn't demand a range of movements. He wanted kids who skied a lot at that age because they would have picked up the movements and wiring they would unconsciously use in racing to react fast and correct without thinking.

"When Franz Klammer was hot," noted Andy, "he could *gain* speed from his mistakes. When you're fast, you're on the edge, and there will be situations that you cannot anticipate and must react fast to correct. This is why I was so impressed with Johnson. He was twenty at the time and had the ski-racing technique of only a fourteen-year-old Austrian, but he was a truly gifted athlete with great reactions and quick learning. I knew I could teach him."

Andy invited thirty-five people, including Johnson, to a 1980 training camp. Assembling the group on largely subjective grounds, he then needed an objective means of elimination. And that was where he'd introduced his infamous testing procedures. Although he had conceived the series of general athletic, ski-ability, ski-agility, and ski-intelligence challenges while coaching in Austria, they remained hypothetical until he tried them in America. In many of the tests, athletes were presented with problems—on dry land and on snow—that appeared lateral to racing but in reality incorporated all the essential elements. Andy felt these showed which racers were too heavily influenced by ski-racing technique and which ones had innate ability.

Based on test rankings, Andy chose fifteen from that original group; some, like Johnson, would never have been allowed on the team based strictly on their racing records. Years later, he conducted statistical tests to see how those skiers had improved. The correspondence was astonishing: in 1980, he had one skier ranked in the top fifty in the world, three between seventy-five and one hundred, and the rest below. By 1983, there were *eight* ranked in the top fifty. He was able to bring more than half the group to this point in just three years, a feat that would likely have been impossible if he'd chosen other people. This was also very scary—it basically said that you could take a group, apply these tests, and toss out many individuals right off the bat because they'd never make it no matter how hard they tried. Not surprisingly, the controversial results were never publicized.

From 1984 to 1988, Andy directed and coached the Austrian women's team and simultaneously conducted groundbreaking research to earn a PhD in Sport Science from the University of Innsbruck. His thesis bore the Zdarsky-esque title *Biomechanical Analysis of Slalom Race Technique*. Predictably, his girls fared well at the 1988 Calgary Olympics, where Sigrid Wolf won the Super G and Anita Wachter took the Combined (in which participants have to race both Slalom and Downhill events).

Andy retired from coaching at age thirty-six, but as one of the winningest ski coaches in history, he was repeatedly sought after to return by the likes of Canada, the U.S., and Austria. Youthful, enthusiastic, and full of anecdotes when I interviewed him, Andy's frequently controversial views on coaching hadn't diminished in the least. His opinions tended toward the magnanimous perhaps because of his acute awareness of the complexities involved in the outcome of not just a single race, but a season or a career.

"What's your favorite downhill course?" I asked.

"You always love the course your team wins on."

"Which athlete did you most enjoy working with?"

"Each athlete represents a unique experience, and I have loved them all equally."

Had he still been coaching the Austrian women in 1999, Andy would no doubt have loved the Vail courses, in which his former paramours shone. He may, however, have wondered if his efforts had actually yielded stronger affinities with racing for the North American public.

ON THE FACE of it, the public seemed to be buying into at least the hoopla end of the Vail World Championships. After five days, the races had been well attended and were

generally running smoothly. Ditto for side events, concerts, and parties. Goodwill and shared purpose abounded
as momentum gathered for the showcase men's Downhill at
Beaver Creek.

Under blue skies, racers assembled atop the Birds of
Prey course, designed by Swiss downhilling great Bernhard
Russi, while stands and sidelines swelled with the largest crowd ever to watch a ski race on this continent (some
10,000 people as compared to 50,000+ for European races).
Music blared, incomprehensible Euro ads flickered on the
JumboTron at the finish, and announcers pumped up the
stands where spectators, faces painted with national colors, rang cowbells and waved flags. Freaky mascots milled
at the finish: purple cows from chocolate sponsor Milka;
an Iowa football team–style Bird of Prey; the Carlsberg
Elephant, and presumably, representing the surrounding
White River National Forest, Smokey the Bear. The crowd
cheered wildly as the first racer freefell over the stomach-
sucking steeps of "The Brink" and the race was on.

Early on, Norway's Kjetil Aamodt stormed into the
lead. Then the indomitable Austrian, Hermann Maier,
flew by, hands driving forward, upper body low as he beat
aside gates and aired perfectly over a roller, always—as the
announcers propounded with what they thought was genuine insight—searching for more speed. At the finish, as
per script, he was in first. Next followed Norwegian rival
Lasse Kjus, the then–World Cup Downhill leader who, days
before had shared gold with Maier in the Super G. Kjus
lacked Maier's speed and aggression in the technical spots
but rocketed through the gliding sections with perfectly
lined turns and efficient jumps, finishing 0.31 seconds
behind The Hermannator. It was more than impressive.

In contrast, the Americans were wild and undisciplined:
one blew up above the final turn, wobbling down favor-
ing a leg; another lost a ski close to the bottom, finishing

the course on a single plank. Unlike Euro prima donnas who might stand, shake their heads, then toss their skis into the woods in disgust, the fallen Yanks displayed John Wayne—esque pride in crawling to the bottom of the run under their own power, which raised a heartfelt cheer from the hometown crowd. Once the last of their countrymen had raced, however, the erstwhile cheerleaders scattered en masse, leaving the stands largely empty and back-of-the-pack dregs from *auslands* like Mexico to their lonely pursuits.

Despite the almost universal technical (meaning race-trained) backgrounds of their big-mountain freeski heroes, most of today's kids simply can't relate to the discipline and single-mindedness of ski racing: the sacrifices of time, money, and opportunity, the long-term goals and low probability of success. Which isn't surprising in a society that bombards us with the message that short-term gratification, fun-hogging, and hollow celebrity-worship are the acmes of modern culture.

What would it take to keep people interested? Or to get newcomers on board? Was it even possible, I wondered, after overhearing various exchanges in the post-race mêlée?

"Where are the kids?" a mom asked.

"Oh," said dad, "they went to the terrain park after the third racer."

Later, at a press conference, European journalists questioned Maier about the minutiae of his run: What was he thinking at this jump? Why had he knocked aside gates like a slalom skier? Local reporters politely and industriously scribbled the answers despite the arcane nature of the information. Finally, one had the courage to raise his own hand.

"Hermann," he hesitated, "I understand your friend Arnold Schwarzenegger is here..."

The floodgates burst.

"What did he say to you?"

"Did you give him your skis from Nagano?"

"Have you visited Planet Hollywood?"

The Hermannator-Terminator story quickly eclipsed the proceedings, the other racers shifting uneasily until the moderator shut down the *Hard Copy* hot seat.

IN THE WOMEN'S Downhill, the story was much the same, only this time it was too dangerous to stand beside the icy course in ski boots. Course officials wouldn't allow anyone onto the mountain without crampons, and because they were scarce, I elected to spend the race in the start area. There, technicians ruled the roost, adding and removing wax layers, brushing, making last-minute edge adjustments, sliding skis back and forth on the snow like dinky toys. When racers finally exited the start gate, days of strategizing and laborious tinkering with equipment went with them. Tension ran high, and a Canadian girl burst into tears after a terrible run, screaming at her techs.

"What did you do to my skis?"

"She eesa queena beetch," pronounced a group of Italian ski techs, erupting into gut-wrenching laughter, humored that she would even *dare* to question a fellow tech's judgment.

Around them, two tottering Milka cows slinging wicker baskets full of chocolates patted competitors on the back in the start tent, lending the scene—as I'd now come to expect—a surreal aura.

Occasionally, a racer would radio teammates at the top after a run.

"The course is super-buff and you should really attack and go for speed," Megan Gerety advised after being the first American to finish.

It was tempting to speculate that the Austrians overheard, but they hardly needed to. They took the contest handily, with Renate Goetschl edging teammates Michaela Dorfmeister and Stefanie Schuster. American reporters seeking reasons for this dominance peppered the trio in the post-race scrum. They missed the obvious, however, which was helpfully pointed out by a European translator: the Austrian women were simply better trained, better equipped, better supported, and the cream of a much larger pool of young talent. In short, they were much better racers, shown not so much by their winning in Vail as by their collective longevity: to a person, they stood on podiums with alarming regularity. The Americans looked stunned.

I asked a credentialed local volunteer what she thought was behind the sweep.

"I don't know," she shrugged, "I didn't even know they *had* snow in Australia."

IF NORTH AMERICAN ski racing was going to build a bridge to the twenty-first century, it appeared that bridge would have to cross the Atlantic Ocean. In other words, successfully selling racing in North America meant having to sell alpine culture as well.

At the awards presentation in Vail Village, the Milka boys, backed by a traditional Austrian band robed in the familiar cow costumes, broke out the lederhosen and danced, clapped, and rang bells for the bemused crowd. In a nod to Euro disco sensibilities, the awards were handed out by a revolving door of officials introduced by an over-the-top emcee, while pretentious FIS pageant and Birds of Prey music (they wrote a frickin' *song* for the race course?!) played in the background. Also like in Europe, a glut of fur fashions crowded the square, solidifying Colorado's place as center of the continent's cheesy ski-clothing universe. Did this scene represent the long-awaited convergence?

Perhaps food was the answer. The Carlsberg beer tent was packed, the Milka cows couldn't keep up with demand for the chocolates they were handing out, and crowds swarmed Grana Padano's many cheese kiosks. Since cheese was integral to the alpine milieu in which ski racing was born and continued to flourish, and everyone loved cheese, perhaps *it* was the perfect vehicle to sell racing. Such unassailable logic was likely at work when the famous Parmesan consortium from northern Italy signed on as a title sponsor. A brigade of beautiful Italian girls employed special cheese-gouging instruments to dispense chunks from massive wheels. It was impossible to ignore the girls' tight T-shirts emblazoned with more beautiful girls and the slogan "Good for the head."

Cheese, sex, racing, cerebral connections: Grana Padano had it all.

I asked the chief cheese chick about the promotion. She told me forty wheels at seventy-seven pounds each were shipped over in a container. That was over 3,000 pounds of cheese.

"Do Americans like it?" I asked.

"They like anything that's free," she said.

"Will they buy it in a grocery store?"

"I hope so," she answered without really caring; she was more interested in driving downvalley to Dillon to buy cheap cowboy hats and boots.

From the volumes being consumed, Americans appeared to like Grana Padano just fine, and maybe they'd even be tricked into buying some. The real question, however, was would they appreciate it? Not likely. The cheese—or at least the process of its production—was a thousand years old, and the wheels themselves aged several years. Contrast this to the 1.6 nanoseconds it took a machine to squirt out the rubbery, edible-oil product known as American Slices, and you see where this argument is going. North Americans are generally far less concerned with where things come from than in obtaining them in a timely and convenient fashion. And there are parallels between the incremental modifications required to perfect a cheese, and the long, dedicated, sifting process required to place a ski racer on the podium consistently.

"Ski mentalities are totally different between Europe and the U.S.," Andy Rauch had explained, "and I think this is reflected by the popular sports in these respective countries."

He was onto something. Compare football and soccer. Both are great sports, but football is short, single actions of several seconds to get to the goal; it's stop, regroup, make strategy, and then go again. Soccer, however, is relatively uninterrupted flow involving strategic buildup—a game can go ninety minutes during which there may be no goal.

"That's *very* different thinking," Andy had pointed out. "Short- versus long-term."

CROWDS FOR THE Combined weren't as large as for other races, but those like myself who had hospitality passes had apparently all shown up. Grazing in the VIP tent began in earnest after the races, where line-ups around the canapé-warming trays rivaled those at the lifts. The food, however, proved far less interesting than the conversations flowing over it: despite my week-long attempt to locate an enclave of race savvy among the local posh, the ranks of the ignorant remained truly astounding.

"What fuckin' languages are *those?*" grunted one Marlboro man beneath his Stetson when official times were read in English, French, and German.

"Snowboarders are the problem," offered another Luddite out of the blue, in a ham-fisted attempt to explain Austrian dominance and American ineptitude. "I'll bet Austrians don't put up with snowboarders. I'll bet they shoot 'em on sight. I know how to solve the problem *here*—make lift-tickets for snowboarding a hundred bucks."

The scene would not have been complete without the costumed cows.

"How about a chocolate?" one leaned in to ask in a thick Scottish brogue, hoping to placate the dude.

A photographer joked about milking the udders of one of the enormous inflatable cows lining the course.

"Go ahead," said a Milka executive with the unabashedly partisan "FANCLUB Hermann Maier" embossed on his jacket, "it's full of Carlsberg..."

Just then, the winner of the downhill portion of the Combined, Swiss Bruno Kernen, was escorted to the VIP tent. Lacking credentials but still dressed in his race suit and number, he was nevertheless hassled mercilessly by volunteer gatekeepers and eventually detained by a beefy State Trooper who had his ear wired to his collar.

"You know *nothing* about ski racing," screamed Kernen's coach. "This man just *won!*"

In the background, the old ladies volunteering their time to check badges squawked like parrots.

"He's got no credentials, *bwaack,* he's got no credentials, *bwaack...*"

The subtext again highlighted the general public's— even the average skier's—disconnect with ski racing. Ultimately, the exact nature of this disconnect would be exposed on break day.

While powderhounds had avoided drought-plagued Colorado that season, and those who'd come had found themselves skidding down surfaces that qualified as race pistes in any other jurisdiction, organizers had been ecstatic with their rock-hard manufactured courses—a reality that continued to confound potential viewers and frustrate host venues. Race surfaces had become *so* unlike any form of natural snow that measurable amounts of the real thing were disasters of the highest order. Thus, while regular skiers prayed for a big dump, race types prayed harder for none. The outcome of this kharmic tug-of-war, if you believed in such things, had been dribs and drabs of snow on an irregular basis. In a perfectly timed coup for skiers, however, and with the collective will of organizers suspended by the FIS-mandated break in the action, the preset weather day dawned stormy, with heavy snow and wind.

For a brief, paradoxical moment, skiing in Vail returned to its natural state. Racers secretly spoke of "freeskiing," a term *they* had originally and appropriately coined to describe what they did when they weren't chasing gates. It spoke volumes about the continued two solitudes, a reminder that although the current freeski movement had at least some roots planted in the soils of technical skiing (albeit mostly in the form of lapsed acolytes), it was powder that continued to solve the soul equation. That night, in what seemed an après celebration to this reality, a good ol' western rodeo ensured that everyone who wasn't racing the next day got very, very drunk.

And so it went for the rest of the week: killer races during the day, killer parties at night. By most accounts, Vail indeed succeeded in staging the greatest Alpine World Ski Championships ever. Victories for the FIS, however, were few.

Sure the Super G duel between Maier and Kjus broke TV-viewing records in Austria, and certainly NBC made a splash with technology that superimposed different racer's images in the same section of the course (this visual helped compare line choice and other factors affecting the infinitesimally small and difficult-to-understand time differences). The bottom line, however, was that NBC did so because North Americans would never *get* ski racing. Here, for a host of reasons, the discipline remained an expensive, elitist pursuit on par with equestrianism and yacht-racing, and the public's notoriously ephemeral interest would continue to ride the four-year sine wave of the Winter Olympic Games, further waxing and waning with the fortunes of the Canadian and American national teams.

But so what? Maybe it wasn't necessary to inspire a huge buy-in. Racing would always be part of skiing, serve its role, and have a core of dedicated fans. Perhaps, in the end, and despite all the imported cheese(iness), the 1999 Alpine World Ski Championships were actually everything anyone could have hoped for. Besides, since ski racing was at least exciting in the moment—a high-speed, hard-object, soft-body blood-sport that made for great television— would skiing *ever* have anything better to watch?

11 | X MARKS THE SPOT

> ... the noises [freeskiers are] making sound
> nothing like fingernails clawing the lid of a coffin.
> They've grown up with snowboarders—roomed,
> road-tripped, partied, and copulated with them—
> and know that neither sport will push the other
> off the mountain. Everything will be just fine if
> everyone just shuts up and slides.
> ROB STORY *"The Planetary Snow Bohemians Will
> Save us All,"* POWDER, *September 1995*

STORMS WERE always descending on ski country, but the one brewing along North America's west coast in the mid-nineties was all-time. A pair of powerful cyclones, driven by the spiraling winds of two independent freeskiing revolutions, were about to merge into the biggest gale skiing had ever known.

The storm of the century wouldn't be enough to blow away the entrenched elements of snowboarding that were taking over the mountain-resort industry, threatening skiing with the very real prospect of extinction. The tempest fed liberally from those same elements, however, and when it settled, snowboarding would find itself sharing every inch of proprietary ground it had smugly claimed with a new and energetic ski culture.

Naturally, we watched on radar from *POWDER* head-quarters, the collective batholith of experience and titanic analytical abilities that we *imagined* we possessed suffi-cient only to understand the system's genesis and momen-tary gravitas, but laughingly unable to comprehend the real forces at work or to predict the breadth of their outcome. Others figured they knew: both *Freeze* and *Freeskier* maga-zines were founded at that time on the premise that some-thing new and big and exciting was happening, and that no existing magazine could adequately represent it. They were right, but one thing was clear to all: the usual peo-ple, places, and powder equation looked *very* different. Two unique visionaries were working from distinct ends of a brand-new continuum. With the venues of Alaska's remote ranges and Whistler's summer freestyle camps spawning both radical new ski designs and unheard of maneuvers, skiing's usual passion for steep faces and deep powder was suddenly competing with artificial terrain parks and spare urban staircases. Similarly, travel-heavy ski movies were now up against a well-funded, fast-evolving new freeski competition that celebrated both the grass roots and the cutting edge, and was beamed around the world by an explosion of multimedia.

How this mix would all come together could never have been guessed; that it *did* is the story of skiing's future.

WHEN I RECEIVED the fax, all I could do was laugh.

Inappropriately but uproariously titled "1998 Winter X Games Fun," it detailed a list of injuries in Skiercross, the snowboard-inspired, Roller Derby—style battle in which four skiers at a time were released from start gates to drop into a snaking, berm-filled course and elbow their way past each other at high speed to the bottom. From what I was reading, it looked like ESPN—the maverick U.S. sports channel behind this new high-action, Gen-X alternative to the regular Olympics—might have created the most dangerous sport in the world. The litany of injured skiers: Tara Bell, blown knee; John Dill, two broken heels; Wendy Fisher, heel damage; Allison Gannet, blown knee (or two); Kent Kreitler, blown knee; Noel Lyons, five broken teeth; Denny Rey, badly blown face; Dave Swanwick, blown knee; Kristen Ulmer, broken heel.

Injuries had put out fully 20 percent of a field of forty-six. If someone had said, "Here's a gun with five chambers and one bullet, aim it at your knee and pull the trigger; you have a one-in-forty-six chance of winning five grand, but a one-in-five chance of a season-ending injury," would any of these athletes have accepted?

Such were the early days of Winter X, the annual Red Bull—fueled, alt-TV sister to the skateboard-and-BMX—dominated Summer X Games, that had quickly come to dominate the aspirations of those caught up in the new wave of freeskiing (now defined as anything different from a traditional FIS event). With safer courses and better athletes, Skiercross would eventually refine itself into an only occasionally bloody gladiator sport populated by ex-racers (after the Vail Alpine World Championships, many retiring national teamsters found a second life in Skiercross) and become popular enough to debut as an FIS-sanctioned Olympic event in 2010 (begging the question of whether it can still be called freeskiing). Winter X eventually added Big Air, Superpipe (a spectacular, extra-large version of snowboarders' cherished halfpipe), and Slopestyle (a variable combination of jumps and rails that riders are encouraged to be creative in hitting) to play both to Summer/Winter X's prime demographic, as well as to the swelling ranks of young skiers weaned on terrain parks.

With television, the Internet, and an unprecedented global youth marketing machine behind them, ESPN's Winter X Games held the power to ultimately define a generation of young skiers. What couldn't have been foreseen, however, was that this power would also remodel an historic town that represented every stale aspect of skiing's old-school, and that the revival would serve as a template for the evolution of the entire global ski scene.

BY THE TIME the millennium rolled around, legendary Aspen, Colorado, home to much of America's classic skiing gestalt—from the experimental early resort scene of the 1940s through the freestyle revolution of some thirty years later—was a cobwebbed shadow of its former self wrapped in a mink stole. Populated by the gentrified wealthy, Hollywood celebrities, writers, musicians, hippie "thinkers," and cokeheads, the town's mainstay mountain, Ajax, was one of only four remaining holdouts on the continent to ban snowboarding. Aspen had passed through Lunn's Spenglerian cycle; it had become an alpine civilization in decline.

Even knowing what Aspen *wasn't*, it was still hard to say exactly what *was* represented by its strange pastiche of snakeskin-banded cowboy hats, turquoise jewelry, diamond chokers, hairdos from another planet, and T-shirts that screamed "Vail Sucks" in one-hundred-point type. (This I granted them: compared to Aspen, Vail really did suck.) On one pilgrimage to the town, my flight from Denver was filled with more animal prints and expensive pelts than a Siegfried & Roy pageant. Then, when the plane pulled up to Aspen's terminal, the woman in front of me reached into a humongous handbag and extracted a tiny, blinking Yorkshire Terrier, its head fur drawn up in a mauve ribbon. "Now that wasn't so bad, was it, Felix?" she muttered. "Mommy's *very* proud of you."

Escaping directly to Ajax, I began by lapping Ruthie's Run, which the speed-loving Euros I'd met in Vail enthusiastically referenced as the best run in North America. Sucking up corduroy rollers at subsonic speed on one of Colorado's crisp, preternatural, blue-sky days painted Aspen's on-mountain experience, at least, as perfectly sane. But later, poking through the surrounding forests for leftover powder, I came across shrines to The Beatles, Jimi Hendrix, Elvis, Bob Marley, Jerry Garcia, and, most bizarrely, Marilyn Monroe, built around framed photos adorned with beads, posters, candles, incense, and vinyl records.

Maybe these had something to do with Hunter S. Thompson and the litany of other sixties-era scions living in Aspen. Thompson, who'd once run for mayor, was known for fomenting insurrection from his seat at the Woody Creek Tavern, where I'd once met him, rheumy-eyed, clutching a Wild Turkey on the rocks and a Marlboro in his signature cigarette-holder. (Hobbled by a degenerating hip, he blew his brains out Hemingway-style in 2005, and his friend Johnny Depp ponied up five million dollars to build a huge cannon from which, as the town watched in reverence, Thompson's ashes were dramatically blasted.)

Ultimately, however, Aspen was lodged in most skiers' consciousness because of the 1993 feature film *Aspen Extreme,* which starred that nice Canadian boy Paul Gross as T.J. Burke, who heads west from his Detroit home to chase the dream of ski-bum-writer-wannabe for—to its eternal shame—*POWDER.* The movie ends with the magazine running one of Burke's stories *and* inexplicably putting him on the cover. Of course, *POWDER* would *never* put a mere writer on the cover (especially from Detroit), but that was only one of the film's far-fetched sequences. In another, Burke's friend Dexter Rutecki falls into a crevasse, though glaciers can't be found anywhere near Aspen.

Nevertheless, the names T.J. Burke and Dexter Rutecki ring with more recognition each year, their costumed avatars populating retro ski days and hot-dogging parties around the continent. The very over-the-top quality that makes a maudlin B-grade movie into a cult classic turns out to be what Aspen is all about. Nothing there is simply extreme— it's *really* extreme.

This was best exemplified by the 24 Hours of Aspen, an endurance race in which two-person teams (largely ex-racers) competed to log as many top-to-bottom runs on Ajax as possible in a twenty-four-hour period. For fifteen years, the event had seen participants skiing through the night, shitting and pissing in buckets in the gondola in lieu of bathroom breaks, and straightlining runs at eighty miles per hour when their bodies were too tired even to stand. By 2001, sponsorship and interest in this event were waning, making Aspen and its appetite for extreme the perfect match for a new sports extravaganza in need of a home. Someone just needed to arrange an introduction.

David Perry, chief architect of Whistler-Blackcomb's late-nineties success story, had moved south at the millennium to bring similar magic to Colorado Ski Country, the state's mountain-resort marketing consortium. By the time he transferred to Aspen as vice president of marketing, he'd already kicked down the Ajax snowboard embargo and brought in the 2002 X Games. He staged an encore in 2003, then inked a deal with ESPN to hold the games through 2012. Suddenly, Aspen was X's de facto home. How big was this? Pundits universally agree that no smarter marketing move has *ever* been performed by a ski resort. Now, each January, ESPN creates a miniature city beside Buttermilk Mountain, with hundreds of technicians, dozens of trailers, and a million miles of cable, while the night-time ski and snowboard Superpipe finals see tens of thousands of fans decked out in as much sign-and-sticker fanwear as the Super Bowl.

After years of catering almost exclusively to an over-the-hill jet set, Aspen was back in the limelight with the continent's youth, just as it had been in the seventies when we papered our bedrooms with posters of freestyle heroes tossing through Volkswagen-sized bumps on Ajax's infamous Ridge of Bell. Unlike the measuredly ephemeral effects of an Olympics, however, the X Games have rejuvenated Aspen and made it *the* place to be again.

Did it simply take a new and radical snowsports showcase to drive an aging dame forward and send resorts around the world scrambling to similarly reinvent themselves? Not quite. Even Winter X had been built on a sea-change innovation that both ensured its success and a future of constant evolution: the twin-tip ski.

ON A WELCOME sunny day in the middle of a rainy June, Blackcomb's Horstman Glacier buzzed with energy. From any vantage above, what appeared to be dozens of ants were digging, building, shaping, jumping, spinning, and following each other over myriad boxes, rails, and jumps that from a distance resembled jacked-up frozen waves. Up close, the insects turned out to be a rag-tag mix of girls and boys, aged eight to eighteen, attending one of several ski and snowboard camps, each dressed in baggy bottoms and over-size jackets of bright stripes and frighteningly busy prints that seemed gravity-bound to pool at their feet. Among them, the spandex-girded legs of the occasional self-conscious race-camp kid were glaringly obvious as they shifted uncomfortably in the T-bar line-up, desperate to be yanked from the crowd's judgmental midst. Ten years after their invention, twin-tips were now the best-selling ski category globally, and the gate-chasers had reason to feel left out.

"Without twin-tip skis, more kids would be snowboarding, it's that simple," longtime Momentum Ski Camp freestyle coach Trennon Paynter summarized. "There'd be *more* snowboard camps up here, and probably more traditional mogul camps since mogul skiing is the only real ski discipline with guaranteed air time and tricks—which is really all kids want."

Anyone who has ever clicked into a pair of skis will concur: powder, pistes, moguls, trees, etcetera, each offers a certain amount of amusement, but jumping is where the real fun lies. And air time is what the twin-tip is all about.

"Somebody would have invented a twin-tip eventually. Skiers were just *itching* to ride in the park," according to snowboard legend and impresario Ken Achenbach, whose ski and snowboard Camp of Champions celebrated its twentieth anniversary in 2007. "It would have taken longer if Salomon hadn't done it, but technology would eventually have caught up to demand."

As witness to both the birth of snowboarding and New School skiing, no one was better apprised than Achenbach. However, his point overlooked the true visionary in this equation: a retired National Team mogul skier from Campbell River, British Columbia, named Mike Douglas.

Whistler-based Douglas had worked his way along the usual ski-bum/shitty job/aspiring-athlete axis into a solid career of international World Cup competition and on through to what seemed the next logical level. In 1997, he was a thoughtful, focused coach for the National Development Team's mogul squad, a static discipline in a waning sport that looked to leave him no comfortable exit strategy. He and his buddy Stephen Fearing, an American in a similar position as coach of Japan's national mogul team, figured that getting skiers into the terrain parks and halfpipes so popular in snowboarding might help rejuvenate freestyle skiing—and yield them some career options. In a scenario of now almost mythic proportions, they sketched out an idea on a napkin for a new high-performance ski that, like a snowboard, would have both an upturned tip and upturned tail: it would spin more easily on snow and you could slide backward (switch) on it, allowing skiers to ride up and out of halfpipes, rotate, then re-enter backward and slide down without digging their tails in. The pair excitedly shopped their barroom-blueprint around to all the big ski manufacturers. Perhaps because incarnations of the twin-tip idea had surfaced before—all the way back to the fifties—but gone nowhere, they were turned down by everyone.

Douglas and Fearing were at the end of the road when Toshi Shimizu, marketing director for Salomon's Japanese division, signed on, declaring he would fund the research and development himself since the parent company in France had no interest. With the requisite manufacturing and marketing muscle to both realize *and* keep the idea from sinking into the kind of gimmick grave that skiing was all-too famous for, the new Teneighty (referring to the Holy Grail of three consecutive 360-degree rotations) went from drawing board to real board in just nine months—the fastest-developed new ski type in history.

By the time the Teneighty rolled out of the factory in February 1998, Douglas and his athletes—J.P. Auclair, J.F. Cusson, and Vinnie Dorion (another charge, Shane Szocs, was skiing on the K2 Poacher, a short, soft, proto-twin-tip that ultimately failed)—were already innovating new tricks daily, reinventing freestyle skiing for an eager press and a voracious worldwide audience. As in snowboarding, the tricks involved a range of different grabs (Mute, Japan, etc.), single and multiple full spins (360, 720, 1080), added half-spins (180, 540, 900), and corked-out (off-axis) maneuvers that weren't even *allowed* in FIS mogul competition. Photos and video circled the globe. Sales exploded. Every ski company had to have a twin-tip. Within three years, the NCAF (New Canadian Air Force— an original Canadian Air Force had competed in traditional FIS aerial freestyle) had changed everything about the way people skied or even *thought* about skiing: the versatile new skis and their photogenic mavens quickly shifted on-hill aspirations to parks, pipes, and trick-filled off-piste freeriding, creating a next generation of skiers that may not otherwise have materialized.

It was skiing's greatest-ever revolution.

Like the original freestyle era of the late sixties and early seventies, skiing's New School (then referred to as park and pipe, or progressive freestyle, and these days as just jibbing) was full of fun, exploration, and conquest—especially in the early days. In the summer of 1998, the first in which they had the Teneighty to mess around with on the Horstman Glacier, nineteen-year-old Quebecer Vinnie Dorion spent his time practicing instead of coaching. He started riding switch into jumps, looking over his shoulder, picking up speed, and throwing unheard-of tricks.

"We were already landing switch sometimes, but taking off that way wasn't on anybody's mind. Too scary," Auclair told me of those days. "But Vinnie didn't have a paying ski deal, so he worked harder than any of us. He was *really* motivated."

Salomon, which fully sponsored Douglas, Cusson, and Auclair, had only paid Dorion lip service. He was given free skis, but the other three—by dint of age, experience, and extroversion—were more easily promotable. Still, when the Summer X Games in San Diego announced a Big Air exhibition of New School skiing to see how it flew (Big Air would debut for real at the subsequent 1999 Winter X Games), Dorion figured he should be there. When Salomon didn't put his name forward as a potential participant, he took matters into his own hands.

"I drive to San Diego dat summer, an' 'ave no credential," Dorion recalled. "Just show up an' act like I should be dere and everyt'ing. And when I see da guy who organize da demo, I was like 'C'mon dude, let me in. I got some sick shit—I suppose to be dere, you know, is just misunderstood.'"

Aided and abetted by other riders, Dorion poached the jump, blowing the crowd away with a smooth Switch 360 (taking off *and* landing backward) and the first 900 (two full forward rotations with an extra half-rotation at the end to land switch). It catapulted him from relative obscurity into the same limelight as his teammates. Salomon sheepishly signed him up, and other sponsors came calling. Dorion soon found himself thronged in hero-mad places like Japan, autographing breasts and car hoods in the mêlée. And that's the way it worked for a series of young stars who became instant pros in a brand-new milieu without definition or limits: show up, throw down, sign on. The bandwagon effect was instantaneous, with virtually every ski, boot, eyewear, helmet, glove, and clothing company out to create a "team" of New School riders to represent their brands. The effect spilled over into the simultaneously growing ranks of big-mountain skiers (more on this later). In the long and storied history of skiing, there had *never* been anything even close to this level of sponsorship available.

A sudden murrain of park-and-pipe rats wasn't the only thing driving the renaissance, however; the easy-riding twin-tip also allowed entry-level skiers who wouldn't otherwise have contemplated entering a terrain park or half-pipe to charge the non-mountainous ski areas where these were the only form of entertainment. The twin-tip also followed the snowboard's rail-grinding incursion into cities, mimicking the urban-infrastructure-smacking revolt of skateboarders and in-line skaters. What really aided the twin-tip's meteoric rise among skiing's youth, however, was that the entire revolution—more so even than Alaska's big-mountain, steep-and-deep breakout—occurred in front of the world at large, a story that owes as much to the grassroots Petri dish of the Horstman Glacier as the televised spectacle of the X Games.

Photographers and cinematographers swarmed the Horstman to watch the NCAF and their followers in action. Kids and coaches from the four corners of the White Planet carried the word—if not an actual pair of skis—home after those first late-nineties summers. The Horstman quickly became *the* place to see and be seen, and hot skiers of the moment were virtually expected to coach at one of its camps. It was a place to work on new tricks and share ideas, identify new talent, and bring them up through the ranks. World-class freestylers like Anthony Boronowski, Sarah Burke, C.R. Johnson, Philou Poirier, T.J. Schiller, Corey Vanular, and Colby West all attended Horstman camps.

Four generations of New Schoolers later, the big pros don't always show up at the glacier camps anymore; they're off chasing the dream and the big bucks that the twin-tip spawned. Summertime sees them busy skiing on photo shoots in South America and New Zealand; making reality TV shows in the States; filming commercials in Europe; surfing in Bali and driving sports cars in Monaco; entertaining the troops in Iraq; and consulting on competitions, ski design, and marketing across the globe. As a result, the glacier itself has lost much of its draw for aspiring freestylers.

"Nowadays," levels Douglas, now a former camp boss himself, "there are *amazing* parks everywhere, so kids don't feel pressure to come to Whistler in the summer just to jump in a good park."

True, but it hasn't stopped pros and wannabes from feeling the pressure to go to Whistler in the winter to ride and film on the resort's Euro-like high alpine or access untracked lines via snowmobile in the surrounding Coast Range backcountry. This drive to conquer the big-mountain world was the second front of skiing's perfect storm. And it, too, had its own commander.

THE LITANY RANG from the stage of Dusty's Bar & Grill in Whistler.

"Ever skied moguls...naked? Then you knew Shane. Ever watched a big-mountain contest? You knew Shane. Ever ridden fat skis in powder? You knew Shane. Ever laughed at a fart joke? You knew Shane. Ever watched birds wheeling in the sky and wished *you* were one of them? You definitely knew Shane."

Thus began the memorial for thirty-nine-year-old James Shane McConkey, who died on March 26, 2009, while filming a BASE jump in Italy's Dolomite Mountains. The James Bond–style stunt required skiing off the 1,900-foot Sass Pardoi cliff, executing a double backflip, releasing his skis, gliding away in a wingsuit, then pulling his parachute. It was a feat McConkey had performed on many occasions. But this time his skis failed to release properly, forcing him to remove one manually and lose sight of the ground. By the time he'd succeeded in jettisoning both skis and maneuvered into flying position, it was too late to avoid impact.

The ski world's Superman was gone.

As the most versatile and influential skier in history, McConkey had ascended the podium in every discipline from alpine racing to moguls to big-mountain to Skiercross to Big Air during a seventeen-year career. He also joined Douglas as one of a handful of technical innovators who proved the doubters wrong by pushing skiing in new directions at the end of the nineties. The first shove came from fat skis, the double-width planks invented when Austrian ski designer Rupert Huber cut a snowboard in half lengthwise to create a powder-skiing tool for non-experts. That ski, Atomic's Powder Plus, was eschewed and ridiculed as an unecessary crutch by most expert skiers, but McConkey saw fat skis as being perfect for steep Alaskan peaks and single-handedly convinced an industry obsessed with hourglass-shaped carving skis—its latest countervail to snowboarding—to embrace the wider ride for off-piste stability and speed. Aided and abetted by Alaska's film exports, the subsequent explosion of fat and mid-fat ski designs boosted the world of freeriding into a different orbit.

McConkey's next push came some years later. Noting that the force exerted on skis by powder snow was akin to that exerted by water, he invented a reverse-sidecut, reverse-camber ski modeled on a water ski—a convex flex pattern that was also wider underfoot than it was at either end. This "banana" ski, the Volant Spatula, was scoffed at even harder; in a natural Newtonian twist, every ski manufacturer now produces a similarly shaped board. As if he'd done all he could for skiers underfoot, McConkey turned to skydiving off stationary objects, or BASE jumping (the acronym derives from Buildings, Antennae, Spans, and Earth), looking to a final threshold in big-mountain skiing. He succeeded in building a new career around this notion of "the close-out line," an aesthetic descent that was otherwise unskiable because it ended in a massive cliff. McConkey would ski the line, fly off the cliff, then pull his chute. It made for compelling footage; suddenly a ski film seemed incomplete without a BASE jump.

"Why not? Why *not* use a parachute?" Steve Casimiro offered in the 2007 wide-release feature documentary *Steep,* of skiing's (possible) next horizon and McConkey's (again) oft-criticized new vocation.

McConkey's inventive and hard-charging persona was, however, tempered by an entertainer's heart. When a season was cut short by yet another knee injury, McConkey invented Saucerboy, a hardware-adorned, plastic platter–riding, Jack Daniels–swilling character who injected hilarity into an otherwise moribund industry. He (and sometimes his alter ego) starred in dozens of films, but *There's Something about McConkey* (2000), *Seven Sunny Days* (2007), and *Claim* (2008) best covered his oeuvre, becoming instant classics and must-owns for any dedicated ski bum.

Survived by his wife, Sherry, and three-year-old daughter, Ayla, McConkey was skiing's brashest, most inventive daredevil. My own friendship with the man had granted me insight beyond my vocation when it came to skiing's ever-present outer limits, but it was his backstory—a tale traversing so much of the modern ski experience that it offered an instructive microcosm of skiing's recent history—that explained why he had ultimate influence on the sport.

MCCONKEY WAS BORN in Vancouver to Can-Am parents who separated when he was three. He and mother Glenn moved from Whistler to Santa Cruz, California, where Glenn turned aside her own opportunities in order to create more for her son; her biggest gift was skiing. When they were still living in Whistler, Glenn had skied while carrying him in a backpack, and he loved moguls.

"Bump, mommy, bump!" he legendarily screamed, shaking the pack whenever Glenn strayed onto smooth groomers.

Like his estranged father, Jim McConkey, a ski-star with eponymous runs in Whistler, Alta, and Park City, Shane on skis was ballsy, big, wild yet controlled, unassailable. His talent on boards was deliverance from schlepping pizzas in Boulder, Colorado, and bussing tables in Tahoe, California, where, like Douglas, he eventually rose above the ski-bum fray to rule a critical mass of skimanship at Squaw Valley, a place, like Whistler, that doesn't suffer pretenders. He came by his talent naturally, but he'd put in the requisite time to hone his craft.

McConkey raced for thirteen years, attending high school at Vermont's Green Mountain Academy and working his way up to Nor-Am level. With racing's strictures and low rate of breakthrough, it was perhaps inevitable that he would tire of it, and that he departed directly for the Pro Mogul Tour was, in retrospect, not surprising.

"Moguls re-instilled the excitement of skiing," he said. "Just like when you're a kid. Suddenly my eyes were open to all the possibilities again."

"Like the time you threw an illegal backflip in a mogul event at Vail, had your pass yanked by patrol, then rushed the course naked, throwing a huge spread-eagle and getting permanently banned from the resort?" I asked.

"You must be talking about someone else."

A rediscovered love for skiing eventually propelled McConkey directly into the heart of the burgeoning big-mountain scene (then still called "extreme" skiing). After his roommate Kent Kreitler won the U.S. title in 1993, McConkey jumped in. When he competed at the World Extreme Ski Championships in Valdez in 1994, he'd finally boarded the train he hadn't known he was waiting for. Soon, he was driving it.

As his star rose, you could catch McConkey on the newsstand staring out from the pages of a half-dozen magazines. In many photos he was upside-down over a cliff, looking ahead to the landing in one of his trademark backflips. But his rapidly expanding universe—five major titles in three seasons—was turned upside down in a real way in January 1997 when he tore his right anterior cruciate ligament, putting him out for the season.

Back in the saddle the following winter, he placed fourth at the Canadian Championships, first at the European Championships, and second at the U.S. Nationals, before blowing the other knee. As testament to his performance to that point, he won the 1998 World Tour title despite not having competed in the World Championships.

Others in his position would have been devastated, but McConkey threw himself into giving back. He traveled to both New School (he was a huge fan of the growing jib scene) and big-mountain freeskiing events, keeping himself and everyone else stoked. He was instrumental in forming the IFSA (International Free Skiing Association), an organization dedicated—in McConkey parlance—to making sure "a really cool sport stays really cool." In practical terms, it functioned to standardize criteria for judging and to lay out rules for course parameters, sponsorship, and television coverage.

The wealth of experience in starting the IFSA, with its people and politics and paradox of regulating something that was, at its heart, anti-regulation, couldn't be emphasized enough in McConkey's mind. He also took the opportunity of a hiatus from competition to re-school on the risk-versus-rush equation with a new course: BASE jumping 101.

"The mental aspect of BASE jumping helped my skiing tons," he told me. "Every little hazard can be life threatening, so you have to note each tiny detail beforehand. As a result, I'm taking a lot more into account in every run now, and it's allowing me to ski far more difficult, exposed lines."

That BASE jumping would eventually claim McConkey was, according to some, mostly a matter of time. There was nowhere else to go, they thought, nothing else to try; but there was *always* the opportunity to fly farther, or in a different way. And that had been McConkey's point all along.

Somehow, McConkey knew that the new energy emanating from a place called X would ultimately flow back to meet the purity of the big-mountain experience. And, indeed, this was where the two storms eventually merged: the twin-tip might have changed everything, but McConkey's overarching influence on freeskiing would even change the twin-tip.

IT WAS, IN the cyclical nature of things, inevitable: in melding the twin-tip with a fat-ski profile, and eventually reverse-camber technology, Shane McConkey, Mike Douglas, and the legions of big-mountain freeskiers and New School freestylers they inspired came together. The new mindset and new equipment that jumped the barricades from terrain park to urban park, back bowls to backcountry, now brought a whole new look to off-piste skiing. Cornices and flutes were the new tabletops and quarterpipes. Big-mountain skiers scrambled to learn park tricks, and park riders scrambled into the backcountry, sometimes actually having to learn *how* to ski (not kidding) to do so.

Few succeeded as well at this confluence as Douglas. From the beginning, his calculated eye and smooth style could always be counted on by the sport's various visual artists, but his reinvention from Godfather of the New School and X Games commentator to an in-demand big-mountain star now pitted him annually against Alaska-honed titans like McConkey and the legendary Seth Morrison for Male Performance of the Year at the *POWDER* video awards. When he won the honor in 2003, Douglas upped the ante for all freestylers. He showed little sign of slowing down even as he crested his mid-thirties to became a filmmaker himself, the only skier of his generation to match McConkey's professional longevity and influence.

Sadly, Douglas became the Last Man Standing in the friendly bet that he and McConkey had famously publicized on film, the two equal-aged friends putting a dollar on the line over whose career could be milked longest; McConkey is gone, but the combined impact of the perfect storm they spawned together rages on unchecked.

In skiing's brave new world, there was no better way to observe this shift than by riding shotgun in the back-forty with the filmmakers, photographers, and cat- and heli-ski operators herding the starmaker machinery. If you didn't know any better, you might even deduce that the only reason the world's top freestylers attended super-duper booter events like the X Games anymore was so they could win enough cash or cachet to heli-lift their injured, aging bodies into the backcountry to ride super-fat, reverse-camber twin-tips in soft powder with those who'd gone directly there a decade ago looking for some peace, quiet, and rail-free space.

Somewhere, McConkey was laughing his ass off.

12 | JUST SHOOT ME

I just want to go ski/Get all my shit for free
(whoa-oh-oh-oh)
Have fun eternally/Or 'til I blow my knee
(whoa-oh-oh-oh)
YOUTUBE VIRAL SENSATION *My Friend Is a Pro*
by Colby West and John Symms, 2009

ON THE dark road to Revelstoke, British Columbia, amid another record stretch of high pressure during a snow-impoverished winter, Mike Douglas's ruminations had descended into prayer.

"I hope the weather and terrain are good enough that we don't have to resort to grinding rails," he said. "And I want to step it up gradually, you know, start with a warmup run, then some mini-golf [short, technical descents of only a few seconds] and get to the big stuff last; I hate throwing down right out of the gate."

He hoped that Salomon teammates C.R. Johnson and Mark Abma were into taking a similar approach.

"By the way," he added, "remind me to buy some Advil when we stop for gas."

In Revelstoke, we found the rest of the crew. Mica Heli Skiing's director of sales and marketing Darryn Shewchuk, on whose tenure we'd be skiing, was secretly imploring that we weren't the same nightmare that other film crews had been. But first things first. "Who's paying for all of this?" he asked of no one in particular, for which he was rewarded with no answer whatsoever.

Swedish sensation Mattias Fredriksson was beseeching the weather gods for sixteen-hour work days so he could bank as many money-making images as possible for his pan-global photo empire. "Uhhh... we better to have an early start tomorrow," he drawled, in his nasal, punctiliously syllabic English. "It's a two-hour drive to the helipad, I have two hundred kilos of gear to transport, and I want to be shooting by noon."

Johnson was bargaining for sleep after arriving directly from a surf trip to Panama. "I'm a bag of shit and can't move," he mumbled, facedown on the floor, fortunate his baseball cap was already twisted sideways when he'd landed there. "There's no way I can ski tomorrow."

California-based cinematographer "Blue State" Ben Mullin, typically occupied with praying that he'd meet a Canadian girl—the closest thing to a female Democrat he would find here—now seemed consumed with Shewchuk's question. "I better call my boss and see if this thing's gonna work," he mused, fingering a worn credit card.

Otherwise, everyone was silently hoping that Abma, en route alone from Kelowna in his dilapidated pickup, would find us. Although it was understood that Salomon was dropping a load of cash on this shoot, someone had the temerity to wonder aloud about the whereabouts of the company's promised test skis. With that on the table, and because the skiing across an area of B.C. the size of Australia had been wiped out by unseasonable warmth and rain, everyone then wanted to know if there was even anything *left* to ski.

It wasn't the most promising start to a trip.

THE STEEP-AND-DEEP ethos of the early nineties and the resulting stories and videos about every new backcountry destination had been a boon to an already multimillion-dollar industry, spawning a further proliferation of touring, cat-, and heli-ski operations. Documenting them—or at least the latest crop of pros riding at them—had become an industry unto itself. A new B.C. heli-operation that claimed to out-Alaska Alaska? Better get there before someone else did. But if you've read this far, you know how tough that was to do.

Back in the day, making a ski film was relatively easy. Filmmakers and producers chose a few exotic locations they were sure nobody else was shooting at and hand-picked a crew of A-team skiers to go and have "an experience." Then they lined up a few deep-pocketed sponsors so they could hire award-winning 16mm cinematographers, and sometimes even invited a top-seeded still photographer and a known writer to help give the movie legs in the worldwide snowsports press.

These days, the accelerated commodification of skiing and resulting competition for dollars have dramatically changed the equation. Wherever a film crew goes, no matter how exotic the location is, it is unlikely to be the first there: the group will find itself fighting over donkeys to transport its gear and a guide named Peligro with someone—probably snowboarders. Most contemporary cinematographers have become award-lacking, impoverished ski bums who shoot with borrowed digital cameras and max out their own credit cards on behalf of one film company, though the resulting footage can, for a variety of political and business reasons, end up in as many movies as there are athletes. There are always a writer and a still photographer with the shoot now, both sure they could do their job better if the film crew disappeared into a crevasse. Meanwhile, the new breed of transcontinental athlete-models are required to bring along their *own* travel and heli-budgets, making them less focused on an experience than on gathering five- to thirty-second moments of inspired (or accidental) bravado that could be sewn together into killer (read also "sick" and "rad") segments for ever more demanding sponsors, and generating the exposure required to renew threadbare contracts that will allow them to spend the following winter in the same anxious square dance, linking arms variously with film, photo, competition, and PR demands.

Somewhere in there, if the athletes even cared—and shockingly, many did not—they would get to ski. For fun. With no lenses in sight. Unencumbered by any worry that their "seggie" wasn't in the can or that someone in an office in Europe was adding up logo-visibility minutes under a column headed by their (very likely misspelled) name.

MIRACULOUSLY, AND with Abma in tow, the next morning we drove to the helipad, shuttled loads of gear and skiers, and moved into Mica's comfortable, isolated lodge high above Kinbasket Lake by noon. It being a bluebird day, we wasted no time in wolfing down lunch and making a test foray into the wilderness of Mica's vast tenure.

Mica Heli Skiing was the latest venture of Dan McDonald, the architect behind Island Lake Catskiing, and like that ridiculously successful firstborn, his latest brainchild had spawned a mag-and-movie circus. McDonald's unique vision included the world's first vacation-property time-share for a backcountry operation—which, frankly, seemed the next logical step in what had turned into a decidedly luxe enterprise. But Mica's major appeal was terrain: seven drainages and 1,000,000 acres of sprawling glaciers, fluted faces, and serrated peaks. Its location on the western slopes of the Rockies was also key. Whereas the Monashee, Cariboo, Selkirk, and Purcell ranges were peppered with heli-ops, they couldn't lay claim to the same diverse terrain and a snowpack that was deeper, higher, drier, and more reliable than even the B.C. Interior. Operating with only eight guests a week, Mica always had untracked—even, we found out, during a snow drought.

Ten minutes' flight from the lodge, at the head of the Harvey drainage, a well-preserved foot of powder sat on a settled base of twelve feet. This discovery was enough to morph a scouting mission into sudden pressure to get something in the can. In short order, athletes and cameramen were dropped in strategic locations across the valley's headwall. Any hope of a warmup evaporated as instructions were shouted, skiers grew quiet, and cameras rolled.

Despite the shotgun start, Douglas hit his first line perfectly, sailing off a flute and dropping thirty-some feet. Abma missed his mark and was flushed from the face by an avalanche of his own sloughing snow. Johnson nailed a sweet line on a rimed face and finished with a huge 360, demonstrating how adept he was at throwing tricks off tricky features.

A second round saw Douglas line up a drop over a bony fin; but when he launched, he disappeared into a cascading Niagara of slough only to magically reappear at the bottom, shaking his head at the good fortune. Trying to avoid triggering the same kind of flume, Abma tripped up in some rocks and cartwheeled down. He had to climb back up through thigh-deep powder to reclaim a ski. Johnson went bigger than before but didn't stick the landing and got to his feet holding his shoulder and screaming in the high register of a young girl. Ouch. We explained to the panicky guide that what sounded very much like catastrophic injury echoing around the valley was merely one of many painful strains that, at the tender age of twenty-one, Johnson had learned to live with.

The harsh realities of skiing professionally exacted a toll, and the rewards were often meager in relation to the risk and physical punishment. When Johnson spent $12K USD on heli-time and other costs for a film, it was in addition to the hefty sum his sponsors had already thrown down to have him appear. And his personal contribution was usually beyond what he'd been given for travel, leaving him perpetually out-of-pocket just to be in movies whose sole reward was a ticket to be in more movies and ergo—following this?—spending *more* of his own money.

I'd scream like a girl, too.

The next day Douglas, Johnson, and Abma were largely on their game, making stylish grabs off knife-edge flutes and affording us the rare opportunity to observe three generations of ski-film stars at work. Fastidious in approach and perennially solid, Godfather Douglas was the most polished, pretty much hitting everything he tried. Johnson wasn't far behind. Once a prodigy teen coached by Douglas on the Horstman Glacier, he was one of the new millennium's biggest superstars. A fantastic all-around skier known largely for stratospheric Superpipe performances, Johnson had also acquired the chops for big-mountain tricking by growing up in McConkey's considerable shadow on Squaw Valley's steep terrain. (Unfortunately, the following year a freak ski collision with a friend would leave Johnson with a brain injury from which it would take years to recover; tragically, the brilliant young skier died in February 2010, the result of a fall at Squaw.)

And then there was Abma, a two-time *POWDER* awards Male Performance of the Year phenom, a park master of smooth, super-booter air who'd surprised on film the previous season with ridiculous big-mountain lines. But at this juncture of his sophomore season in the spotlight, he was struggling; lacking the experience to pick lines best suited to him, he also suffered from self-induced performance anxiety, so meteoric had been his rise. Emblematic was the backstory to the savage opening line he skied in Matchstick Productions' (MSP) *Yearbook*.

"I got called into a shoot in Bella Coola because someone was injured. I'd just arrived and was rushed into a helicopter with [Whistler's Quebecois sensation] Hugo Harrisson and Shane McConkey," he recalled, pausing to let the specific gravity of the company sink in.

"They'd been there before and knew what they were looking at. Hugo told the pilot, 'Drop me here,' and then Shane said, 'Drop me off here.' So now I'm all by myself in the heli and I just kind of look around without really thinking and say, 'Drop me off *there*.' Once I was on top, there was no turning back; I was super-gripped but before I had time to think the radio crackled and they're saying 'OK Mark, you ready? Three, two, one...'"

That instant, in which Abma put every iota of experience, technique, and guts on the line to hurl into the abyss, proved the stuff that action-sport magic was made of. But it could easily have gone the other way, where blowing a first chance at big-line bravado meant a quick ticket to ignominy. It helped that usually supersonic Harrisson spent the winter cartwheeling through his own *Cirque de désolé* and that McConkey was riding ponies down the comeback trail, but Abma had quickly proved he was the real deal.

BACK AT THE lodge at the end of the day, a debate opened over whether wireless Internet in the wilderness was a good thing or not. Mullin walked into the common room one evening to find everyone tapping away on their laptops.

"Jesus," he muttered, "this is just like Starbucks."

And why not? After all, we are all businesspeople—earning our keep, staying in touch with bosses and clients, lining up future business, engaged, like the rest of the world, in making money both for ourselves and those who employ us.

The fact that, at least to outsiders, the commodity in which we trade seems an intangible balance between risk and recreation matters not. It is strictly business—albeit a dangerous, often short-lived one built around the fine line between whimsical "extreminating" and mortal exterminating, where one small mistake in the former could result in the latter.

There were other reasons for staying connected. Like any business, the ski-media industry was a shark tank of fissioning loyalties and fusing partnerships driven by an ever-evolving vision of what was "core" and how it should be represented. Witness the rise of *Freeze* and *Freeskier,* which from the beginning cultivated a friendly but smug rivalry with POWDER. Animosity ran more deeply among moviemakers, some of whom weren't even on speaking terms and slagged each other publicly for sport.

"The asshole factor in this business is *huge,* and the only reason we don't kill each other is because we get to ski in all the most amazing places in the world," said Mullin. "Powder snow is the Great Pacifier."

Unstated competition also lay at the heart of Fredriksson's approach to his craft. One of a handful of shooters who beat others to the punch with sponsors and magazines, the one-time editor of Sweden's national ski magazine *Åka Skidor* was widely recognized as one of the world's best outdoor photographers. Talent, dedication, and a farmer's work ethic helped boost him to this echelon, but a hyperkinetic personality and business savvy kept him there. He was so hard-working that the athletes secretly joked they could only truly relax when Fredriksson was asleep. Given the overarching role of photo incentives in their lives, however, he was, in every sense, their meal ticket. Thus, when Fredriksson complained that motion-camera setups were interfering with his work, or when we all had to carry so many rolls of film for him in those pre-digital days that he didn't even know where the unexposed rolls were, athletes didn't say, "Thank God," They said, "Let's find that film, goddammit!" and "Where do you want us to go... sir?"

It was a parternship that had produced an enormously successful four days for everyone. Of course, in ski movies, many behind-the-scenes partnerships figure into the success equation—even the one between the guided and the guide.

"LAST MINUTE TO take a crap!"

Like a blender full of beer caps, the grating voice echoed from the kitchen, out through the parlor, past the stuffed cougar, and washed over the pool table in historic Tweedsmuir Lodge near Bella Coola, British Columbia. Ostensibly a timely reminder that the toilets would soon shut down so that repairs could be made to a water system damaged in the latest of an endless series of storms, the effect was quite different.

None of the assembled skiers, photographers, filmers, writers, cooks, and guides could contain themselves. They choked back laughter, fell to the floor clutching their aching guts, and wiped beaded tears from their cheeks.

Infamous guide Pete "Swede" Mattsson had struck again.

One of the ski-film industry's most influential players, Swede and his cinematographer partners Christian Begin and Beat Steiner had incorporated Bella Coola Heli Sports just after the millennium and now controlled the world's largest single commercial heli-ski tenure—some 2.56 million acres at the head of a tortured network of islands and fjords, sixty miles inland from B.C.'s central coast. Straddling the edge of the coastal rain forest, the mountains there annually pulled down an average fifty to sixty-five feet of deeper, drier snow than areas closer to the Pacific. Deceptively chiseled peaks dropped 8,500 feet to the valley floor, yielding massive powder aprons, filled-in routes through convoluted glacial seracs, and an abundance of lengthy, inviting couloirs, just like Europe. In sum, Bella Coola offered a different look and another horizon, and it had quickly become heli-skiing's new nirvana. (Interestingly, this was exactly the type of terminology both local Nuxalk Native legends and the first white visitors used to describe the lush, treed valley of meandering rivers and abundant wildlife.)

Having a six-seat helicopter land only a hundred feet from your bed at 6:45 a.m. goes a long way toward taking the edge off the morning scramble. Within minutes of Swede's pronouncement, it seemed, three heli-loads of eager skiers had been sprinkled across various unnamed peaks, dug and evaluated pits, and were each submerged in neck-deep contrails. As Head's international team of sponsored skiers submarined down slope after slope, moviemakers and photographers were suddenly in their glory. Bella Coola indeed seemed the perfect setup.

"Of course it's the perfect setup," barked Swede through a mouthful of tobacco. "That's why I'm here!"

Crude, rude, and standing just under six feet, Swede was the most in-demand guide of the global snowsports film industry that frequented his adopted home of Whistler. He likewise serviced the huge advertising, television, and feature-film juggernaut that regularly rolled into town from Vancouver, Toronto, New York, and Los Angeles.

Growing up in Uddevalla, Sweden, he'd skied local hills, then spent three years managing a restaurant in Åre, Sweden's version of Whistler. He partied hard and skied his ass off, but wasn't ready to stay put. He attended restaurant school, worked on cruise ships, spent winters in the Alps and summers at Scandinavian sailing resorts, moonlighted as a chef in Steamboat, Colorado, and Gothenburg, Sweden, and finally emigrated to Whistler in 1981, where he ran a restaurant and bar.

"I had a really professional job with a lot of responsibility and would hire my ski-bum buddies to help out," he recalls. "They were hard workers but never showed up on time if the skiing was good. Pretty soon, even I couldn't show up on time and had to give up on the restaurant lifestyle because I wanted to ski and climb more."

After spending a winter at Apex Mountain in the B.C. Interior, he returned to Whistler followed by two greenhorn skiers—Eric Pehota and Trevor Petersen. They all fell in with a crowd that loved to climb as much as ski in the uncharted territory of the Coast Range and off the newly opened Blackcomb ski area. The small group of off-piste adventurers included Pehota, Petersen, Beat Steiner, Steve Smaridge, and the infamous Peter Chrzanowski. Stories of their exploits were legion.

"We skied hard and partied harder because there wasn't much else to do. There were no girls, and it was like a cowboy town, the Wild West. Even the mayor was a coke dealer!"

They were also climbing big peaks, kayaking new rivers, and flying off to remote places to rack up a huge list of first ski descents.

"We were living wild, doing things no one had done before. Adventure *was* life. It was pretty much like a movie," he concludes.

It seems only natural, then, that he ended up in the movie business.

Extreme skiing was big in the early nineties, so Swede and Petersen started No Wimp Tours to mine the growing market of those who wanted to be guided deep into the mountains. One of their first trips was to the Pantheon Range near Mt. Waddington with POWDER's Steve Casimiro and Blizzard of Aaahs star Mike Hattrup.

"Those guys were *shitting* themselves when we got dropped off," laughs Swede. "The only camping spot was this small green patch surrounded on all sides by hundreds of grizzly tracks."

The trip, however, was a success, and in a now-familiar scenario, the subsequent story and photos helped launch the young business. Swede was doing most of the guiding because Petersen—a big-name skier by that time—was busy with family, sponsors, and film trips. He also guided for several Whistler heli-ops and even ran Paul Freemont-Smith's springtime heli-ski operation in Greenland for a season. Somewhere in there, he started guiding for filmmakers.

"My early film jobs were guiding snowboard film crews. There weren't many people making movies back then, and it wasn't common to take on the expense of a guide, so at first we were just hired to do safety. Nowadays we do a lot more. We don't even call ourselves guides—now it's film *coordinators*."

In true Alaskan tradition, Swede was a cowboy guide who let skiers ride stuff no one else would. He'd give his opinion—even when there was sure to be trouble—but he'd tell riders how to manage it. Then he'd stuff a rubber chicken in their pack when they weren't looking and howl at his own joke when they found it. His attitude and brio had a huge influence on the ski-film industry.

In Bella Coola, however, the slap-happy Swede's respect-ful approach with the local community had also won much praise. He held informational meetings with Native leaders and brought their traditional artists and dancers to meet heli-ski groups at Tweedsmuir Lodge.

On our fly days we made massive, glacial runs to valley-bottom lakes in the morning, then flew over inlets to shoreline hot springs in the afternoon, where we soaked, beachcombed, picked mussels, and watched whales, seals, and eagles. During one grounding because of bad weather, we found our way to a rope tow and circular cabin once used as an observation post at Mt. Robson. We towed in to the Tweedsmuir Ski Club on snowmobiles through stunted forests, and with no one on the 200-foot hill, we fired up the rope-tow and lapped gleeful runs. Other down days we visited Native mask- and totem-carvers, hunkering in dark studios listening to rain and the spirit-animal legends that drove local mythology—not to mention Swede's constant pronouncements.

Ultimately, Bella Coola's potent draw married deep and mysterious history with unfathomable ski terrain, endear-ing characters and an incredible breadth of activity, some-thing that was unique in heli-skiing. Which made it unique in a ski world where unique had quickly become king. Espe-cially when it came to movie fodder.

IN THE SKI-PHOTO-AND-MOVIE business, skiing a shot usually takes a backseat to a shot of skiing, as I'd been both sadly and comically reminded on the Mica Heli gig with Douglas, Abma, and Johnson. On a final, relaxed after-noon, while we whiled away the hours waiting for sunset's alpenglow to light the next series of shots, Abma—who'd sat morose and silent for an hour before spontaneously booting up the ridge above us and disappearing from sight—suddenly launched from the top and cleaned a crazy triple-drop on the sketchiest line imaginable, apparently solely to exorcise some personal demon. It was a short, sharp, masterful piece of skiing that few of us even caught.

"That was *unfuckingbelievable!*" Johnson had said. "But since it wasn't on camera, does anybody care?"

another gathering storm

13 | A DEATH IN THE FAMILY

> I actually felt sorry for the kid... Imagine every
> year all those yahoos start talking about your
> dad and reminding you of how great he was and
> drinking a beer... It's freakin' morbid, if you ask
> me. Let the kid live his own life. Let him get on
> with it.
> GLEN PLAKE in Bill Kerig's *The Edge of Never*, 2008

THE MOMENT of arrival could not have
been clearer. On a gray January day in
1998, during the finals of the Canadian Freeskiing Championships in Whistler, twenty-two-year-old Jeff Holden
dropped from the clouds—and obscurity—into the lap of
recognition and a rocket ride to the top of the big-mountain
freeski world.

Living in a squat and working nights as a bootfitter, the
sleep-starved Holden had wrestled many demons over the
prospect of taking his soul-skiing ethic into competition.
But following the tack that any form of freeskiing was pure
self-expression, he'd worked his way into fourth place,
causing a mild stir as one of several locals stepping up to
the plate against American superstars like Gordy Peifer
and Shane McConkey. Then came the finals.

Dropping into the vastness of Diamond Bowl, Holden cut skier's right into an area no one had dared consider. With a bemused crowd and a phalanx of photographers expecting him to realize the error and bail at any moment, Holden skied past the point of no return, dropped twenty feet onto a hanging snowfield, and, with total commitment, lined off a seventy-foot cliff without the slightest hesitation, landing some hundred feet downslope and skiing boldly away. Though he ended fifth that day, the move was forever etched in the minds of those present.

Not surprisingly, whenever "Hold-on" left the gate the following season, there was many a watchful eye. And his audiences saw plenty. He won the 1999 Canadian event; placed third at the U.S. Freeskiing Nationals in Snowbird, Utah; won again in Andermatt, Switzerland; and, despite a twenty-third-place finish in the absurd one-run World Championships in Valdez, he, like McConkey the previous season, had amassed enough points to take that year's IFSA tour.

Holden's introspective approach made his biggest challenge in competition balancing a line that sprang joy from his soul with one that might win. He was nothing if not genuine, and his biggest moves continued to be those he prospected for alone, in the massive glaciated terrain surrounding Whistler.

"If a photographer happens to be around, great," he'd always said with a sincerity you had to respect, "but I'd ski those lines anyway."

And he had. Freeskiing with friends his second day in Alaska that year, the guy who'd channeled the sentiments of every dedicated skier when he'd once asserted from the podium that it was all about flying, launched a 150-vertical-foot air out of pure gratitude to those who'd helped get him to the World's. He labeled the drop Full Support, a dedication that typified the Holden approach. Then there was the famous photo of a hundred-foot air off a cliff he named Nanny after a beloved great-grandmother who'd recently passed away. His inspiration and creativity on that jump also included construction skills honed in his Kootenay hometown of Fernie: he built a wooden-plank bridge over a chasm to reach the launch point.

An IFSA crown opened many doors in those heady days, and the opportunities that came Holden's way were of the type that elevate starving painters when they suddenly become known—an apt metaphor for a guy who, in line with Lunn, saw skiing in the light of artistry and expression. Was he finally enjoying the true freedom to create in the mountains that we all sought?, I asked during an interview.

"Well," he'd offered somewhat demurely, "I'm not pounding nails this summer."

Holden, in fact, was the vanguard of a squadron of infamous big-mountain locals such as Jen Ashton, Hugo Harrisson, Dana Flahr, and Ian McIntosh who were stacked over Whistler like planes waiting to land at a busy airport. One by one, these skiers would descend to dominate the North American freeskiing circuit for years to come. With its terrain parks and summer glacier side by side with big-mountain, big-snow backcountry terrain, the resort had become the center of a rapidly expanding snowsports universe. It was a California-like place where "bum" was never a pejorative term, anything seemed possible, and trends found footing to ripple out across the White Planet.

Implicit in that milieu were limits to be tested and mistakes to be made. It was the harsh new reality of the mountains that saw skiers living on an edge that Norheim, Zdarsky, and Lunn could never, in their wildest dreams, have imagined.

IF YOU'D SEEN the jump in the summer, tucked high in Whistler's tony Taluswood neighborhood, the first thing you probably thought was *holyfuckingshit*. And that might have lasted a bit, while you drank in the height, densely forested in-run, steep out-run, and, of course, the road. But then, if the machinations of the last two decades had inculcated any hint of big-mountain skier in you—a world ruled by the equation of massive terrain, deep snow, and gravity—your vision might have changed.

You'd have begun to see the possibilities: the fact that the ramp angles matched for takeoff and landing, the way the jump would work with snow, and, turning away from the cliff, the notion that you could escape Earth's grasp and fly, if only for a few seconds, downvalley toward the embracing panorama of the Tantalus Range. And you might want it. Not in a frivolous, careless way, but in the spirit of creating something where once there was only empty space.

Brett Murray Carlson *wanted* the Taluswood gap. It was *his* hit. He'd scouted it throughout the summer of 1999, keeping it secret from all save Damian Cromwell, the friend he'd moved to Whistler with from Calgary as a teenage ski freak. Then they waited for snow.

January 17, 2000, was the best powder day Carlson and Cromwell had seen yet that season. As usual, they were skiing Whistler's Peak Chair with friends. It was beyond epic. Brimming with the kind of stoke that Dolores LaChapelle fingered as existing *only* in the world of friends-in-powder, and in search of the perfect denouement, they made a decision: it was time. Word spread. Friends assembled. Nobody really knew what was up, but they knew it would be cool.

By the time most arrived, Carlson was fine-tuning the launch. Travis Tetreault of Heavy Hitting Films, who'd been shooting Brett for the upcoming *Parental Advisory*, was called in. When he saw what his friend had in mind, all he could do was shake his head and chuckle. The mood was light. After a couple of in-run checks, Carlson pronounced the launch ready. Ten heads turned uphill.

Carlson shot off the lip tucked up tight and focused. But halfway across, sixty feet above the road, his flight had stalled.

"No," he said simply, and in a regular voice that everyone heard.

Still, Carlson held his tuck as he dropped, extending slightly at the end, the same way he'd stomped the landings of countless big jumps. His body took the impact but his head followed the momentum, through his skis and into the pavement.

A woman screamed. Birds flew away. Tetreault put his camera down, unable to comprehend. Everything moved in both fast and slow motion. Cromwell cried and held his friend. Others applied first aid, but it was too late. At twenty-four, Carlson was gone.

He had hit the road less than a ski-length shy of high-fives for life.

THESE ARE THE horrible facts, but anyone living in a mountain town knows the extended story. Someone dies in a risky venture, and an uninformed public convulses looking for someone to blame, looking to answer "Why?" Only there is rarely anyone to blame and no answer, save "Why not?" Naysayers pronounced on the stupidity of the venture. Yaysayers debated the idea of stunt versus accomplishment.

Absent from the fracas was most of Whistler's core ski community. They understood that those who fly too close to the sun in the mountains are the sacrificial lambs of our collective ambitions and how easy it was to die doing what you loved. Although life would never be the same for those who were there that day (it took years for some to process the events; others never will), all ultimately found strength in Carlson himself, and the passion that touched everyone he knew.

At the wake, the energy—like Brett—was infectious. Everyone, including the resort, pitched in for a party that saw hundreds of attendees, and venerable Dusty's Bar went Richter. His death had come on the cusp of a new zeitgeist in skiing, and everyone understood that something larger was happening. More parties ensued. A Brett Carlson Memorial Fund was established in Vancouver and Calgary to bring inner city kids to the mountains. A massive fund-raiser in April was the biggest party of the year in a town with the biggest parties on the continent. Over $10,000 was raised to build a backcountry cabin for youth-at-risk programs.

It may have been his unabashed love of skiing, his inno-cence, or simply the prevailing energy of the revolutions rocking the ski world, but somehow Carlson's death gained a life of its own: though he'd never sought attention, he didn't slip away unnoticed.

A couple days after the wake, Cromwell rode alone up Peak Chair with Carlson's ashes in his pack.

"Just me and him," he'd told me. "One last ride."

At the top were family and friends, waiting to celebrate one last run for Brett. Most skied Whistler Bowl, but Cromwell and another friend, Joe Lammers, cut around the back of the peak to West Cirque and the line they'd last shared with their friend that fateful day.

"That," recalled Lammers of his descent with Cromwell, "was the most amazing run of my life."

NOBODY BUT CARLSON knew what actually went wrong at the Taluswood gap: high takeoff, short in-run, slow snow. It didn't matter. It was simply miscalculation in a game we all played with the laws of the universe, and Carlson paid the unstated price that hung over each of our heads every day in the mountains. In the end, some would always see his death as stupid and senseless. But then, they probably saw us all as stupid.

I'd moved to Whistler only a month before, and though I'd met him on occasion, I never knew Carlson well. For the remainder of that season, however, he was everywhere around me. As an editor, I'd lost writers, photographers, athletes, and friends in the mountains, but this was my first up-close view of a ski death and its personal connections. Stoically absorbing these other losses, I'd never shed a tear, but I found myself doing so often over Brett, seeing in his story many I knew, and even, on occasion, my wide-eyed young self in that first winter of eternal promise with Merl in Banff.

You could visit ski towns or hear about losing friends in the mountains, but ultimately, you had to live there to really know.

NO MATTER HOW you sliced it, DOA was a complete mess. The infamous, thousand-foot pencil couloir cleaving the southwest aspect of Blackcomb Peak had seen a few too many rays and a few too many skis before freezing solidly at day's end. Awash in muted pastels, the line lacked nothing aesthetically, yet no skier with any modicum of sense would consider such a crud-choked luge track at this time of day.

But there we were, stepping gingerly into the throat, picking our way down snow ramps chocolate-chipped with pebbles, sideslipping hourglass constrictions with ski tips and tails brushing rock. Swede, Christian Begin, photographer Bruce Rowles, skiers Dan Treadway, Johnny "Foon" Chilton, and I were but a few of the dozen or so strung along the length of the chute, leapfrogging each other in a halting descent. It wasn't just conditions that were giving pause, however; there was also the kid.

Where the adults were hobbled by narrowness, chunky snow, and the lingering effects of flasks and joints that had circulated up top, eleven-year-old Kye Petersen was skiing DOA with panache. His body position was perfect, hands low and forward, eyes down the fall line. He dropped several feet on each turn, grunting occasionally but always grimacing—his face drawn into an incredibly focused, specter-inducing look that had us all riveted.

If you were a skier who read magazines, watched videos, or even glanced at a Rossignol ski poster anytime during the late eighties and early nineties, you'd seen this look before. Trevor Petersen, Kye's father, was one of Canada's greatest ski heroes. Handsome, blond, and pony-tailed, he was possessed of an extra-large personality and enthusiasm to spare. Arriving in Whistler on the coattails of Swede, he and partner Eric Pehota had gone on to redefine extreme skiing (a term the pair once comically derided on film in favor of "severe" skiing) in North America by following the European example of first climbing the routes they planned to ski. They were poster boys, magazine staples, and film stars until Trevor was tragically killed in an avalanche in Chamonix on February 26, 1996. He left behind his partner, Tanya, five-year-old Kye, and Neve, then three.

Coping with the loss was difficult, but somehow as he grew, Kye had come to exhibit the same spirit and fierce determination that had characterized his father. He also had a similar thirst for outdoor pursuits: already he made slick bottom turns on a surfboard, basked in fame as a skateboard standout, and consistently turned heads—in a town where heads weren't easily turned—as a pint-sized ski sensation in the terrain park. He was pushing the boundaries of backcountry travel for kids, though he still had much to learn of the dangers and risks that his father—though all too aware of—had succumbed to. Kye had a style, drive, and even facial expressions that eerily resembled Trevor, but his peers around the halfpipe saw him simply as a shockingly talented, well-sponsored ripper with a tiger in his tank.

It was the spring of 2001. Rowles and I were watching some pros session a huge quarterpipe during Whistler's World Ski and Snowboard Festival when a scuffle broke out near the finish area. Several competitors were trying to help Kye—who had been barred from the hit because of his age—poach the pipe. Diminutive Vinnie Dorion, perhaps channeling his own struggle to get into that first X Games, had even donated his bib, hoping the officials might confuse the two. But the insurance-leery organizers weren't stupid and quickly turfed Kye from the event.

"Does your mom know where you are?" joked one as he escorted Kye from the jump.

It made me ponder the dilemma of parents with a child possessed of aptitude and ambition in a dangerous pursuit. How do you nurture talent while managing the risks required to improve? And, in this case, how do you keep past tragedy from exacerbating your concern?

"I read somewhere that [Canadian race legend] Nancy Greene's parents never told her to be careful, just to concentrate," Tanya told me. "So I just tell Kye to stay focused and not push it. I hope he learns to be careful through that."

But Kye was old enough to move on his own outside of parental circles or structured programs, and he frequently exercised his own idea of what focus and "not pushing it" actually were. Which is why Rowles, by dint of time spent shooting the young skier, had become somewhat of an on-slope caretaker and backcountry mentor.

"I saw him in DOA one day with no avalanche gear and realized that he was getting out there," he said of the time he spoke with Tanya about giving Kye a transceiver and a backcountry bitch-slap.

They'd agreed that education and knowledge—like teaching hormone-charged teens about safe sex rather than telling them to abstain—was the key to staying out of trouble. Nevertheless, he was still a kid, and Tanya was rightly protective, not wanting him to get a swelled head, be pushed by sponsors, or hurt himself.

"He needs to grow into his boots and develop as a person, enjoy the sport, not pressure himself," she explained. "I want him to go slow so he has a long career—not the typical short life of a pro."

There was, however, no slowing Kye's progress. He was a sponge, soaking up in a year what probably took Douglas and the NCAF three to learn. And he was *always* thinking about the next trick.

"He was already throwing backflips in January," related Rowles, "and by February he threw his first Flare (backflip with a 180) in the halfpipe. Everyone went wild when he landed it."

Around Whistler, many had their eyes open and ears to the ground when it came to Kye. And they endlessly debated the question of nature versus nurture. Although genetics weighed heavily, there was surely an equally natural element of imitation. There was no denying that Kye had the burning drive and determination of his dad, the need to prove the world wrong by going at the impossible twice as hard, but he'd also grown up surrounded by billboard-sized photos of Trevor in Whistler buildings, endless skiers pointing out where his father had skied and what he'd accomplished. Kye was hyper-aware of this legacy, pride alight in his eyes when he spoke of Trevor. When I spent time with him, however, I was always cognizant of the light you *couldn't* see: despite the encouragement, praise, and love that surrounded him, Kye's reality would forever be a child's little heart yearning for its father.

Skiing was a tangible path to that intangible, something that would lead Kye, at age fifteen, on a remarkable journey to Chamonix with author and filmmaker William Kerig. There, he would meet and be briefly mentored by one of his father's heroes, ski-mountaineering legend Anselme Baud, who'd watched his own son, Edouard, die in a fall down the infamous Gervasutti Couloir the previous spring. That 2005 trip would culminate in Kye skiing the Glacier Rond—the run on which his father was killed—with Trevor's friends Glen Plake, Mike Hattrup, and Scott Markewitz, under the tutelage of the famed guide Stéphane "Fanfan" Dan, who himself came close to dying in a dramatic crevasse fall the following day. The gripping tale of Kye's eye-opening pilgrimage to Chamonix would result in Kerig's 2008 book and eponymous feature film, *The Edge of Never*.

Though these vehicles provide a fitting legacy to the Petersens' story, probing the elusive connections between the dead and those left behind always leads back to heart-rending reality and the question of whether the risk of many outdoor pursuits is worth the payoff. The truth is that peril, whether it's physical or psychological, economic or cultural, is everywhere in skiing, even in a seemingly benign substance like snow, whether that risk might be in skiing it ... or selling it.

14 | INVASION OF THE POWDER SNATCHERS

> Yesterday's tracks had vanished. Straight, steep,
> deep—it had returned to perfection. I looked up
> at the other instructors, to their poised bodies
> and dark eyes behind goggles, and saw hawks
> peering down from high perches. Predators.
> RICK PHIPPS, *Skiing Zen*, 2006

IN NAEBA, Japan, the snow fell in waves, sifting from the sky as if an unseen hand was periodically shaking it loose from the clouds. Mesmerized, Shane Szocs and I gazed into the steadily descending curtain, reveling in it after a long winter of record cold alternating with heartbreaking rain in Whistler. There had been few chances for my beloved Creekside Crew to meet, and when even a few inches of snow had materialized from the murk, the battle had been ferocious: thousands of frustrated riders tracked it out in no time. In Naeba, there was never a fight for fresh tracks. And, it seemed, Japan—vast and tiny, forested and groomed, steep and flat, futuristic and antiquated, home to some five hundred ski areas—was perpetually covered in some of the planet's deepest snow. Yet now, it appeared, this was all up for sale.

A LITTLE KNOWN fact: Japan first invaded the United States in June 1942, when it occupied two of Alaska's Aleutian Islands, Attu and Kiska. Given the islands' remoteness and horrendous weather, it took American forces a year to eject the interlopers. This small and doubtless miserable cadre was the first invading force to have set foot on American soil since a bunch of drunken pre-Canadians burned down the White House in the War of 1812.

At the end of World War II, when U.S. Army Chief of Staff George C. Marshall was installed as Secretary of State and de facto overseer of war reparations, he made it known he had no intention of pursuing the "negative course" his country and other victors of World War I had taken. (The Treaty of Versailles, designed to punish and humiliate Germany, succeeded all too spectacularly, driving that country's subsequent turn to Hitler.) The Marshall Plan saw $22 billion USD in reconstruction aid sent to Europe, including loathed Germany and Italy, while General Douglas MacArthur supervised a similar rebuilding of Japan. Today, all three states are solid democracies and staunch allies in most global matters.

When it comes to business, however, international relations are more complex: it's still a story of surreptitious imperialism in which invasions and counter-invasions continue under cover of feigned allegiances, partnerships, and compliance. And none has succeeded at this shell game better than Japan.

After Japan's defeat, cries to hang Emperor Hirohito as a war criminal were ignored by MacArthur, who rightly believed him more useful alive. Indeed, the revered symbolic leader of this honor-bound nation made it known to his subjects that although they'd fought nobly, it was their duty to obey the victors. Powerful fealty to the emperor (and possibly the atom bomb) meant no distracting insurrection or internal struggles, allowing the Japanese to turn their natural industriousness to reconstructing their nation and their economy. They had learned from the Americans that if you built a better mousetrap, the world would beat a path to your door; they then used their considerable creative enterprise to, in most cases, go one better and reinvent the wheel—including ski lifts, skis, boots, and clothing.

Although the Japanese held no focused resentment, their unprecedented, weaponless, slow-motion invasion of the Americas hit where it hurt most—in the wallet. Over the next three decades, Japan successfully exploited the West's true vulnerability, consumerism, while rigorously protecting its own cultural traditions. Ballooning trade deficits and tanking domestic auto and electronic industries in North America spoke to their success; "Made in Japan" was a commonly bandied joke here, but the joke was on us.

By the dawn of the eighties, Japan's self-sufficiency and mastery of the Western economy was complete. It was importing mostly raw materials, from industries such as mining, forestry, and pulp and paper in which it had stakes, and exporting a range of high-demand manufacturing such as cars, electronics, and sporting goods. Japanese plants sprang up around North America, and Japan's technology-licensing agreements kept many flagging domestic companies alive while Japanese multinationals grew to planetary proportions.

Japan also bought hard into North American clothing, transport, hotels, and ski resorts, while tightly regulating foreign investment in its own economy, so it was mostly Japan that profited from its own affluence. Money to burn at home meant money to travel abroad, enough to take over the very travel sector it used; while fortress Japan stood strong, it established beachheads in western Canada and Alaska, the closest Pacific Rim destinations to the Land of the Rising Sun. To this day, the Japanese constitute the biggest foreign cultural presence in places like Whistler and the Canadian Rockies.

In 1990, however, the economic bubble would burst in spectacular fashion, and a major decade-long contraction would begin. It would hit hardest in those places that saw the most frivolous bandwagoning and over-extension, including skiing and snowboarding.

THE ROLLOVER BELOW the summit of Naeba, where Szocs and I made our first turns, was also where we found our first face-shots; blinded, our mouths and nostrils filled with so much fluff that our laughter failed to dislodge it.

With few others riding the powder and only 10 percent of the ski area's actual terrain utilized, we started naming the unused areas. We dubbed our initial run Keep Out in honor of the first sign we skied past. Dummy was a line under the gondola that during a previous visit had been home to a red-jacketed ski-patrol mannequin holding a *Warning!* sign. Off the summit was an amazingly consistent pitch we dubbed Overhead. Afterward came Double Overhead, North Shore, and Pipeline—the latter rolling down through an aisle of arcing trees into silent forest. Surf-related names seemed appropriate: each lap, our tracks filled like a returning tide while we rode an eternally breaking wave of the best snow imaginable.

But if morning offered the best in Japanese yin, afternoon demonstrated that, as anywhere in the ski world, yang was close by. We rode the world's longest (3.4 miles) and most pointless gondola to the world's flattest ski area, Tashiro, and from there on to Kagura, where, unbelievably, it was snowing harder and was noticeably deeper. We were shocked to find many off-piste tracks in Kagura and a large tour group from Colorado claiming responsibility.

This unusual commercial enterprise begged a question: was North America finally contemplating a full-scale invasion of Japan's powder, or was Japan finally waking up to our appetite for it?

Certainly more stories about Japan's incredible powder skiing were appearing in the worldwide snowsports media. And with powderhounds continuing to scour the globe in search of the next steep-and-deep Shangri-La, it was only a matter of time before the Japanese ski industry's annoying but pervasive mantra of "hands off the off-piste" caved to the pressure. Or some foreign investors made them an offer they couldn't refuse.

There was only one problem: this enticing but uncontrolled bounty wasn't all ice cream and balloons. And I knew its hazards all too well. It was here that I'd first seen the White Dragon lash out. As we skied Naeba that day I couldn't chase the memories. Szocs figured it was time to eat the dragon.

We crept onto the slope carefully. We weren't supposed to be there, off piste near where the patrol scarecrow once warned trespassers away. But the fresh, thigh-deep snow and steep, widely spaced hardwoods were irresistible. Just like before.

"We have to do this," insisted Szocs.

ON MARCH 4, 2001, Szocs and I were in Naeba where athletes from around the world had gathered for the Core Games, Japan's version of the X Games. It was snowing hard, and with competition canceled for the day, many *gaijin* (foreigners) had been skiing the bottom of a steep, forested off-piste slope all morning. The snow was stable, the slope well cut.

During a very late lunch, as snow piled deeper, several of us eyed the steeper, untracked, upper face, but in the

end, only three had declared the legs for it—me, cinematographer Ben Mullin, and photographer Flip McCririck.
Lulled into complacency by the morning's safe passage, we
unwisely left our packs containing avalanche shovels and
probes in the lodge, unaware that conditions were changing.

One last tired run. Geothermal vents and uneven terrain.
Heavy snow and rising temperatures. Unknown objective
hazards. A dangerous slope in dangerous conditions. It was
a formula for disaster, but we were neither particularly
worried nor vigilant.

"Spread out and watch each other," I remember saying as
we pushed off at the top, but no one heard. We'd already
been whooping our way downward. It was so deep all you
could do was steer. Mullin was somewhere to my right,
McCririck to his.

Suddenly, I was forced to make a sweeping right turn to
avoid the sardonic maw of a steaming sinkhole. Out of the
corner of my eye I glimpsed Mullin's head protruding from
the snow. It hadn't seemed right. Had he fallen? I continued
toward him but he wasn't there when I stopped.

"I must be in the wrong place," I thought.

But I wasn't. Snow flowed past the tips of my skis like a
deep, fast river. I couldn't see to the other side in the dim
light and falling snow; everything was the same color. The
sounds were ethereal: sand running through an hourglass,
a shower of glass beads, the clack-clack of drumsticks, an
axe hitting a tree, metal on metal—all muffled, distant,
ugly.

Finally realizing what was happening, I pushed onto the
polished running surface that the snow had vacated. I heard
myself calling Mullin's name but knew he wouldn't answer.
It seemed a long way down to where the snow had pooled
like a lake of porridge, 150 feet across, three feet deep. I
skied onto the front edge of the debris in eerie silence.

I tore off my avalanche transceiver and started pressing buttons. An error message appeared and I tried again. Same error message. I started panicking, cursing non-stop. I could hear my heart, see my hands shaking. I told myself to breathe, and finally I got the sequence right. A signal appeared immediately: Mullin was somewhere in front of me.

I remembered being on my knees, tearing at chunks of snow with stone hands. I'd uncovered blood-matted hair, but no skull. Then, Mullin's head pushed up near my other hand; he was semi-conscious but groaning, in total shock. I dug him out, flopped his scalp back on, and pulled my hat over his head to hold it in place. His face was a mask of blood, chin hanging off. McCririck arrived, and we propped Mullin against a tree. Then McCririck kept him steady and awake while I skied off for help. It took an hour. Mullin had a punctured lung, twenty-four skull fractures, and had to have his scalp and chin sewn back on. He looks great now and you'd never know.

Years later, I would know how terrified I had been that day. I followed Szoc's lead through the murk, feeling more than seeing his movements. Until that day, I'd resisted remembering details of the avalanche in favor of vague platitudes sufficient to gloss over the story in barroom recounting. Being here forced remembrance.

Szocs and I skied from the open into denser trees, stopping on a large convex roll. Predictably, the snow collapsed around us. This was where it had started; McCririck had skied across the top and Mullin below, the section between them letting go. Still, it seemed too innocent. I searched for an obvious lane through the trees. There were many.

I heard something and glanced up abruptly, sucking in air. There was nothing. When I turned back, Szocs held my eyes. He knew.

"Wind," he smiled softly, dropping in.

We skied the slope in sections, alternating leads, ending at safe zones the way we should have that first time. A hundred turns, and we carried onto the bench where the slide had buried Mullin.

It had been an incredible run, but I was spent in an unfamiliar way and realized I'd been holding my breath. I had a vague urge to celebrate, yet chatter seemed violate. We remained quiet. Snowfall closed in again.

"You had to do that," said Szocs, finally.

"Yup," I agreed, sure now, breathing deep, knowing Mullin would have skied it with us if he was here.

No scars, no patrol dummy, no superstitious prohibition would have stopped him. Powder was the sweet we all craved, and Japan was a giant confectionery.

THE JAPANESE ARE nothing short of bold when it comes to engineering but fairly cautious when it comes to the natural world. Whereas North Americans appreciate the wild side of the sport—trees and chutes and cliffs and powder—the Japanese have always preferred orderly and manicured aspects like moguls, racecourses, and groomers. But they also enjoy fashion and trends, and voraciously consume magazines and videos. They know what's going on. And though they've adeptly turned the iconography of most Western culture into abstractions and caricatures, not so with skiing and snowboarding. Now that fat twin-tips were king and big-mountain skiing was in fashion, Japanese attitudes about off-piste riding were finally evolving.

There were more tracks through the woods than ever in Naeba, suggesting it was game on for powder with Japanese skiers, which was both bad and good news for gaijin. Bad because it would mean more riders on the slopes, and likely more avalanche accidents; good because we'd no

longer be the only easy-to-spot outlaws, and it would edu-
cate the masses by forcing ski areas to practice avalanche
control and rescue. Of course, once Japan's ski industry
catered to outsiders, the issue of powder access would be
moot. In that event, it would be exploited for every penny
possible.

A warm island adrift in a cold ocean, Japan comes by
its ridiculous snowfall honestly. This bonanza graces the
steep terrain of the Japanese Alps and provides some of the
best tree-skiing in the world. The wide-open hardwood
forests, with their quiet solitude and room to turn, are a
potent draw for any powder-starved populace within striking distance—like Australians.

There are Aussies at every ski resort in the world, as
ubiquitous as the beer that sustains them. However, this
lot was putting down roots. The general economic down-
turn of the nineties and a global squeeze in the snowboard
industry left Japan's domestic ski industry on the ropes.
Visits plummeted, and resorts as well as dozens of soft-
and hard-goods companies closed. (Repercussions were felt
all the way up the food chain: in a nationally scrutinized
scandal, a businessman who owned fifty-some ski resorts,
including Naeba, was indicted on tax fraud and jailed.)
With nowhere else to turn, Japan was finally entertaining outside investment. Lodges were on sale for as little as
$50,000 USD, ski areas for half a million. And Oz reckoned
to be first in on this fire sale, mate.

Australian tour companies had been frequenting the
Hokkaido Island powder haven of Niseko for a while, but
when one outright bought the Hanazono ski area there,
many felt it was the beginning of the end to Japan's culturally rich ski scene.

"We brought a group in under the auspices of an Aussie operator," Jill Dunnigan of Extremely Canadian World

Tours told me in her Whistler office. "I wouldn't do it again. They supplied a coordinator for our group because each Aussie operator is vying to be the one who cracks the North American market. My clients were all, 'Get that Aussie bastard away from us—we don't want to see him again.' He was culturally insensitive and ruining their Japanese experience."

The Aussie vibe got so out of control in Niseko that other visitors began looking for Aussie-free zones. It isn't that Australians aren't nice people, it's just that they were loud, obnoxious, and taking over. So it was no surprise that locals welcomed polite Canadian skiers who experienced and appreciated their culture, often spoke some Japanese, weren't afraid to eat all manner of oceanic goop, and could even use chopsticks.

"Most of the core locals, like pros and patrollers," explained Dunnigan, "immediately recognize when you have a level of respect for the mountain—and by association their culture."

How long this cultural sensitivity might last was anybody's guess. The Australian takeover of Niseko was a weird reality, but only one of Japan's many weird realities. After all, to get to anything genuine in Japan you usually had to wade through a tsunami of absurdity. It was a place where everything was a study in contrasts.

DESPITE THE ZEN directive to live in the moment, Tokyo's twenty-eight million citizens cared less about the present than melding past tradition with a *Jetsons*-like future. As such, the city was riddled with monuments to both: cavernous wooden temples filled with burning incense, knotted prayer papers, and scuttling monks squatted below gleaming steel-and-glass towers packed with revolving doors, tiers of umbrella racks, and blue-suited workaholics. Dull office complexes and avant-garde edifices, like the space-station headquarters of Japan TV and a neighboring convention center of inverted pyramids, mixed with rabbit-warren design in space-adapted buildings with broom-closet apartments; hotel rooms with wraparound bathrooms you practically wore; and vertical parking garages designed with huge, revolving sprocketed chains on which the cars are stored. Add this to a world-leading system of tunnels, bridges, and bullet trains, and it was clear the Japanese weren't afraid to build anything: no technical, political, or financial hurdle was too great.

Nor any inanity. Ubiquitous vending machines dispensed everything from corn soup to Jack-and-coke, dry beer, "sex-water," fifty kinds of canned coffee, and cold green tea that tasted like an infusion of lawn clippings. Why? Because people were too busy to wait in stores while teams of fawning, white-gloved clerks in sixties stewardess-style pastel dresses and pillbox hats methodically assembled purchases with clinical patience, packed them carefully into a bag, and handwrote a receipt. *Prease to thank you so much for buying our sex water!*

People rushed through Tokyo's labyrinthine subway, streaming through portals, down escalators, and onto platforms, spreading out like molasses. Similar crowds flowed through the infamous Shibuya Square intersection in six different directions, beneath three-story-high video screens and towering neon signposts that displayed the ultimate in trendiness, including images of New School ski celebrities like the NCAF. In vertical malls accessed by escalators, storekeepers hectored, lights flashed, and every cubby blared its own incomprehensible beats. Little of this mash-up made sense outside of Japan, and some of it not even there: what could you make of a T-shirt that read "Seeking their own personality, it is good to be sticky about things, isn't? Glittering curiosity."?

The dizzying downtown kaleidoscopes were hard on the eyes, but nothing compared to the overcharged aural landscape: so many cell phones rang at once that it resembled music, and calliope and carnival sounds filtered through the subway so that even the train-changing chaos sounded like a circus. If you felt like bolting screaming from it all, you could run but never hide: all doors opened automatically to an annoying *beeeeeep*.

It was enough to make you want to go skiing.

JUST WHEN WE thought it couldn't get any better, Szocs and I arrived in Nozawa Onsen, a small village built around hot water that bubbled like blood from the Earth's volcanic skin. From historic architecture to unique regional foods and *sake* street vendors, from snow-god shrines and fastidious guesthouses to geothermal heating, hot-spring baths, and a foot-soaking trough in the village center (where you could doff your ski boots and kick back with a beer), it offered the kind of cultural immersion required to understand and appreciate Japanese tradition.

There was new snow from a recent storm and it was sunny, cold, and stable. Off the top of the highest lift sat one of the best chunks of terrain we'd ever seen: a mile of knife-edge ridge led to an endless series of steep, protected, north-trending chutes and valleys—pure Japanese Alps. We skied with Nozawa guide Katsu Kono and two local park riders, Take Sakamoto and Toru Tachibana. Although not used to skiing their native deep powder, they were happy to follow us. Eventually we traversed far out along the backbone to drop into the steepest, craziest section: roll-away ridges flanked by funneling chutes flowed into a valley that showed evidence of constant filling by avalanches. Sure enough, by the time we arrived, the sun had the overloaded trees dropping bombs and west-trending faces shedding snow into the lower chute.

Skiing a stand of trees near the bottom, something stirred beside me. I looked up to see a strange animal dolphining down the chute accompanied by Kono, who was cranking powder turns beside it like a cowboy chasing down a calf. The *kamoshika* is a deer relative whose look and size was best described by Szocs's riotously accurate moniker of pig-sheep-goat-fish-llama-dog. In this predator-free environment, the animal was curious about who was disturbing its peace beyond the piste. As it ambled away, it stopped often to peer back at us, at one point even walking back along Sakamoto's track toward him.

In that moment, I realized that aside from big-time avalanche danger, the widespread opening of Japan's powder stashes would come with another cost.

After a long day on the hill and a traditional Japanese dinner of infinitesimal choice, we'd done what any visitor should—visited the *onsen*. A few minutes in the scalding waters of these natural hot springs and we felt like boiled gaijin. Afterward, there were toasts long into the night celebrating our dubious connections with Japan. Beer was at the top of that list, and next day all but Kono were too hungover to function. After a few runs in warming conditions, we'd pulled the plug on further turns.

Instead, Szocs and I dressed up in straw *Shogun*-era rain costumes plundered from a nearby museum for a photo shoot at the base.

"We look like idiots," I said, catching our hay-bale reflections in a window.

"It's impossible to look like an idiot in Japan," Szocs countered. "Nothing is too strange here. We could walk around downtown Tokyo dressed like this, and no one would notice."

He had a point. An interesting tolerance for sideshow humanity seemed strange in what could often be a rigid society, but it was part of the rich, evolving tapestry there. And it was something that a guy like Ricky Lewon, who had spent years living and ski-racing in Japan, could appreciate.

On one Extremely Canadian trip, Lewon and Dunnigan's husband, co-owner Pete Smart, finished a smuggled forty-ouncer of whiskey on the plane and made a hundred friends in the process. In Niseko, however, Lewon almost got in a hundred fights with rugby-minded Aussie drunks who didn't appreciate his fluent Japanese and the attention he drew from locals. Then one night the EC crew went to a hostess bar in Sapporo. The hostesses were so enamored that afterward they took the group to their favorite transvestite club, where one of the young women asked Lewon, Smart, and Dunnigan if they wanted to see her new vagina, which was then displayed on the bar and the delicate surgery explained.

For the time being, it seemed, Japan's surrealistic identity crisis—powder included—was intact, but Dunnigan held out little hope of preservation on either front.

"I really loved this traditional lodge that was for sale in Niseko, and wanted to buy it, but I was worried about this whole Aussie and North American thing," she said. "Globalization of the ski industry is going to bring cookie-cutter resorts here and destroy the fantastic culture."

She had reason to worry. An invasion by North American resort sensibilities would result in a ski product that, in the phrasing of a malaprop banner Szocs had seen hoisted over the stage at the launch of a Japanese clothing company's new international initiative, was "World Class Bland."

However, it was too late to turn back the hands of time, and the invasion of Japan's mountain kingdom was already on. It was time to either get on the train or be run over by it. In our waning hours in Japan, Szocs and I had decided there was a way to do this without ruining what existed.

A Marshall Plan for the Japanese ski industry that they could rebuild and profit from: we would buy a funky, forested resort and bring prescreened experts over for powder skiing. We'd run lifts but limit the clientele so the terrain didn't get too tracked out. We'd drive snowcats powered by biodiesel made from tempura grease along the endless ridges of the Japanese Alps, plumbing the thousands of available lines. We'd have our own traditional village, farm our own food, brew our own beer and sake. In honor of Japan's abstract fixation with pop culture, we'd call it "Bam Bam Super Funski Powder Resort!!!" We'd have a special Bam Bam Powder Club après bar with Lewon as master of ceremonies, as well as a first-of-its-kind, foot-soaking, Nozawa-inspired place called the "Supersoaker Fancy Free Bar," which would raise (or lower, depending on your perspective) après to new levels while your feet dangled under the tables in hot water. We would sell fun Jinglish T-shirts with slogans like "Fuck Off—I has enough friends" and "No War! Let's Peace Up the World."

No war. And a soft invasion. Like snow falling from the sky.

15 | SPACE, THE
FINAL FRONTIER

Where there is snow, there is skiing...
STEPHEN POOLEY, *The World Atlas of Skiing*, 1990

THE GYPSIES danced into the night. By a river, on the edge of town, silhouetted like kindergarten cutouts by a towering bonfire, their marionette figures circled the flames, swooping flutes, pounding drums, and weaving an ancient rhythm whose metronome rivaled the house-techno leaking through cheap, porous brick from a local club.

We stood apart from the dancers, separated by a concrete ditch we hadn't anticipated as we'd stumbled toward the fire over rubble-constellated ground. It was emblematic of a deep cultural chasm—or at least a divide that we were too drunk to cross. From our wavering vantage, it seemed we were peering back through the centuries, a vignette that also foretold an oddly possible future: skiing handed off by its longtime Western caretakers to the open but confused book of rising economies and ancient cultures. This was Bulgaria.

I'd heard that some crazed riders held an annual big-mountain contest in the unheralded but impressive highlands here. A Whistler posse was heading over to do battle, so I'd convinced *SKIER* magazine to send me. That everybody and his dog already seemed to know about the event—such that writer Sam Moulton and photographer Paul Morrison, withering in the cold to my right and working on a story for rival *Skiing* magazine, were but the tip of a significant media iceberg docked in the town of Bansko—soon became clear.

That night, however, was merely the eve of Lent, and the gypsies were enjoying a final toxic binge before their forty-day fast. They swigged homemade, grappa-like *rakia* from soda bottles passed by hands otherwise occupied with music dating to the Ottoman Empire. We watched as the last empty bottle was end-over-ended onto the pyre. On cue, the wind picked up and snow bore down over the ragged, pyramidal sill of the Pirin Mountains. The gypsies' notes spiraled on Vesuvian sparks, drifted over the garbage-strewn ditch, settled onto frozen ground, and rushed toward us like cold air under a door jamb.

Our Bulgarian hosts watched impassively. Moulton scribbled in his notebook, Morrison squeezed off one last shot, and I pushed my ungloved hands into a backpack to fight the growing chill. What I found there was warmth of a different stripe: a half-finished bottle of rakia. It was going to be another *very* long night.

THEY CALLED THEM The Magic Trees, and they were. If you imagined 3,000 vertical feet of powder on forty-degree slopes under perfectly spaced Douglas-fir trees, you'd have the *bauplan,* or blueprint, for this chunk of Bansko Resort. It was an eternity of forest between the main peak, Todorka, and the groomed rollers of a ski area that had recently morphed from a funkified, Soviet backwater for local sport aficionados to an ultramodern destination with a lengthy access gondola, high-speed lifts, and computerized snowmaking.

The mantle of huge trees was one of the last old-growth forests in Eastern Europe and one of the big reasons the area was also a national park. Another was wild goats.

Our first run had been through an inch or so of new snow over a krummholz tangle of Macedonian pine. Our next lap found us in an open, sweeping bowl battling changeable conditions and crust, which is when the Bulgarian Extreme and Freestyle Skiing Association (BEFSA)—represented by Krasi Petrov, brother Ilian, and Ivo Altanov—decided to show us The Magic Trees.

"Watch for goats," said Ivo. "They hide in forest."

"Will they run away or charge?" I asked, recalling that BEFSA's big-mountain contest was titled Mad Goat Ride, and posters featured a crazed-looking ungulate.

"Maybe. I don't know," said Krasi, pushing off. "They are crazy."

We followed under the canopy, amazed at the living-room legroom, slightly perturbed by icy, rattling conditions, and on high alert for marauding goats. We saw none, though it's likely they saw us crashing through crust and tumbling under the protective evergreens. As we loaded the chairlift, four otherworldly ice sculptures rose like sixty-foot stalagmites to end in sharp, disemboweling spikes. So bizarre as to somehow oddly belong, they threw shadows across the snow like sundials.

"What are *those?*" I asked Krasi.

"I don't know."

"They're there *all* the time?"

"No. From vodka promotion."

"You *do* know. Are they sculptures?"

"I don't know."

"What should we know about Bulgarian vodka?"

"Is drink like water."

"Hmmm... can you drink tap water here?" I asked, suddenly interested.

"Yes. It is very good. Although maybe not so much in Bansko. You might have stomach disorder. I am developing disorder last time here. It is very bad. So, no, do not drink tap water."

We'd first become entwined with the brothers Petrov at the airport in Sofia, Bulgaria's capital, where the smiling pair had been sent to pile Moulton, Morrison, myself, and a mountain of luggage into their tiny vehicle. Then we ventured into the city to kill time until we could meet up with Ivo (BEFSA's vice president) for the drive to Bansko; Sofia had offered a discount lesson in Eastern European history.

Bulgarian communism sailed into the sunset during a bloodless 1989 coup, leaving the familiar hourglass stratification of post-communist society—an ultra-rich class that had always capitalized (pun intended) on the hidden economy of communism and pounced after privatization; a tiny middle class that should, theoretically, grow; and legions of working poor caught out by the sudden, titanic changes. Bulgarian and Russian Mafia controlled the economy, using bombings and assassinations to keep the populace in fear.

"Just like government," explained Krasi.

No kidding. As of 2008, there'd been over 130 contract killings since communism's collapse.

Although the country was some 1,300 years old, its capital offered little of the cultural hubris usually found in European cities; anything that survived communism's architectural homogenization had been quickly whitewashed by the new capitalist influx. Squat, columnar buildings and Soviet-nik statues mixed with the inevitable hallmarks of American economic imperialism—McDonald's, KFC, and

Dunkin' Donuts. The suburbs were an oozing wound of decrepit post-Stalinist apartments scabbed over by a patina of unfinished construction. On the roads, a scourge of brightly painted but barely operating vehicles that offered a much-appreciated counterpoint to the brown-gray landscape was being reseeded with black, navy, and gunmetal Audis, Mercedes, and BMWs—the smoked-window fleet of corruption and instant wealth. It was enough to encourage French partners to invest 600 million euros in an improbable destination ski resort.

Were criminals and laundered money the new face of ski development in the twenty-first century? You had to wonder: who else in these duct-taped economies could afford to build such infrastructure-heavy frivolity—not to mention the cost of skiing at them. You could practically hear The Scorpions' post-communist anthem, "Wind of Change" playing in your head, loaded with new irony.

Ironically—or unfortunately, depending on how much rakia you'd had the night before—you could also hear "Wind of Change" playing each morning at breakfast, looping through the dining room on the same Euro-rock soundtrack. Each day, the first iteration of "Gorky Park" in the chorus would cause Moulton and I to break out the lighters and sway... until they switched to techno played so loud that the thumping base caused more wincing than the inevitable slab of sour cheese centered on a plate between two greasy eggs.

Krasi was only mildly amused by our concert emulations. He was too busy instructing us in Zen and the Art of Bulgarian Yogurt: there was thick yogurt, thin yogurt, liquid yogurt, sour yogurt, sweet yogurt, sheep yogurt (very special), and, I suspected, wild goat yogurt traded under the table by BEFSA operatives.

"What do you think of this music?" I asked.

"I don't know."

"Do you like this song?"

"Yes. Maybe. No."

BACK ON THE chairlift, I contemplated Bansko, 3,300 feet below, lodged to one side of a broad valley, centered on a centuries-old trade route between Turkey and Europe and used by all manner of peoples, including the Ottomans, who controlled the area for half a millennium; there were enclaves in the Pirins that had always resisted their rule. Those mountain dwellers were Bulgaria's first skiers.

The east–west-trending Pirins received weather from both south and north, and near Bansko lofted toothily to some 10,000 feet. Steep, consistent fall lines were everywhere, and the resort seemed to combine the pistes of Sun Valley, the alpine of Whistler, the backcountry of the Rockies, the powder and tree-spacing of Japan. The requisite veneer of a perfect Next Big Thing.

Above The Magic Trees rose Todorka Peak, a stark, 1,600 feet of couloirs, cliff bands, sloping shelves, and hanging snowfields. Bisected by fracture lines indicative of a sketchy snowpack, the entire western face had slid off two weeks prior, which is why the BEFSA crew felt it perfectly safe to climb above the top lift and lead us across some serious exposure on that same face. Moulton, Morrison, and I stared anxiously at rock-solid, edge-resistant *verglas* that funneled hundreds of feet down heinous chutes to a hanging valley while the BEFSA crew skipped across the scoured gutters like it was a walk in Gorky Park.

After traversing the chutes, we found decent, buttery turns in the first couloir we came to. That wasn't good enough for Krasi, who insisted on dropping a fifteen-foot cliff on twice-repaired skis held together with Krazy Glue.

"Will your skis hold?"

"I don't know."

"If they don't?"

"My brother glue them back together."

Sibling rivalry apparently dictated that older brother Ilian then drop a *thirty-foot* cliff onto hardpack. Watching this feat explained Krasi's shattered secondhand slats, as well as Ivo's paternalistic approval of the Petrovs' compliance with tradition.

Ivo moonlighted as a marketing specialist when he was not skiing or attending to BEFSA biz. This I'd discovered on the drive from Sofia a few days back when, as Moulton and I were writers and Ivo a subject, it had been determined we would ride with him.

"How are you doing?" I asked as we pulled away.

"I am already crazy."

"How's the contest looking?"

"We are still negotiating."

I took this to mean shitty, yet to realize that negotiating was less issue than custom.

We drove south toward Greece, as invading Macedonian armies once had. Tiny, disconsolate lights marked scattered taverns, farms, and billboards in the Cyrillic alphabet; intervening blackness concealed valley, plateau, forest, and finally, a mountain pass. Cresting it, the lights of Bansko hovered like a space station below a void of stars.

Our hotel was a bizarre complex of interconnected stonework cottages located strategically outside of town. It was owned, we were told, by a "credit millionaire" (read: loan shark). In the smoke-filled lobby, worried-looking folks crowded both sides of the desk, waving cigarettes, pointing fingers, and shouting. The BEFSA braintrust seemed unperturbed that months of careful preparation was suddenly hostage to the whims of an intransigent desk clerk with heroin-hollow looks and a death-row disposition.

"Hotel room?" I asked.

"We are negotiating," said Ivo.

"Lift tickets?"

"We will negotiate."

"I thought this was all arranged."

"Yes, but ... situation change ..."

Bulgaria had mountains, sure, but could it overcome the communist hangover to stage a legitimate contest? Sixty-plus contestants from ten countries were banking on the answer being yes. Me? I was just banking on some normalcy.

IN BANSKO WE'D sampled several traditional taverns, or *mehanas*—their waitstaff costumed in black boots, puffy pants or skirts, lacy white blouses, and wielding menus that featured something called a "meat-boat"—but gravitated most often to the Eagle's Nest, a local skier hangout considered too ghetto by the Bulgarian nouveau riche. Rheumy-eyed, leather-vested waiters and overflowing squat toilets didn't help that atmosphere, but the food was fast, plentiful, and sometimes good, and the rakia, at the equivalent of twenty-five cents a shot, was as cheap as it got.

One night we'd occupied a long central table with several Mad Goat riders and a smattering of BEFSA brass. In a corner booth sat *POWDER*'s Dave Reddick, Porter Fox, and a film crew. It was strange enough that we'd all found ourselves in this Black Sea outpost at precisely the same time, but on the bar's lone TV, live from Sofia, American skiers Kina Pickett, Wendy Fisher, and Hannah Hardaway were explaining to Bulgaria's top talk-show host—a manic, skinhead cross between David Letterman and Conan O'Brien—how they'd come here to shoot a Warren Miller film segment but been skunked by bad conditions. It was too bizarre to watch.

Throughout the nineties and early in the new millennium, feeding frenzies of writers, photographers, filmers, and athletes were common in places like Engelberg, Whistler, and the heli-ghettos of Alaska and B.C., but seldom did they convene *before* a place had been vetted in the snowsports media. Indicative of future developments, however, the Bansko story belonged to the Internet.

The BEFSA guys had been e-mailing the European ski world for years, generating interest in their offbeat area and their contest. Their website linked to other key freeskiing sites, and that, more than anything, had drawn the sea of freeriders we found ourselves swimming in. How the timing of this particular cluster came to be so exact was anyone's guess. Only Fox had really known anything about the place: he'd visited Bulgaria on a whim in 2003, hitting good powder and catching the resort in predevelopment glory.

"It was like Jackson Hole circa 1978—steep, deep, and hardly anyone riding it," he'd told me.

"Wow. Jackson... *really?*"

"Well... not entirely. Someone tried to sell me an AK-47 my first day here."

That night, Fox thought they went bowling. Or at least that's what he would write in *POWDER* months later. Arriving at the shiny-new alley ourselves, we recognized immediately that despite the setting, the *POWDER* crew—inexplicably dressed in costumes ranging from Frankenstein and Dracula to a headless man and Amish farmers—was simply and famously drunk. Clearly they were trying to exorcise some demon of the day. It eventually got sloppy, and bottles of rakia tumbled from people's coats. As we shared the last of a bottle, Reddick leaned in.

"What *is* this place?"

"Bulg..."

"Um... Oh, God—the helicopter; I've never been so wigged out."

"Sketchy?"

"So bad. The pilot... too scared to land on a peak. Straight off the farm... skis tied to the skids with shoe-laces... I can't even..."

"Have a drink."

"What *is* this place?"

Good question. Finding the gates locked back at the hotel, I hopped the fence with reckless abandon only to find myself in the arms of a large greaseball in a tracksuit with a piece of cold steel in his hand. Our credit millionaire was home, doubtless pursued by his own creditors and in need of 24/7 protection. Only the humorous titter of my drunken English kept me from having my head blown off.

On the mountains, at least, it was snowing again.

ALTHOUGH IT DREW few stars, the Mad Goat Ride achieved its goal of a true multinational enterprise. And it was unlikely heroics from a twenty-three-year-old University of Calgary mechanical engineering student on a year-long work term in Zurich that took the prize. Brandon McLean got a pat on the back, a check that would just cover the cost of his trip (if, in fact, it proved cashable), and a bellyful of rakia from an international contingent that celebrated by invading a decrepit former Communist Party hot-springs resort *en masse*, chasing local farmers from their daily soak in the outdoor pool.

The festivities started slowly at that night's party but picked up when shots appeared on the smoky bar; by midnight the brothers Petrov were in full swing, having liberated themselves from all clothing, doffing shoes in favor of ski boots. They wore headlamps and slid sideways on their boots at people; their lights made them look like trains hurtling across the dance floor. Krasi, a non-drinker, seemed particularly out of control, having consumed an uncharacteristic two orange sodas with his usual yogurt.

"I am wild and crazy guy," he said by way of explanation, forehead strobing absurdly.

"He *is* crazy guy," said a woman who worked with him at the Sofia Hilton, offering me a shot of something that tasted like stove fuel.

I looked around. Was this *really* the landing strip for skiing's next major airlift? Eastern Europe still seemed too messy and isolated to command anything but novelty status. Skiing had now spent a decade firing off in all directions with equipment, styles, sensibilities, venues, and competition, but where were the sport's *geographic* horizons? As Krasi—still reaching for a comprehensible metaphor for his behavior—leaned in to tell me he was "mad as goat," I noticed the tag on his headlamp: Made in China. It was prophetic.

As it turned out, when it came to skiing, everyone and everything *was* going to China. Long before this wishful big-mountain circus had debarked in Sofia, the ski industry had, in bit and part, already boarded the Orient Express. Skis were now made in China. Clothing. Goggles. Helmets. Someone in Guangzhou was probably even tooling up a factory to make knock-off European lip balm. And recently, this telling tidbit had hit the newswires: in a nod to Western affluence and affectation, the Chinese government had *mandated* the creation of a domestic ski industry.

In my mind, I imagined a glitzy, red-lacquered lodge where a giant gas fireplace sizzled beneath an enormous wok stirred by a jolly chef dishing out short orders of house pets to dozens of smiling skiers whose cast-encased legs were propped on a hearth of plastic, knock-off rock.

It wasn't far off.

WHEN OUR SALOMON/MSP film crew arrived at Mr. Lorie's Shangguang Hotel and Wanlong Ski Area at 3 a.m. one

February night, he greeted us in trademark white track pants, white slip-on sandals, and white knit T-shirt, a gold chain around his neck. He showed up the same way at breakfast, proving that the outfit wasn't a set of pajamas. He rocked the emaciated Pillsbury Doughboy look all day, lurking in the shadows, shouting into an earwire. And again that night when we'd crowded around a traditional round-table with the equally mysterious Mr. Ko to feast on seafood hotpot, five-spice pork, sliced duck, chili wheat noodle, and soy-sugar walnuts.

Mr. Lorie also sported this very un-Chinese color in photos hanging throughout his hotel. Spotless and smiling through his ragged Ho Chi Minh beard, sandwiched by smudges of grim, dark-suited businessmen, government officials, and foreign dignitaries, he resembled the center of the knock-off Oreo cookies that ski stars Sammy Carlson and Simon Dumont had subsisted on for days. Coincidentally, Mr. Lorie was trying to do something about just that.

In Wanlong's bright, airy cafeteria, below a menu proudly displaying a photo of boiled dog, Mr. Lorie hovered like a ghostly grandmother, plying the boys with cryopreserved sandwiches and sickly sweet rolls. They were having none of it, standing firm on Oreos. But his largesse suggested why Mr. Lorie dressed like a steamed bun and why he was rich enough to build a modern ski area from scratch in record time, with an army of laborers, in a place it never snowed: he owned a bakery. A large one. With over 4,000 outlets.

Mr. Lorie should have been standing outside on the world's largest lodge deck, gazing through a string of fluttering fish-kites at the commerce engulfing his glorious slopes. Instead, he was playing nursemaid because our group had split along generational lines: veterans Mark Abma and Mike Douglas conducting ambassadorial duties outside, teenage prima donnas Carlson and Dumont—officially over the "lame" terrain park—stationed inside.

The boys' lack of diplomacy signaled that they clearly didn't comprehend *guanxi*—China's central concept of connection in which one person is able to prevail upon another, or be prevailed upon, to perform a favor or service. They did, however, have a point.

The woebegone terrain park had been built to specifications passed by Douglas through Japanese intermediaries. The result—echoing the miniature version of Stonehenge in the mockumentary *This is Spinal Tap*—reflected the difficulty of translating "large" through three languages while holding your hands apart. The jumps, which the Chinese considered enormous, were far too small to safely execute serious tricks on, so the cat driver took another crack at beefing up the launches. And, undeterred by their petulance, the benevolent Mr. Lorie took another crack at feeding the young pros he'd imported to christen the good ship Wanlong.

WITH CHINA DANGLING from a thousand price tags and dominating the media just shy of the Beijing Olympics, no amount of knowledge could have prepared us for what we found there. Starbucks might have been the first thing we saw in Beijing's ultra-modern airport, but it was an over-polished caricature of the real thing. Everything else was alien, starting with the "control" ambience: pressing crowds were countered by steely-eyed police strolling the marble halls with bone-white earpieces and batons in hand, like security at a Guns N' Roses concert. The airport was also where the yelling started.

"*Ni how!* Mike Dugrash!" screamed a guy leaping spastically in a bright-red ski jacket plastered with nonsensical logos, as I pushed a caravan of luggage through Arrivals.

"No, I'm not Mike, he's behind me."

"Hi, hi, hi!," said another, poking me hard in the arm and executing a foot-grasping pirouette that looked like ice dancing but was probably an attempted Mute 360. "Mike Dugrash...? Freestyrrr skate?"

"No, Mike *skier,*" I replied, unconsciously forsaking unnecessary grammar. I pointed over my shoulder to Abma and Dumont. *"Those* figure skaters."

"Figurrr skaturrr? Ahrrr..." Much nudging and loud discussion in harsh Mandarin. The metallic words cut the air like cleavers.

Using humor, however, was pointless. He just poked me harder.

"Mike Dugrash...? Freestyrrr...?"

His pleading eyes telegraphed both China's hunger for outside knowledge and the collective determination propelling Chinese tourists abroad in great chattering waves. In his persistence I saw the boiler-room of the world's fastest-growing economy, the pride of an emerging people, and the cultural aspirations of half-a-billion nouveau riche who had become the latest, greatest prey for a host of voracious ski-tour operators. Finally, in his desire to emulate at all costs, and, having witnessed firsthand in Whistler the recent influx of Chinese armed with mothball-impregnated jackets and a penchant for fugly stuffed animals, I saw this: the end of skiing as we knew it.

THAT CHINA IS hell-bent on creating a domestic ski scene is no longer news. That it will look very little like skiing, might be. There are some two hundred ski areas in China, but only thirty have functioning lifts, many salvaged from the vast mechanical junkyard of Japan's disintegrating industry. Elsewhere, donkeys deliver skiers to the top of tilted farm fields. Although they are devoid of infrastructure or services, it serves some mute purpose for the Ministry of Sport to list these as ski areas.

Mr. Lorie and Mr. Ko had decided to build a Western-style ski resort about five hours northeast of Beijing. Since the cheapest things in China are land and people, they secured a chunk of worthless mountain covered in hard-scrabble forest on the edge of the desert, and started an access road. Although bitingly cold in this part of Hebei province, it rarely snows, so they required a massive snow-making system. That there wasn't much water to feed it also posed no problem; peasants downstream be damned, they built a dam and coaxed several anemic, spring-fed creeks into a lake. The ten-mile road, heavily excavated runs, four lifts, snowmaking, parking, and stylish hotel were finished in nine months by a workforce of thousands laboring 24/7, qualifying Wanlong as one of the Seven Manmade Wonders of the Ski World. Right up there with Bansko's ice sculptures and Chamonix's Aiguille du Midi tram.

When China wants something—witness its repurposing of gold-medal gymnasts for gold-medal freestyle-skiing aerialists—it gets it. The only large country with the power to motivate an entire citizenry in a single direction, it has decided that the bourgeois sport of skiing is now an official state-sanctioned activity. Thus, the Chinese will ski not because they particularly like the outdoors but because it has cachet and is Western; even if there's no real mountain and only ersatz snow, they'll happily enjoy a knock-off version of inferior aesthetics.

Mr. Ko, Salomon's man in China, clearly had a vested interest in creating a market for hard goods. Powerful guanxi with Japan's beneficent Toshi Shimizu, the driving force behind the Teneighty twin-tip, meant that the invasion of China would be launched from Japan, using the celebrity of North American ski stars as leverage. Before dropping them behind communist lines, however, Toshi arranged a Japanese boot camp: Abma, Carlson, Douglas, and Dumont trained in secret for a week at two relatively unknown ski areas in the northern part of Honshu. On the soaring volcanic ring of Hakkoda and in the forested, labyrinthine canyons of Hachimantai, the boys spun back-country gold from crusty snow and aging powder, dropping chutes and savaging spines for the cameras, jibbing rime-encrusted trees, and launching massive booters into deep landings, each rider bringing individual style to the kind of freewheeling, uncontrolled show the Chinese *should* have seen.

EYES PRESSED TO our bus windows on the way north from Beijing to the resort, one thing had been clear and, apropos of skiing, immensely worrying: China wowed with enter-prise but strangled with monotony. Neo-capitalist facades couldn't hide the glut of low, gray buildings of communist practicality and central-committee frugality that clut-tered each city outskirt; every boulevard featured identical whitewash-gilded trees; the clay-brick houses and walled-in yards lining roadways were all crumbling in a strange uni-son; and every dilapidated truck seemed dilapidated in pre-cisely the same manner—dusty, bald-tired, leaning heavily to one side, its clanging metal gate hanging like a shirttail.

Although the Chinese will bring zeal and focus, they also bring a franchise mentality to the sport (if you own 4,000 bakeries, you can own 4,000 ski areas). They might all look the same but hell, North America spent the past four decades creating its own version of McSki-ing, and look at all the fortuitous outlaw innovations *that* had engendered—freestyle, snowboards, twin-tips, parks and pipes, the powder and backcountry explosion, fat skis, big-mountain skiing. If China bakes up a giant (fortune) cookie-cutter ski industry, it can only lead to mo' better evolution in the sport—right?

Unlikely. In China, few protest. And few disobey rules simply because there might be a better, more fun way to do something. If Chinese skiers develop even a modicum of proficiency in any discipline, it will be because of their skill at emulation.

Skiing, however, has always flowered in the soils of individuality, so it will be extra-hard to beat sameness out of the Chinese model. For instance, when Abma threw a neat ski trick for the cameras, off a wall near the hotel onto a dirt-encrusted pile of spindrift, it drew only quizzical looks and a nervous hush from hotel staff. Was it some form of subversion against Mr. Lorie? Did Mr. Abma not understand that the ski run is over *there?* Will he not be arrested?

On that sunny Saturday, Wanlong's parking lots were filled with people who'd driven from Beijing to rent identical skis, boots, poles, and red ski jackets, then line up for half an hour to load the beginner's chair, a conveyor belt of disaster moving at the speed of Zen but nevertheless pouring skiers off in a continuous slapstick carnage that resembled ski-film impresario Warren Miller's famous comedy segments.

I took the lift to the top of the ski area, where wind-and-sun-ravaged Tibetan prayer flags were strung from a wooden hut named "Finland House." Beyond the ski hill, ragged, undernourished horses grazed in a cold, windswept desert. I wiped a patina of Mongolian dust from my goggles and made several runs on long, steep, race-graded pistes. They were fast, groomed to perfection, and artificial enough to bring a smile to the face of any FIS official. They were also empty because even those Chinese who *could* ski couldn't forsake their social nature for even a minute; they wanted to be where everyone else was—at the bottom crashing into each other.

Meanwhile, the terrain *parkette* had been retooled, and Carlson and Dumont were lured from the cafeteria to session it as best they could. A handful of Chinese mutely observed as best *they* could, unsure without a frame of reference what they were watching, but certain it was, in part, the madness of capitalists with too much time on their hands. No argument there.

The performance started with various tricks on a rail before the boys moved on to the thirty-foot booter, throwing a dozen different 540 combos of increasing quality before Dumont's 180 Truck Driver—a pike-position rotation in which the skier leans forward to grasp both ski tips like a steering wheel—finally drew applause. To make things interesting, all four skiers hit the jump together, choreographing spins in opposite directions so they wouldn't collide. They wrapped up with a wall-ride session topped by Carlson's executing a 180-to-stall atop the wall, then spinning 540 off it in the opposite direction. The boys had at least earned their Oreos.

BACK IN THE cafeteria, a woman in a white, Elvis-style one-piece replete with rhinestones swept in with her entourage and plunked herself down beside us. She had skunk-dyed hair; wore an endangered snow leopard coat, Chanel sunglasses, and pounds of makeup, and held a cigarette holder between lipstick-stained teeth. She was Cruella de Vil, a one-woman Chinese Aspen, and a friend of Mr. Lorie and Mr. Ko.

"Very, very rich," said Toshi. "*Three* private jets!"

"She like your pants," allowed her companion to Toshi, pointing to his faux-leather leggings, "and invite you all to traditional Chinese dinner in Beijing!"

Toshi thanked her with hands clasped and head bowed. Then, as she walked away, he turned quickly to me.

"I don't think we can survive something like that. What kind of Chinese dinner do you think it will be?"

"The scary kind," I offered, certain.

"I know," said Toshi, "that's what I'm afraid of."

Considering the things I'd seen Toshi eat in Japan, this was *the* most frightening thing I'd ever heard.

Over the next few days we worked our way back to Beijing, absorbing The Great Wall—the world's most aptly named structure, a many-thousand-mile amusement park that included an eponymous single-run ski area—then Tiananmen Square and the Forbidden City. Somewhere in this whirlwind of sino-conography I began to think that maybe we hadn't really been brought here to ski after all: we'd been brought here to *understand*. Something. Perhaps a lesson in seismology before the tourist tsunami hit North America? But with the level of inscrutability from Mr. Lorie to Mr. Ko to the friggin' bus driver dialed up to eleven, who really knew?

Soon enough it was time for our dinner. We dodged indescribable traffic through shimmering, glass-walled canyons of Olympic-inspired, futuristic architecture, which was ironic given our destination. Beijing Fangshan Restaurant in Beihai Park, a formal imperial garden built in the days of Kublai Khan, offered exquisite food from various Chinese dynasties. Stunning hostesses in period garb held paper lanterns as we were led through a scene straight out of the Qing Dynasty: we passed the famous White Dagoba, sitting above a Jade Islet on a tranquil lake; the Nine-Dragon Screen, built to ward off evil spirits; and Five-Dragon Pavilion. Our private dining pagoda was an indescribable crucible of lacquered ceilings and traditional Chinese art. Water bubbled from a spring in the scale-model village adorning our etched-glass table. We drank hundred-year-old tea.

The fourteen-course dinner included lobster sashimi plucked from the live animal. Each time someone lifted a slice from the platter, the lobster's eye-stalks swiveled around in what seemed like mild annoyance but could just as easily have been excruciating crustacean pain. There was chewy turtle, chewier geoduck, camel's paw, and flayed deer penis.

Dumont and Carlson knew enough to be honored and actually sampled some of the fare (though Carlson gripped a half-eaten McDonald's cheeseburger—fetched for him by Cruella's minions—under the table just in case). Stars from Beijing's Chinese Opera appeared from behind hidden panels to perform for us in full costume. It was otherwordly and culturally humbling enough to make skiing seem shallow, frivolous, and hedonistic. A worthy target for callous mass manufacture compared to the 5,000 years of culture and tradition on display.

Perhaps *that* was the point.

The meal ended with a plate of steamed buns of various shapes, each decorated with small bits of colored sweets. We all picked one, while Mr. Ko's wife explained how each represented a certain personality. She went around the table, describing each of our fortunes based on the bun we'd chosen. When she got to Mr. Lorie she simply bowed her head and moved on.

I got it. After all, the buns *were* white. And white was the color of Mr. Lorie's fortune.

In the winter mountain world, however, white could also be the color of *misfortune* and much schadenfreude. Like when there was too much of it and people didn't know what to do with it. Or if you were maybe fighting a war in it. Or if nobody and everybody was in charge at the same time. Like a bureaucratic whiteout. Like India.

And it wanted to be a ski country, too.

AS WITH MOST things in India, it was a fight to get on
the gondola. It wasn't so much the usual powder-day jostling—though twenty inches of new snow and two days
without access to the upper mountain ensured there was
some of that. No, it was more of a personal battle for Paul
Morrison, a guide, and me to muscle ourselves and packs
and skis through a half-open, thigh-width clamshell. Fortunately, the Stage II Gondola in Gulmarg, India—well rusted
before it opened in 2006 (actually, the yellow, egg-shaped
1960s cars were already ancient when they arrived from
France in 1989)—was crawling through its bottom station
with requisite dharmic purpose (i.e., slowly enough), and
we managed to jam ourselves in, sweating, before the doors
clamped shut on our skis. These remained comically thrust
out of the gondola for the remainder of the halting ride up
Mt. Apharwat to just over 13,000 feet.

During our passage, we had plenty of time, given how
many times the gondola ground to a halt, to drink in
Apharwat's pristine slopes. So pristine they were devoid
of anything resembling a piste. Ahead we saw squadrons
of skiers and snowboarders dropping from the summit plateau onto bifurcating ridges whose toes were peppered with
ancient Himalayan birch. The place was being shralped so
thoroughly it almost seemed like a real resort instead of the
La Grave–style death trap it was: Apharwat revealed *the*
most dangerous avalanche gullies I'd ever seen, their hazard barely balanced by the relative safety of the intervening
ridges. During one stop, I drank in the serrated grandeur of
the Pakistani Himalaya hovering above the pool of diesel
and woodsmoke cloaking the Kashmiri capital of Srinigar.
I unconsciously ticked off each of the visible 26,000-foot
peaks: Nanga Parbat, Masherbrum, Gasherbrum I and II,
Broad Peak, and was that the tiny pyramidal icon of K2
wavering on the northwestern horizon? I was suddenly

distracted in this task by the guy in the "J & K Ski Rescue" jacket sitting with his back to us, who filled the tiny cabin with acrid cigarette smoke and repeatedly adjusted the AK-47 slung around his shoulder so that the barrel was somehow always pointed at my head. I wish I was kidding.

"Jesus Christ," I mumbled.

"God almighty," said Morrison.

"Allahu akbar," said our smiling Kashmiri guide, Ashref, believing he was joining us in joyful prayer.

For a change, it was sunny and clear, and everything had been on the move early today, even the fuzzy, animated gargoyles lining every rooftop. The monkeys had taunted and hurled garbage down on us as we'd ambled along the road toward the gondola station from Highland Park Lodge, a hilltop warren of rustic cabins buried so deeply in snow they were only apparent by the smoke curling from their stone chimneys.

As short as the walk was, it revealed much about the contrasts of the place. In one direction, a parade of Hindis from New Delhi was fashionably dressed in colorful, diaphanous saris, scarves, faux fur, and Elton John sunglasses. Scrunched knee-to-ear on traditional hand-carved wooden sleds drawn by indigent, drab-smocked Islamic men, they slid morosely by on bulky sled runners greased with rancid mutton fat. In another direction, aspiring skiers often wearing two different—and different-sized—boots or skis and a single glove stumbled toward the valley's short rope tow. The massive military presence everywhere made Lebanon's weaponry display seem like a carnival concession. (The only *real* military danger, however, was the chance of a bald-tired taxi colliding with one of the many army convoys wrapping around the convoluted access road—or a gun-toting soldier squeezing into your gondola.)

Miraculously, we had intercepted the notoriously evasive ticket seller under a stairway, obtaining lift passes without being caught in the usual multilingual brawl that followed him everywhere. It was like winning the lottery, and the 100-rupee ($2 USD) tickets had even resembled prize checks—giant fluttering papers someone might knock on your door to deliver. We'd handed ours to the cadre of smoking, shouting lifties who eyed them with suspicion (what else could they be?) before starting up the mountain.

At the top, we had to fight our way *off* the gondola past shivering, poorly outfitted Kashmiris and heavily armed Indian Army regulars who were arguing forcefully over who was responsible for cleaning the squat toilets of several nearby barbed-wired, sand-bagged military posts aiming their not-insignificant artillery at Pakistan. We slipped into a sea of slouching patrollers decked out in familiar but faded Whistler-Blackcomb ski patrol jackets and found ourselves staring at Indian ski guides wearing bright, bi-colored WB mountain host and ski school outfits, as well as soiled-black WB mountain-ops clothing on guys with "High Altitude Warfare School" baseball caps. A group of Brits was being hectored by guides from the Whistler-based Extremely Canadian tour company. Half a dozen languages reached our ears, again overshadowed by loud Australian. To top it off, as we slid tentatively past the line-up of retro Whistler wear and gun-toting soldiers to drop into one of Apharwat's 3,000-vertical-foot powder gullies, we were suddenly in a scramble for first tracks with a posse of Whistler snowboarders and their film crew. We found ourselves wishing, *inshallah* (God willing), that they would be conveniently avalanched out of the way. Just like at home. Was this *really* India?

THE OVERWHELMING Whistler presence was easily explained: in 2006, the global snowsports media had collectively declared Gulmarg a Next Big Thing, but this newfound notoriety came in part through the efforts of

Whistler riders, in a trail that traced back to an Israeli-Canadian snowboarder named Ido Neiger.

A land-mine clearer by trade, Ido had in 2000 passed through Gulmarg, which is lodged in the Pir Panjal Range on the infamous India–Pakistan Line of Control. War had raged intermittently over the Islamic territory of Kashmir since the partitioning of India and Pakistan in 1948, and the area was both messy and dangerous. Still, Ido had fallen in love with the place; he wasn't the first.

Gulmarg, which means "meadow of flowers," was named in the sixteenth century by Sultan Yusuf Shah. He and other Mughals made annual summer migrations to Gulmarg to escape the stifling heat of the plains, as did the subsequent British Raj, who ultimately introduced the gentlemanly pursuits of golf and skiing; at one point, 500 British mountain-warfare troops were stationed and training there. When Ido arrived, however, the only skiing was on a short slope through gentle trees off the Stage 1 Gondola (installed by the Indian government during a window of regional peace in 1998) or a brutal climb to the summit of Mt. Apharwat. Neither option was an experience to inspire foreign riders, though this was precisely what Indian tourism authorities had hoped for—as had two locals, Hamid and Yassin, who'd grown up in nearby villages and had been making the eight-hour climb up Apharwat through waist-deep snow for years. Staking their fortunes on optimism, Hamid and Yassin operated a cluster of shops where hash-filled hookahs and interminable arguments bubbled outside darkened doorways that offered everything from guiding services to clothing to rental gear, fragrant cardamom-spiked Kashmiri tea, food, film, and carpets.

When we'd met Hamid—who was permanently installed behind dark aviator glasses—he'd opined over the impending development that he hoped would deliver them modernity.

"In the future, *inshallah*, things are better," he'd said. "Last year I make the foundation for my guesthouse and this year, *inshallah*, I will build it. There will be more options of ski. More lift. But not so much crowd... or pollution. Gulmarg is still very special place."

"But it's still a *dangerous* place, right?" I'd asked.

"No... religion no problem in Kashmir: Muslim, Christian, Hindu, Sikh. All here no problem, all like snow and mountain," he'd told me with a smile, while over his shoulder I eyed the campus of the Indian Army's High Altitude Warfare School.

Yassin, however, was too busy to offer opinions. As Gulmarg's permanent traffic cop, unofficial mayor, and chief prevaricator (a national skill), he was constantly on his cell phone, gesticulating wildly so that the dirty orange ball cap he wore seemed to be bobbing while he orchestrated a host of on-mountain chaos.

"No, we do not have guides today," he would tell someone apologetically.

"Yes," he would offer with enthusiasm to another caller, "we have many guides today."

"Do not come today because maybe the gondola does not open," he would say.

"Come, yes," he would then tell someone else. "Of course the gondola will open."

"Yes, we have any equipments you are needing," he assured a caller, then, in the same instant, to a person standing outside the shop, "We are finished with equipments."

Ido figured he could help smooth out this scene by throwing his lot in with Hamid and Yassin under the banner of Kashmir Alpine. He helped direct international business their way and spearheaded Mission Gulmarg, a project to promote and assist in professionalizing the ski operation.

After some fundraising and political maneuvering, Ido arrived for his fourth season with over 1,800 pounds of secondhand WB clothing and gear, plus an international team of professional mountain-rescue volunteers to train Gulmarg's nascent patrol. The team included Canadian ski-mountaineer and planetary snow bohemian Ptor Sprice-nieks, who'd also fallen in love with the place during a visit in 2004.

"Kashmir was legendary to me after [John] Falkiner and the Clambin guys came here," he'd later tell me, "so it was always on my list."

Indeed, one of Team Clambin's most infamous exotic telemark skiing missions was a 1989 spring fling in Gulmarg. They'd danced down the lower slopes, dropping knees through towering pines in a compelling video that cycled endlessly in ski-town bars around the world. It was no *Blizzard of Aahhhs,* but surfacing during the height of both the telemark and adventure-ski revolutions, the short flick had had an impact on the minds and missions of many a young skier.

Between enjoying local ski-touring, curry, and abundant hashish, Ptor and company buckled down to training. While Indian bureaucracy and corruption made this goal equally rewarding and frustrating, *inshallah,* important baby steps were achieved in inculcating mountain safety, first aid, and avalanche awareness in the eager Kashmiris. Some challenges couldn't be overcome: avalanche control had to be accomplished "organically" by ski-cutting dangerous slopes because the Indian military either wouldn't provide ordnance for snow control or were worried that any explosion might draw fire—or an air strike—from Pakistan.

At the end of the Stage II Gondola's first season of operation, adventure-skiers worldwide were all talking about Gulmarg. But who was actually there? To start, a random bunch from Buffalo, New York, that we'd run into in the Highland Park Lodge.

"We saw it in a Warren Miller film," one said, "so we came."

"Yeah, but now we're kinda scared," said the other.

"About the mountain," I asked. "Or all the guns?"

"Mostly the food."

"And the monkeys. They're freaking us out."

MORE SNOW OVERNIGHT meant another morning fight to get on the gondola. Arriving at Stage II base, we joined eighty or so keen riders who awaited the gondola's opening, each hoping to make their cold-smoke dreams come true in Himalayan powder and notch another exotic destination on their boards. If Gulmarg took hold as a new ski-adventure locale, each could say they were there "when."

In the line-up was a motley crew from Australia, New Zealand, Japan, Canada, the USA, Britain, Austria, Sweden, Norway, France, Germany, and even Peru. Most were dressed in the fashion-forward technical clothing that is the uniform of serious freeriders, accessorized with shovel-laden packs and stickered helmets. There were, however, exceptions: there was the dreadlocked dude in leopard-print pants calmly rolling a massive joint in front of unperturbed police and a pair of helmet-clad Brits wearing local knee-length wool smocks over their gear (and their shovel packs over their smocks), absurdly standing in the snow holding cups of tea on saucers while the The Moody Blues' "Knights in White Satin" crackled out of the tinny, bullhorn speakers overhead.

All of the Indian skiers milling around were clothed in international hand-me-downs—outdated suits and even more ancient skis and boots that had likely survived years in some Euro rental program before landing here. Gulmarg wasn't the White Planet's only garbage dump, but between its fixer-upper gondola, WB's donations, and the rest of the ski-related debris littering the place, it was certainly the largest.

Despite the crowd, skiing the mountain that day wasn't to be. To start, the ticket seller had once again vaporized. And, as the crowd stared dumbfounded from below, the "ski patrol," practicing organic control, cut off one big avalanche after another, mostly on predictably risky sun-facing aspects but also, scarily, on the shadowed, north-facing lines we were all expecting to ride. In one comically perverse scenario, a patroller who'd just traversed out of a significant slide stood at the bottom of another slope on the same aspect while one of his compatriots made a ski-cut several hundred feet *directly* above, an ungodly breach of safety and common sense. Miraculously, both arrived alive at the bottom to yell at each other and the lifties, then go up again. It recalled a conversation I'd had the day before.

"It is only since few years we see probes and shovels here," Hamid had said, "but *inshallah* is more safety now."

"What?" chimed in Yassin indignantly. "Many years I am climbing to the top and skiing snow to here [he'd hit himself in the chest] and checking for avalanche only with my poles. We don't need more safety than for the gondola to open."

Still, we remained, baking in the sun, hoping the gondola would crack, the avalanche danger actually *increasing* while we waited. Like some sort of high-altitude hologram, the ticket guy coalesced out of the heat-shimmers rising from the snow, and there was a brief but intense scramble around his kiosk. Many Westerners had paid Indian guides or stand-ins to buy tickets for them, and, in service to their sahibs, fistfights broke out and bloodied noses abounded. But it was all for naught. After four hours of watching 3,000 vertical feet of tantalizing snow rot in the sun and giant thermals billow up from the bowls—and after eating an unnecessary and disgusting meal in the Restaurant Cum Waiting Area (a real name)—it was official: the gondola would not open. The disconsolate crowd dissipated toward the base and we were the last to leave, keeping a hopeful eye on the gondola in case someone changed their mind. They didn't.

It was probably just as well. The thermals had quickly crowded into a violent tempest, the kind that kills a dozen climbers at a time on peaks like Everest and K2, and it was snowing heavily again.

Instead of heading down with the rest, Ashref suggested we hike south across the Kongdori Plateau on which we stood, then make a forested descent to the town of Tulmarg. I was more than game—it was the very route depicted in many a recent film. Snow sifted down as we marched away from the gondola station, slipped past a café, cut a traverse across a short slope, then set a track toward the forest. We were soon followed by another guide and a group of snowboarders. When we reached the point where the plateau's edge broke over into a series of treed gullies, visibility in the falling snow was zero.

"Here?" I asked, peering into the dense flakes.

"Hurry," said, Ashref. "We must go before the others are poaching these best snows."

Again, like at home, we were in a dogfight with a crew of Whistler snowboarders. And, having learned his English largely from ski bums, Ashref had endearingly appropriated the term "poach."

For an hour we plunged down steep, gladed lines under monstrous arbors that recalled Bansko's Magic Trees, finding deep snow on the right aspects but more than occasionally feeling the tug of underlying crust. It was gorgeous and quiet in the snowy woods. Maybe too quiet. At one point, alone in the vertical bowling alleys, I pondered whether the snow leopards that lurked there—known to carry away dogs and even children from the village—had perhaps learned that clueless skiers occasionally stray from their group.

Eventually, we spilled into a valley of house-sized river boulders decorated in fat marshmallows of snow. Chattering monkeys scrambled up from the river and swung into the pines, admonishing us for the interruption. We crossed a bridge, lashed our skis to our packs, and hiked for twenty minutes to a trail that we skied down to a road where, in theory, we would be picked up. After an hour, a jeep appeared, its rattling tire chains lashed on with every conceivable fastener including butcher string. What ensued was a terrifying high-speed ride down a jeep-width road cut deep into the snow (what if someone was coming the other way?); it was clear why no vehicle in Gulmarg had side mirrors.

In Tulmarg we downed Kashmiri tea and mutton curry at the Downhill Restaurant while contemplating how, the year before, Kashmiri separatists had thrown a grenade into a bus full of tourists there. Outside, TV trucks and busloads of wide-eyed tourists and athletes pulling in for India's fifth annual Winter Games jostled for position on the road with plows, military convoys, and hundreds of smock-draped men smoking and yelling for no apparent reason. The chaos followed us on the swerving, halting drive up the switchbacks to Gulmarg. Along the road were dilapidated bank-cutters, ditchbound delivery vehicles, disheveled riflemen, Hindi strollers, monkeys, and dozens of men wielding picks and shovels, ostensibly fixing a road that they'd so far only made more impassable.

Surprisingly, the entire parade reminded me of Chile. And Mexico. Japan, New Zealand. Lebanon and Greece. Austria, Switzerland, France, Italy. Iceland and Greenland and Scotland and Newfoundland. Even Bulgaria and China. It was this notion of humans of every stripe forging their way into the mountains by whatever means that put me in mind of what many a philosopher has loftily posited: we take to the Earth's heights as a springboard to spiritual discovery, to summit, as it were, our very souls. While this was possibly true, our vertical spirituality-seeking was harder to quantify than the fractious and often farcical enterprise that dodged and swooped behind it like a kite tail. That would be skiing.

IT WAS WINDY at the top, but there were good turns to be had on the leeward north-facing slopes where powder had sifted in, albeit dangerously, for days. At least the gondola was open, and we got on it. On our first run we skied fall-line flanks, traversing around the nose of each ridge and skiing the fall line again. This routine netted us tons of vertical on wide-open terrain. Near the bottom, we whipped over a knoll and bagged a few deep turns in a lone copse of giant trees. Our second run wasn't as good. We climbed above the top station for fifteen minutes, struggling in the thin air at 14,000 feet, then traversed a gully onto the next ridge. Unable to find anything good to ski on the wind-hammered slope, we made guerilla turns down a steep, blown-in face, plates of crust disintegrating in our wakes like crackers crumbled into soup. Traversing a knoll, I dropped tentatively over its convexity, only to have the entire slope crack under my weight and drain like water into the adjacent gully. It was the kind of slide that killed the unwary here every season. I avoided being swept away by exiting quickly right, yelling back up the slope to warn the others to follow the ridge down.

As we regrouped in safety under some twisted birches, a mad, smiling Kiwi on a pair of K2 Pontoons—the McConkey-designed, China-made model that was the archetype for the new wave of super-fat rockered skis—screamed straight down the gut of the adjacent chute, passing us, like a dolphin at Marine World, in a full tail-stand salute, his poles trailing behind. The improbable sight emphasized the fantastic nature of what was occurring in Gulmarg: spores from the four corners of the international ski community raining down in the middle of Himalayan nowhere to ride the latest wave of big-mountain gear in the kind of terrain and conditions it was developed for. It was almost heart-warming—until the slope the Kiwi had just ripped down ripped out under our feet and almost flushed all of us down to Tulmarg. This place required constant vigilance; it was like skiing on eggshells. (Gulmarg continues to be a dangerous place for avalanches. In February 2010, seventeen soldiers from the High Altitude Warfare School died in a massive slide that buried almost sixty of them.)

Still—and only a surfer who'd just survived a dangerous big-wave pounding to paddle out again would understand—we decided on one more descent. Again we climbed above the top station. This time it took us an hour to the summit, where we scanned awesome ridgelines and chutes on the hidden peak behind, leading into the unknown of Pakistan. Maybe we'd be back one day to ski them. Skiing was happily pregnant with such possibility—there was always a next time, another descent, better conditions.

We turned our attention back to Gulmarg. While the others traversed into the steep bowl via an easier route, I dropped a more difficult line off the top below a cornice, reveling in exquisite high-speed movie turns from one side of the bowl to the other in cold, fast snow. I was careful to spend as little time as possible crossing the concave center of the bowl, in case a billowing cloud of white death was funneling down from behind. We regrouped on a safe knoll and rode powdered ridges for hundreds of vertical feet, the umber smog above Srinigar our backdrop, Morrison's clicking camera the soundtrack. Again we plunged into the trees, finding beautifully deep blow-in for a few dozen turns until the slope flattened out to face the sun and conditions got nasty.

Calling on the unconscious skills acquired over a lifetime on snow, we muscled downward through sastrugi, breakable crust, and frozen tracks, splitting up when we reached the forest plateau, each thinking we had the best line back to the lodge. I meandered off through towering pines, tracking the smell of curry on the breeze. But I angled too far left, hitting a road that spelled at least a half-hour's walk back. I didn't care; the fight to get on the gondola that day had been worth it. Monkeys screamed as I shouldered my skis, and the sky darkened with a plague of ravenesque birds streaming back into Gulmarg as they did each afternoon to roost comfortably near hotels and squawk obnoxiously until sundown. I was thinking about these often odd rhythms of the mountains when a lone figure popped out of the forest ahead and dropped to the road.

His name was Pierre, and I knew him casually from Whistler. The last time I'd seen him was two years before, as I was getting off a bus one evening in La Grave after twenty hours of traveling from Vancouver.

"Hey," he'd said in La Grave, "how's it going, eh? I'm doing a slide show at the bar tonight. You should come." Then he'd disappeared into the gloom.

This time it was triple the distance from home and double the exotica, but neither of us made the slightest allusion to either. Again it was understood: White Planet, small world.

"Hey," he said, "how's it going? Pretty good skiing, eh?"

"Yeah," I said. "Pretty *damn* good."

"Well, maybe we'll catch you at the party later," he nodded, striding off in the other direction. With the tribe, after all, there was always a party brewing.

"Or up top tomorrow," he tossed over his shoulder. "It's supposed to snow tonight. *Yee-haw!*"

Standing alone in a dark Indian forest, I caught myself smiling, giddy at the prospect like it was the first time. And in the spaciousness of that moment, I finally understood what it all meant, what this feeling *was*. Like love, powder came and went from our lives. We enjoyed it when it was there, craved it when it disappeared, and, ultimately, survived on the belief that it would one day find us again.

EPILOGUE:
LEGEND

The artist and the sportsman know that
their work is a justification in itself, and they
will continue in it, not because of its effect on
civilization or international politics, but because
it enables them to break through the barriers
of this material world, and to taste, if only for
a moment, the happiness which lies beyond.
PETER LUNN, *High-speed Skiing*, 1935

LIKE A medieval aerie, the village of Mürren hugs the edge of a 2,800-foot cliff
above the Lauterbrunnen valley in the Jungfrau region of
the Swiss Alps. From the spacious lounge of historic Hotel
Eiger is a view of its namesake peak, so imposing that even
if you're alone in the room it feels like someone is sitting
beside you.

The rest of the panorama is redolent with mountaineering history: to the Eiger's right lean the Mönch and
Jungfrau, giving way to the massive wall of the Schwarz-
mönch, and below it the great gash of the Trümmelbach
Gorge. Behind the hotel, trams rise first to Birg and then
to the 9,650-foot Schilthorn, where famous scenes from
the James Bond film *On Her Majesty's Secret Service* were

filmed. Directly in front sits the cliff-hugging rail station that disgorges passengers who've taken a tram up from Lauterbrunnen to ride the quaint, wooden train from Gimmelwald to Mürren. Horse-drawn sleds and golf-cart taxis wait outside the station to whisk arrivals over snow-covered roads and past outdoor curling rinks to their hotels, as the streets, in winter, are never entirely cleared of snow. It is merely tamped down so skiers can meander off the mountain and through the village to their favorite après bar without removing their equipment, an alpine idyll that has lasted a century.

Outside the train station stands a monument to Sir Arnold Lunn.

The ever-intrepid British discovered Mürren as a summer destination in the 1840s, the wealthier pilgrims being carried up rocky paths from the valley on sedan chairs. It wasn't until 1910, however, that tour operator Sir Henry Lunn convinced local authorities to keep their alpine-accessing cog railways open in winter, with a promise to deliver snow-tourists. And deliver he did, spawning a spate of hotel construction to accommodate the growing numbers who came to take the air and slide around on skis, which were rare in the Alps at the time. Sir Henry's son Arnold was convinced that this activity held huge promise to tourism, and the instruction and competitions he initiated—including the first-ever slalom race in 1922—brought shape to the sport and a label to this nascent sector of the travel industry: the ski resort. There are other cradles of skiing—China's Altai region, Norheim's Norway, Zdarsky's Austria—but Mürren, where utility, sport, recreation, competition, and organization finally found footing and commerce together, is the birthplace of modern ski *civilization*.

In January of 2010, I was in the Jungfrau region on an assignment, retracing the steps of the dual fathers of ski journalism—Arnold Lunn and James Riddell. I'd spent the first few days skiing in Grindelwald under the Eigernord-wand—the storied north face of the Eiger—and catching the eightieth running of the famed Lauberhorn World Cup Downhill in nearby Wengen, along with 58,000 riotous fans who'd ascended the network of trains and trams to the vehicle-free village. Many of them would remain there, drinking, singing, and celebrating a win by countryman Didier Cuche until dawn. I'd watched from several junctures along the course with a Swiss friend, amazed, as always, with the speed and technical skill of the racers, but also enjoying the ambience of a face-painted, flag-waving, schnapps-guzzling crowd so dense that it eventually stripped the mountainside of snow. Everything about the experience—including the plentiful cheesiness—was intensely genuine; should I have been sad that I would never see such a sight in North America (especially if you couldn't drive to it)? No. I'd come to understand that tradition ultimately lives where it belongs and that attempts to recreate it elsewhere never succeed. In the same vein, you couldn't lament that a European version of the X Games might never draw the crowds it does in North America.

I'd moved over to Mürren the following week to witness (there's no other word) the Inferno, the world's oldest and largest amateur downhill race. Inaugurated by Arnold Lunn's Kandahar Ski Club of Great Britain in 1928, the Inferno ran from the Schilthorn some 8,500 vertical feet and nine-plus miles down to Lauterbrunnen. In those days, a handful of participants had to climb up on skis three hours from Mürren and spend the night in a hut, then climb three more hours up to the Schilthorn in the morning. In 1928 the winner took an hour forty-five minutes to reach the valley; the next year, with more skiers beating down the snow and following a known route, James

Riddell did it in forty-five minutes. These days the fastest racer takes less than fifteen minutes, but with one of 1,900 participants leaving the gate every twelve seconds, the race is now pure madness—and occasional carnage. A friend in the tourist bureau told me that Peter Lunn, ski-racing icon, author, and son of the late, great Sir Arnold, still lived in the Hotel Eiger each winter. I hoped to bump into him and have a word or two about the good ol' days—perhaps tea in the Eiger's lounge?

The day before the race, Mattias Fredriksson and I were taking photos in the resort's Sonnenberg area when a smallish man, hunched over with intense concentration, face sprung with an ivory tuft of chin-whisker, snow-plowed past under the watchful eyes of a middle-aged man and woman. It was ninety-six-year-old Peter Lunn, escorted by his son Stephen and his daughter-in-law. I was awestruck, but perhaps should not have been; at age ninety, Lunn became the oldest person ever to have skied the Inferno, a record likely to remain in perpetuity. Noticing that the group pulled up at a local restaurant for a coffee in the sun, we pulled in as well.

Improbably, I found Lunn sitting on the deck beside Niklas, an Engelberg-based Swedish freerider whom I'd met only once in Bulgaria, the pair of them intently watching "speed fliers" on the face of the Schilthorn. In this new breed of BASE jumping meets kite-flying meets skiing, the skiers were wearing small parachutes and skipping down the mountain face, touching down only where they felt like it—or where it was safe. (McConkey had excitedly circulated a YouTube URL of speed fliers descending the Eiger in 2006.) It was pure invention and mountain art, and that intergenerational moment of shared awe tied everything together. I greeted Niklas—it had been four years—then turned to Lunn.

"I'm delighted to meet you, sir," I said, carefully shaking the hand that stretched out slowly below a slack face. "I've read *High-speed Skiing* cover to cover."

"That was my *first* book!" he responded immediately, his face animating with delight.

"Yes! And *you* were the first person to write an entire book about going fast on skis. Was that what attracted you—going *fast?*"

"No, no," he answered, still smiling. "It was because..."

Lunn seemed suddenly lost. The élan of speed fliers swooping bird-like off the icefalls and cliffs above had hitched his thoughts, perhaps, a quick ride back to *The Mountains of Youth,* the apt title of one of his father's books. I likewise had my own memories: Banff, Killer Hill, Don Valley. We had different recollections, but our intent was the same: it was all about gratitude.

Over the years, the act of sliding downhill on boards has found endless ways to leave me bloodied but smiling— a comical crash, a psychological rout in the backcountry, a tough story to report, or the endless battles of running a magazine. Whatever the circumstances, I've always been grateful for the opportunity to experience, study, and dissect why people chuck everything to go skiing. Or bother to write about it. And I've found a few answers to the question, but only one of them was simple enough to account for skiing's past, present, and future of constant evolution. It was the first one I'd hit upon with my mother all those years ago, and it was precisely the thought that Lunn retrieved to finish his sentence: "...because it's fun."

I guess we were all still flying.

NOTES

1 Steve Casimiro, *POWDER*, January 1992, 13.
2 Peter Shelton, "Whither the Ski Bum," *Skiing Heritage*, December 2006, 10.
3 Maia Rodman, "The Oldest Ski Bum in the World," *Sports Illustrated*, January 1962, 58.
4 Arnold Lunn, *The Mountains of Youth*, 2nd ed. (London: Eyre & Spottiswoode, 1949), xiv.
5 Ernest Hemingway, "Cross-Country Snow," *In Our Time* (New York: Boni & Liveright, 1925), 110.
6 Dianna Waggoner, "Speed Champion Steve McKinney's 120-MPH Runs Make Downhill Racers Seem Snowbound," *People*, January 1979.
7 Lunn, xiv.
8 Delores LaChapelle, *Deep Powder Snow: 40 Years of Ecstatic Skiing, Avalanches, and Earth Wisdom* (Durango, CO: Kivaki Press, 1993), 32.
9 Lunn, 31.
10 John Allen, "Mathias Zdarsky: The Father of Alpine Skiing," *Skiing Heritage*, March, 2008, 8.
11 Steve Barnett, "It's Gone Too Far," *Cross Country*, October/November 1981, 73.